The British question

The British question

Arthur Aughey

Manchester University Press
Manchester and New York
distributed in the United States exclusively by Palgrave Macmillan

Copyright © Arthur Aughey 2013

The right of Arthur Aughey to be identified as the author of this work has been asserted by him in accordance with the Copyright, Designs and Patents Act 1988.

Published by Manchester University Press
Oxford Road, Manchester M13 9NR, UK
and Room 400, 175 Fifth Avenue, New York, NY 10010, USA
www.manchesteruniversitypress.co.uk

Distributed in the United States exclusively by
Palgrave Macmillan, 175 Fifth Avenue, New York,
NY 10010, USA

Distributed in Canada exclusively by
UBC Press, University of British Columbia, 2029 West Mall,
Vancouver, BC, Canada V6T 1Z2

British Library Cataloguing-in-Publication Data
A catalogue record for this book is available from the British Library

Library of Congress Cataloging-in-Publication Data applied for

ISBN 978 0 7190 8340 2 hardback
ISBN 978 0 7190 8341 9 paperback

First published 2013

The publisher has no responsibility for the persistence or accuracy of URLs for any external or third-party internet websites referred to in this book, and does not guarantee that any content on such websites is, or will remain, accurate or appropriate.

Typeset in 10.5/12.5pt Sabon
by Graphicraft Limited, Hong Kong
Printed in Great Britain
by TJ International Ltd

Contents

Preface and acknowledgements   vi

Part I   Histories   1
1   Providence   3
2   Endism   24
3   Dry wall   44

Part II   Themes   63
4   Identity and allegiance   65
5   Instrumental politics   84
6   Fifth nation   103

Part III   Agendas   123
7   Institutions and directions of travel   125
8   The matter of England   145
9   Respect and independence   165
10   Concluding remarks   185

Bibliography   193

Index   223

Preface and acknowledgements

The idea for this book was sparked by a question in a session at the United Kingdom (UK) Political Studies Association annual conference in Manchester in 2009. At that session there had been excellent presentations on devolved politics and administration in Wales, Scotland and Northern Ireland along with reflections on the state of English public opinion. The question asked was a simple, perhaps naive, one: where in all of this interesting work was the UK? Perhaps it was too large a question to receive a satisfactory answer on such an occasion – it was not addressed, never mind answered – but there was a disturbing intimation that perhaps one effect of devolution would be to conjure the UK out of existence (as it was once said of Lloyd George and Ireland). A collection of essays (Gamble and Wright 2009: 1) published later that same year began with the line: 'These are difficult times to be British.' The answer the editors gave to the question why this should be so was straightforward enough. The state which had underpinned that identification was no longer the solid and confident structure of earlier times. Here were a number of challenges which presented themselves to anyone wishing to confront the British question: to say something meaningful about the 'whole', to reflect on what remains solid about the state and to indicate where the UK is in devolutionary times. There is no presumption that others have not addressed these matters. The contributions by scholars such as Charlie Jeffery, Michael Keating, James Mitchell, Alan Trench (to name only a few) have been central to our understanding, as has the research of the Constitution Unit. Equally, Vernon Bogdanor's work on the changing constitution must be the starting point for anyone wishing to understand what has taken place in British politics since the 1990s. As this text demonstrates, the original work of Richard Rose was a particular inspiration. The justification for the book is that by synthesising such insights, but providing a distinctive perspective, it may go some way towards answering the Manchester question.

There is another reason for approaching the subject in this manner. I was very conscious of the rich academic research which has been done already on the politics of Wales and Scotland by those with a more direct, intimate and subtle understanding of particulars than I could ever have. For example, scholars such as Laura McAllister, Jonathan Bradbury, Roger Scully and Richard Wyn Jones in Wales and Nicola McEwen, David McCrone and Ross Bond in Scotland – along with those others cited in this text – have produced work of specific and comparative significance upon which this book most gratefully draws and acknowledges. An exception was made for England which has been comparatively under-researched and which requires separate treatment if only because it is still the anomaly in post-devolution UK. What struck me in the course of writing the book is that Northern Ireland which for most of recent history had been taken to be the exception to all British rules has become more and more like the rule. This may appear an outrageous exaggeration (and it is, of course) but the frequent framing of issues in terms of the national question, the presence of devolved institutions, the effect of distinctive party identities are some features of Northern Ireland politics which are no longer alien to what used to be called 'normal' British politics. To speak of what is exceptional about Northern Ireland today requires a delicious and provocative sense of irony, for constitutionally Northern Ireland has become one of the most stable parts of the UK. The fact if not the value of the Union has become more deeply entrenched there as both the fact and the value of the Union have come more openly into play elsewhere, even in England. Long immersion in the study of Northern Ireland, however, helps one to develop an ear for the exaggerations, anxieties and fantasies of politics and when the temptation is to arrive at immoderate conclusions, perhaps the lesson of experience is to cleave to what Colin Kidd (2008) called the middle ground of interpretation about the UK. Or as J. G. A. Pocock once put it (2000: 46), modification does not always mean liquidation and if the rhetoric of dissolution formerly used in relation to Northern Ireland now seems strange, it may also come to seem so in the rest of the UK. On the other hand, Northern Ireland experience suggests that you never can tell.

The book is structured in three parts. The first two chapters of Part I, *Histories*, consider the way in which (to use Seamus Heaney's words) hope and history rhyme in narratives of the UK, either the Whiggish one of benign constitutional adaptation or the nationalist one of the end of Britain. The third chapter proposes an alternative understanding which more clearly renders unto history what is history's and unto politics what belongs to politics. The intention is merely to demonstrate the point that neither Providence nor the *Zeitgeist* are really very good or sensible guides to what are ultimately questions of political choice. This first part is designed to highlight the inescapable truth that to maintain the UK or to secure its undoing requires political intelligence and wise judgement. Chapters 4 and 5 in Part II, *Themes*, look at matters such as identity, purpose and function which are frequently thought to be deep-rooted problems for the territorial management of the UK. Indeed, the reason why these are difficult times to be British and the reasons for the less than solid and confident structure is because of questions about the identity, purpose and function of the state. Acknowledging the force of these questions, Chapter 6 tries to identify the affective and effective character of the UK after more than a decade of devolution. The first chapter in Part III, *Agendas*, examines the institutional challenges to the integrity of the UK and the political and administrative sensitivities required to accommodate the sovereign authority of Westminster and the democratic legitimacy of the devolved Parliament in Scotland and the Assemblies in Wales and Northern Ireland. Chapter 8 addresses the matter of England and it how it now relates to the new and changing institutional shape of the UK. The final chapter assesses the legacy of Labour government, the adequacy (or not) of the Coalition's 'respect agenda' in the face of Scottish National Party control of policy in Holyrood and the threat that poses not only to Scotland's place within the UK but to the very meaning of the UK itself. Some concluding remarks reflect on the state of the UK today.

In an enterprise such as this one accumulates many debts, too many to acknowledge in every instance. Cooperation for a number of years with members of the Constitution Unit at University College London was an education in itself and I owe a lot in terms of both support and intellectual direction to Professor Robert Hazell. The Unit provided the opportunity for stimulating association with other academics which makes scholarship such a pleasant occupation. Members of the Unit who went on to other posts, such as Guy Lodge at the Institute for Public Policy Research and Akash Paun at the Institute for Government helped to keep me informed of new trends in politics and administration. A very large debt is owed to Alan Trench whose understanding of the intricacies of devolution is unrivalled. His blog *Devolution Matters* is by the far the best commentary available, combining uniquely legal, financial and administrative knowledge as well as an understanding of the comparative politics of territorial policy. Shortly before he died, the late Sir Bernard Crick was kind enough to comment on some of my ideas and to suggest new directions of investigation. Of course all the limitations of interpretation are mine alone.

At the University of Ulster I would like to thank for his support the Dean of Faculty of Social Sciences, Professor Paul Carmichael, who was responsible for asking that question at the PSA conference in Manchester, as well as Dr Cathy Gormley-Heenan, Head of the Institute for Research in the Social Sciences and Ruth Fee, Head of School of Criminology, Politics and Social Policy, both of whom were unfailingly kind and helpful, as were other colleagues in the School who enabled me to talk through some of the awkward questions. Tony Mason at Manchester University Press showed consistent encouragement and I thank him for his faith in the project. Nothing would have been possible without the generous support of a Leverhulme Trust Senior Research Fellowship which allowed me the time and space to reflect on the subject. The members of staff at the Trust were always helpful and sympathetic throughout the period of the Fellowship and remarkably efficient in response to every query and request which came their way. To paraphrase Cecil Rhodes, being awarded a Leverhulme Fellowship is like coming first in the lottery of academic life. My thanks are sincere and enduring.

Finally I would like to thank Sky Aughey whose developing interest in politics helped to keep me up to the mark and Sharon Glenn for her patience while this book was being written.

Part I
Histories

1

Providence

On 19 February 1938, Raymond Chandler (2007: 7) began his notebook with what he called his 'Great Thought'. For Chandler there 'are two kinds of truth: the truth that lights the way and the truth that warms the heart. The first of these is science, and the second is art. Neither is independent of the other or more important than the other'. He believed that without art science would be useless but without science art would be just 'a crude mess of folklore and emotional quackery'. He summed up his great thought with the line: 'The truth of art keeps science from becoming inhuman and the truth of science keeps art from becoming ridiculous.' Students of politics will recognise the force of Chandler's great thought. In the normal run of things, political argument in a society the highest values of which are free speech and open debate must ground itself (or at least, try to ground itself) in the first sort of truth. There is a requirement for 'scientific substance' to any policy proposal and for any claim to serious public attention. The truth that is intended to light the way will be open to dispute, of course, but to argue heatedly on any subject – 'emotional quackery' – without light is to risk being condemned to obscurity and accused of obscurantism. On the other hand, to be in command of facts without conveying what George Bush Senior once called the 'vision thing' is also a political failing. Without it, argument is inclined to appear 'inhuman' if only because it does not connect with stories of people's lives and fails to warm their hearts. In other words, political argument means not only giving the people facts but also making those facts a necessary part of their own stories. As the accomplished narrator, Chandler knew well (2007: 40) that intelligence and the emotions function on different levels. Emotional reactions are often 'independent of reasonableness' but though emotional imagination is very intense, it is also very short. The politics of the everyday, then, is about formulating – or attempting to formulate – persuasive narratives which serve both to light the way and to warm the heart, narratives which are grounded in realities but which also give meaning to those realities. These narratives proclaim effect because they also call upon affect. One could argue that the balance between light and warmth is quite different in the matter of national allegiance and identity. Here the issue is not primarily with policy but with legitimacy, not what we should do but with who we are. It is not so easy – and perhaps it is inappropriate – to distinguish between truths which light the way and those which warm the heart – or, to put that slightly differently, between truths which should light the way and which should warm the heart because nationhood is also the subject of competing narratives about the past, present and future. This is not a failing for it would be 'inhuman' for a subject of such public significance to be discussed entirely dispassionately. T. S. Eliot once remarked (1972: 94) that culture cannot be planned because it is the unconscious background of planning and something similar might be said – and has been said (Canovan 1996) – of the nation.

Of course, there are those who see in the warmth of national discourse little other than the crude mess of folklore and emotional quackery and who argue that the truth of politics – and history – is to be found elsewhere. This was once the role of left-wing criticism, especially Marxism, which narrated a story of scientific politics with the warmth of proletarian solidarity. The collapse of faith in that narrative since the 1990s has meant that national questions – by historical circumstance and by intellectual conviction – have moved again to the centre of political argument. In the UK, the nation appears to some as the truth which will light the way to a more prosperous future, a recovery of heart-warming truths about popular political capacity which will bring emancipation from the folklore and emotional quackery of the old (multinational) order. That has been the central proposition of the evangelist of neo-nationalism, Tom Nairn. And since all discussion of the nation involves discussion of origins and the past, questions of history are at the heart of the matter. Peter Mandler (2006: 282–3) observed how, after a long period when it was eschewed in favour of class and gender, nation 'has over the last fifteen years become a subject of rapt fascination'. This was a 'renaissance' and not a revolution in historical writing though the circumstances, of course, are unique. Mandler's objective was to explore the relationship between definitions of 'nation' by historians and by social scientists and to suggest how they might be brought a little closer together.

This was something which fascinated J. G. A. Pocock. He once wrote (2009: 187) that since societies exist in time they conserve images of themselves and the consciousness of time which individuals acquire is 'in large measure' consciousness of society's continuity. The image of continuity and the understanding of time is an important part of national self-understanding – 'of its structure and what legitimates it, of the modes of action which are possible to it and in it'. Consequently, he thought there is a point at which historical and political theory meet such that 'every society possesses a philosophy of history' which is intimately 'a part of its consciousness and its functioning'. Pocock's essay, first published in 1968, was an essay on how historical consciousness can lead to distinctive forms of political self-awareness. It attempted (187) to illustrate how ideas of institutional legitimacy and illegitimacy arise, function and develop in the particularities of history but also how they 'may be studied as part of the science of society' – one could say at the point where warmth meets light. Pocock here was engaging specifically with the meeting of historical and political theory in the work of Michael Oakeshott, in particular his notion of 'tradition'. For Oakeshott (1991: 59–63) a tradition of behaviour was famously 'a tricky thing to get to know' but one could, by examining the underlinings it makes in its history, grasp how a society 'constructs a legend of its own fortunes which it keeps up to date and in which is hidden its own understanding of its politics; and the historical investigation of this legend – not to expose its errors but understand its prejudices – must be a pre-eminent part of political education'. What such an investigation would likely detect, Oakeshott thought, was 'a flow of sympathy' linking past and present and that such a flow of sympathy was an important element of political stability. Of course, Oakeshott believed that there was a fundamental distinction between *history* as a mode of experience and the *practical past* as the sort of truth which tended either to warm the heart or chill the blood. It is a distinction which all self-respecting historians acknowledge (history versus myth) but it is not one which most people would necessarily recognise. According to Pocock (2009: 216), there is a constant discussion and redefinition of the links between past and present; and how the past can give to the present its structure. 'In that dialogue the past is to the present something more like a wife: an other self, perpetually explored' and it would certainly be 'inhuman' if that self were explored without emotion of some sort. This is not to suggest that modern conceptions of professional history are unimportant because popular history usually feeds off its ideas. It is merely to note, as the quintessentially professional historian J. C. D. Clark (1990: 97) once wrote, that the significance of history outside the academy addresses the great question to which a credible answer is sought in each generation: 'What sort of Britain is worthy of our patriotism?' The possessive pronoun is used intentionally because engagement with narratives of the 'national' past is engagement with a past which, for good and/or ill, is also part of us. To which one can add the question: 'Is Britain worthy of our patriotism at all?'

This chapter considers the sort of Britain which was once thought worthy of patriotism. It does not suggest that this was the only understanding available, which is clearly not the case, merely that there were some important historical assumptions just as vital in their un-spokenness as in their being openly expressed. This is what Colin Kidd (2008: 302–3) has called 'banal unionism' which represented a 'form of casual and unquestioning silence on the topic' even though 'this inarticulate loyalism was punctuated by moments of intense creativity'. This was a conservative disposition which, by subscribing implicitly to the myths which underpinned it, helped to sustain the integrity of the UK. However, it was not Conservative in the party political sense because these historical myths were shared, albeit in different measure, across the parties. When historical science met historical art it produced a powerfully imaginative British narrative, the ghost of which lingers still in public life. The warmest of heart warming historical myths assumed that the county embodied some higher purpose.

Providence

The opening lines of poet Stephen Spender's autobiography *World within World* (1951) captured a distinctive British sentiment. 'I grew up', wrote Spender, 'in an atmosphere of belief in progress curiously mingled with apprehension' but his dominant feeling was that he 'had been born on to a fortunate promontory of time towards which all other times led'. Here history revealed a benign disposition, a history implicitly graced by civil liberty, industrial creativity and parliamentary government though one haunted by impending loss. That sense of benign favour was not the exclusive property of the English middle class. National achievement bound up with notions of the British constitution and empire 'was said to be a people's story' and it was a story eminently believable (Colls 2002: 28). Though the weight in the scale of human happiness given in Spender's Liberal household to the policy of Home Rule for Ireland seems curious today it contains a certain irony. The progressive faith which Spender imbibed was proclaimed with a rather different emphasis on the banners of Ulster Orange lodges opposed to Home Rule. Some of them still display the mid-nineteenth century painting by Thomas Jones Barker – *The Secret of England's Greatness* – which hangs on the wall of the National Portrait Gallery in London. The painting represented that secret as the combination of reformed faith, constitutional monarchy, wise parliamentary counsel, creative moral discipline and material success, which together constituted a civilising mission that made the country specially favoured. And 'England' here meant 'Britain' as every Ulster unionist knew. This English narrative of dignity and greatness was part of a larger historical British self-understanding and when faith and history rhyme like this, intimations of providence are at hand. It was not war, law or religion alone which helped to foster popular identification with Britishness but their historical relationship in a providential setting (Clark 2000: 274). Herbert Butterfield (1944: 81–2), whose reputation had been made on the basis of his criticism of this providential history, distinguished between the truth of that system and its political effect. Respect for the past, he thought, was actually combined with 'what one might call a sublime and purposeful unhistoricity' and the past that had been clung to was one 'conveniently and tidily disposed for our purposes'. This was truly heart-warming history with an appropriate political message, confirming in the UK 'the happier form of co-operation with Providence' which was in contrast to the continental tradition of revolution and reaction. On this point the Conservative, Liberal and Labour parties agreed.

Only the very naive, of course, ever believed that God had arranged the Pennines where He did so that Lancashire would become the centre of world cotton production and Yorkshire of wool; or carbon deposits where He did to make South Wales the centre of world coal production. Yet such providential naivety was an element of British consciousness and one which required regular ridicule. The most famous literary sketch is Dickens's Mr Podsnap in *Our Mutual Friend* (1865), whose declamations to the poor 'foreign gentleman' linked together the virtues of character, constitution and (to use a Hegelian term) British world historical significance, all of which had been most favourably bestowed upon the country by providence. Though, as the 'foreign gentleman' justly replied to Podsnap, that seemed a 'little particular' of providence since the frontier of the country was not large. While the popular depth of this self-understanding is difficult to assess – which is why it obviously lends itself so readily to un-serious treatment, famously by Sellar and Yeatman (1930) – its extent is clear and its effect reasonably enduring (Finn 1989: 181). Some eighty years after Mr Podsnap, A. G. MacDonnell (1942: 147) could still make fun of the belief that things worked providentially in the favour of British (again described as English) interests:

> 'A glance at the history would shows how the enemies of England have always collapsed unexpectedly and mysteriously, whether owing to the sudden uprising of a southerly gale to drive the invading galleons from

Gravelines to the Pentland Firth, or owing to a trivial miscalculation which isolated the wing of an army in the obscure Danubian village of Blindheim, or owing to a Spanish ulcer, or to the sinking of a *Lusitania*, and it cannot be supposed that these incidents were all fortuitous.'

The ironical suggestion of MacDonnell's reflections is that these examples of historical fortune just happened to coincide not only with British self-interest but also with acts of British power ('in the days of coal, every coaling-station was English' and 'in the days of oil, the only oil-wells that did not already belong to people who wanted selfishly to keep them for themselves, became English'). One supposes that God helped those who helped themselves and MacDonnell arraigned a generation of literature and public speeches which had lauded the providential design, trust, burden and duty of the British imperial mission. It was difficult for people to see their history honestly because of all those heart warming providential tales, something which outsiders are apt to point out (Yapp 2011). However, MacDonnell also illustrates the ambivalence of providence in British history, an ambivalence vividly explored in Bernard Porter's *The Absent-Minded Imperialists* (2004). Porter noted how a deeply influential current in British political and economic thinking could indeed subscribe to the notion of providence and the favoured characteristics of British national character and still be hostile to the *ideology* of empire. This was the deeply held belief in free trade which saw not only empire but also nationalism as regressive, a belief which was in tune with the suspicion of popular enthusiasm we find both in utilitarian logic and aristocratic prejudice (Dicey 2008: 329; Mandler 2006). Here was the faith (Porter 2004: 95) 'that free trade and the better world it promised would evolve naturally and inevitably, simply because it was self-evidently beneficial to everyone, whatever some of them might think now, so that it need not be spread by (imperial) force. The word often used for this was "Providence" (with a capital "P", aligning it with "God")'. This vision of progress considered improvement inevitable and ordained such that it could not be considered imperialism (which *did* involve directed acts of power). As Porter pointed out, this heart-warming vision of non-imperialistic righteousness can be an unreliable guide to what was actually done in the name of free trade. In line with MacDonnell's light-hearted but also serious imagination, Porter (96) agreed that providence 'can also be used as a cloak to cover some very *un*providential acts: you can see the direction history is leading, so you help it along. That was exactly how many British colonies came to be first established during the course of the nineteenth century'. And it is interesting to note how providential thinking of a different sort, suggesting inevitability, historical direction with the injunction to help things along, recurs in contemporary nationalist argument (see Chapter 2). Therefore it would be wrong to assume a simple, unchallenged imperial ideology at the core of British self-understanding which somehow permanently constituted its character or bequeathed to it an indelibly reactionary or manipulative mentality. The historical evidence is much more complicated as Chandler's two truths imply.

The sense of providential performance could be related to moral duty as much as to historical self-interest. For instance, in a book which warmly celebrated British national character (Barker 1927: 280–1), we find openness to what, in post-imperial times, would be called the 'world community' or 'liberal internationalism', openness rooted in that older sense of historical mission which today is treated with cynicism as if it were merely imperialistic spin. By the providence of empire and the trust it entailed, it was thought that the UK had given something to the world. Barker (like Stanley Baldwin) believed that the country owed far more than it had given and nations together needed to school themselves anew to 'undertake missions', mainly this time 'under a system of international co-operation'. And though we may think the argument about providence has been consigned to the dustbin of history this is far from being the case. It informs David Marquand's history of the British imperial legacy where the legend of providence is declaimed as a continuing curse because it has led and continues to lead the UK into dangerous international escapades. 'The British were not only uniquely oceanic and freedom loving; they were a providential people, summoned by a higher power to fight for freedom against slavery, and for good against evil' and this is the sort of 'rhetorical trope' which Marquand believes has echoed down the centuries 'and to which Tony Blair was to give his own special gloss at the start of the twenty-first century' (Marquand 2009: 13). Of course, and repeating the sub-text of MacDonnell, the real 'truth' which Marquand implies is neither heartwarming nor patriotically progressive but is convicted of dark acts of exploitation and power. Yet his history is not the truth of 'science' either and artfully promotes another sort of providential story, this time a European 'vocation'.

What gave a renewed lease of life to the sense of miraculous good fortune in British history was the experience of the Second World War, which sense of self-satisfaction was to become once more the subject of satirists in the 1960s. And it is possibly testament to the popular endurance of the providential myth that the public impact of the argument in both Linda Colley's *Britons: Forging the Nation* (1992) and

Norman Davies's *The Isles: A History* (1999) was to be found in their repudiation of such heart-warming faith, if only by calling to mind the (non-providential) contingencies of British history and the contingent future of the UK itself. However this merely helps to illustrate the point that ideas of purposeful historic continuity have functioned as a vital repository of British self-understanding. And if much of this history happened to be *English* history it did not detract from its emotional force and political effect. English history, as Grainger (1986: 53) noted, tended to define paradigmatically the pattern of British thought and it was the English, above all, who thought providentially 'of themselves as something more than "just another nation"'. And there is a history to this relationship too, from at least the Union of the Crowns in 1603 when older English myths took on the character of 'British'. If the magic of nationalism is to turn chance into destiny (Anderson 1991: 11–12), then the narrative recounted here was a very peculiar form of magic. Indeed, as one critic of Gordon Brown (Lee 2006) was to point out, his heart-warming celebration of British virtues in the twenty-first century was sustained by historical illustrations which were almost exclusively about England and Englishness, charged moreover with an undercurrent of an older notion of providence. In defence of Brown, it can be observed that to demarcate so finely what is English and what is not is characteristic of *nationalist* thinking which is concerned to make proprietary distinctions. This was not and is not characteristic of *British* thinking which is much more territorially promiscuous and less concerned to make absolute national distinctions (for one view of this see Jenkins 1975).

Certainly, none of this undoubted Anglo-centric bias ever meant that the Scots, the Welsh or the Irish were mere shadowy presences in the story. Christopher Harvie's impressive *A Floating Commonwealth* (2008), for example, recounts a story of the industrial, commercial but above all, intellectual, intercourse across the Irish Sea and its Atlantic connections through the North and St George's Channels. His non-metropolitan focus helps us to understand the historical texture, vibrancy, energy, creativity and significance of that British life where Ulster, Scotland and Wales were not dismal backgrounds of cultured melancholy but could be said to be, as some residents of Belfast's Shankill Road would still say, at the 'heart of the British Empire' – though perhaps that epithet should be given to Govan (Devine 2011). Not only did their ships, ropes, engines and coal help pump the commercial lifeblood of that empire but also their intellectual influences contributed as much to the character of the country as did the playing fields of Eton. This, of course, is a world that has now passed, an industrial-commercial complex the character of which has been changed and changed utterly, just as its religious controversies and theological disputes have been lost to modern culture. For Harvie, 'a sense of "world" is required for the distinct 'parallel worlds of politics, business and culture' to work. That the 'world' of this littoral floating commonwealth has diminished along with the collapse of faith in the providential British story suggests that these two worlds, the material and the spiritual, were indeed intimately linked in the notion of providence. There has been an attempt to recapture the spiritual element of this story (see Bradley 2007) but the decline of popular religious observance, the modern religious diversity of the UK and, not least, the association of religion with illiberal attitudes and sometimes with 'fundamentalism' make it virtually impossible. Believing in Britain, in short, has lost that vital providential force and neither public discourse nor popular culture can take it seriously. It does not light the way and no longer (so openly) warms the heart. Sustaining the UK today clearly requires argument of a different order. If there is a kernel of truth in the providential inheritance it could possibly be expressed in this way. In reviewing Anselm of Canterbury's celebrated motto *credo ut intelligam*, Karen Armstrong (2010: 131) translated it to mean: 'I involve myself in order that I may understand.' Having faith in the UK would now mean two things: feeling oneself involved with its fate in order to understand it and with that understanding, believing it is important to sustain it. Where providence still plays a role is the often banal and inarticulate assumption that it will survive, naturally and inevitably, an assumption which could now be a fatal error, for it is that very involvement and understanding, naturalness and durability which are contested today. And the other side of that banal assumption is the truth that sometimes things often fall apart and for no reason at all (Torrance 2011a).

The character of the UK

Intellectual involvement with its fate produced valuable understandings of the character of the UK polity. Perhaps the classic example can be found in the work of Sir Ernest Barker who as an 'establishment' intellectual (Stapleton 2001: 3) articulated, in what may be called the dialectic of tradition, an enlightened but also heart-warming vision. The British nation according to Barker (1942: 10) was 'an amalgam of the different species and stocks which have wandered into our island' and there appeared 'always a mixture from whatever angle you look', a view which calls to mind Oakeshott's comment that politics is about attending to the arrangements of 'a set of people whom chance or choice have brought together' (1991: 44). Almost in the language of contemporary literary postmodernism (and postcolonialism) Barker noted, following Samuel Butler, that in the UK one was always 'crossing' and 'bridging'. His description was of the UK as a 'union state' long before that term became popular with academics and he believed there was no certainty that the existing union would retain its integrity. Writing at one of the lowest points in British fortunes during the Second World War, even the generally optimistic Barker admitted that it was 'a question of the future whether the contained nationalities will aspire to any system of autonomy or Home Rule' (1942: 14). In short, he acknowledged that the future was uncertain, a view which should be compared with the fashionable assumption today that the Second World War represented some high point of British unity from which there has been only inexorable decline (for example, see Weight 2002). As Richard Rose described it later (1982a), the UK is a 'Crown of indefinite domain' and that domain, as the secession of Irish Free State in 1922 had demonstrated, was of contingent extent. The qualification of such historical and compositional contingency was Barker's assumption that, for all their distinctions, the nations of this multinational Union complemented each other and shared a flow of sympathy. Here was a dual benefit strategy. On the one hand, it was through political representation at Westminster that the common interest of the 'contained nationalities' was properly secured. On the other hand, it was through the accommodation of diverse and distinctive institutions, practices and cultures that national identities were sustained. This is what Barker called the British 'mixture of unity and diversity', one which he thought was bound to baffle and puzzle the inquirer and one which Keith Robbins (1989) was later to describe as a 'blending'. In this perspective, each individual nation contributed to collective strength and each nation got more 'by being included in the wider scope of the United Kingdom' than by being separate (Barker 1942: 14). Moreover, Barker was certain that the great danger which faced the Scots and the Welsh was that the nationalist path 'might segregate them in isolation, of autonomy and Home Rule'. Two points may be made about this observation.

Firstly, this was not a very positive recommendation of Northern Ireland's devolved status at that time, implying that it was already segregated and in isolation. Like many old Gladstonians, Barker's sympathy with Ulster unionism was limited to say the least. Of course, the intent of Ulster unionist politics under devolution had been to mitigate the worst effects of its isolation and to operate a self-denying ordinance on its autonomy. This was done symbolically at the British Empire Exhibition at Wembley in 1924 when the Ulster Pavilion was deliberately situated adjacent to that of 'Great Britain'. As the *Belfast Telegraph* confirmed at the time, this had been 'chosen to preserve the idea that Ulster, although enjoying political autonomy, is still an integral part of the United Kingdom' (cited in Loughlin 2007: 192). Ironically, whereas for most of recent history Northern Ireland was always taken to be the exception to the British rule (which by turns gratified and horrified Ulster unionists) today it *is* the rule (which may horrify everyone else) insofar as maintaining the UK requires the reconciliation of degrees of devolved autonomy with British integrity. Secondly, the bias in Barker's reflection is an Anglo-centric one since the measure of isolation and autonomy for Scotland, Wales and Northern Ireland was defined by the distance from and relationship with England or even London. Autonomy was tantamount to being cut adrift from the source of *English* energy and progress, perhaps lost to providence. Fortunately for everyone, Barker thought that nationalism in Scotland and Wales continued to be arrested as yet at the 'stage of a vague and academic ideal' which did not represent the 'general feeling' of either country and he was convinced that it was better if things stayed that way. As an external examiner at the University of Edinburgh in 1933, he wrote that (Stapleton 2006: 214): 'All the young Honours candidates...cry up the Union, and pour scorn in their answers on Scottish nationalism. That seems to be the correct attitude', a comment ironically reminiscent of Edward Cooke who, as Under-Secretary for the Civil Department in Dublin Castle in October 1798, had argued that the proposed Irish union would have to be 'written-up, spoken-up, intrigued up, drunk-up, sung-up and bribed up' (cited in Connolly 2000: 399). And that remained true for most of the twentieth century. As Roy Hattersley (2006) recalled: '50 years ago, when I first went to Edinburgh, Scottish nationalism was an old lady giving away leaflets in Princes Street on a Saturday night'. It is certainly not true today.

If Barker's was a heart-warming description of the multinational *fact* of the UK how did he explain that fact? What indeed was to be said of a nation that was not a state and a state that was not a nation (Barker 1927: 16)? Barker had defined the character of the UK by way of a critique of the old Austro-Hungarian empire, admitting (1927: 131) that the 'multiplicity of our system (if it can be called a system) may remind us of the multiplicity of the old Austria-Hungary'. He thought that that there was one fundamental difference. 'Austria-Hungary had no common national fund which could contain, without abolishing, the separate national funds of the Austrians, the Czechs, the Poles, the Magyars, and the Southern Slavs.' In the British case (17), however, the Union combines 'separate national funds with a common national substance' and no line had been artificially drawn between the 'social fact' of nationality and the 'political scheme' of the state. A dynastic state like Austria-Hungary could only unite under the single will of the monarch a number of nations that are required to remain as mere social groups. This was no longer possible in British politics because a *democratic* state 'which is multinational will fall asunder into as many democracies as there are nationalities, dissolved by the very fact of will which should be the basis of its life – unless, indeed, as we have somehow managed in our island, such a State can be both multinational and a single nation'. Here the difference between the British and Austrian experience may be explained partly by that old legend – that Britain had only one Ireland while Austria-Hungary had nothing but Irelands. The Irish contrast may be taken as a concrete historical illustration of the obligations which Barker (however reluctantly in the Ulster case) believed characteristic of this multinational polity. In an insightful examination of the distinction between Habsburg dynastic politics and British parliamentary politics, Dominic Lieven (1999: 188–9) argued: 'Not "Austria" but Franz Joseph negotiated the 1867 settlement with Hungary, which helps to explain how the large German community in Hungary could be abandoned to Magyar rule with no qualms or difficulty, in sharp distinction to Westminster's agonies over the Protestant community when Irish autonomy came onto the agenda.' In other words, there was a 'flow of sympathy' which could not be ignored because it had constitutional voice at Westminster and popular recognition in the press. The difference between British history and the history of Austria-Hungary seemed clear – the UK was characterised not by resistance to change but by the accommodation of change (Sked 1989: 264–9). Recently in the British academy there has been a more sympathetic consideration of the Austria-Hungary model. John Gray (2009: 115), for example, challenged a tradition of British prejudice by calling the UK 'a mini version of the Hapsburg Empire' but his conclusion has a familiar ring to it. Being British 'does not demand that one surrenders one's past or beliefs, only that one accepts the shared practice of peaceful coexistence'. To try to make Britishness into an ideology is absurd because it is a description (120) of 'a way of life in which people with different views of things have learnt to rub along'. That is a more attenuated description than we find in Barker, of course, and whether it is adequate as a heart-warming or even enlightening narrative today is moot, even though Gray's remains a traditionally English way of discussing the subject of national identity.

This notion of the UK as both multinational and a single nation was a subtle one which worked in a fit of absence of mind – so absentmindedly that most people had difficulty describing it properly. That Barker's description of it is distinctly Anglo-centric does not necessarily mean that this was how everyone thought of it or even how it was. Something of that larger spirit can be found in the reflections of George Santayana. Though he appreciated the social qualities he found in England, Santayana (1922: 4) never had 'the least desire or tendency' to become English. Nationality was one of those things like religion and love that were 'too radically intertwined with our moral essence to be changed honourably, and too accidental to the free mind to be worth changing'. Though an Englishman like Porter (2004: xiv) could admit – and not entirely tongue-in-cheek – that like 'many English people, I wish I was Irish', self-respecting Scots, Irish and Welsh would never wish openly to be English, which is not to say that there are not English qualities they admire. What may be called the 'Santayana factor' conveys the ambiguity of relationships in the UK because it captures the significance of national identity as well as its banality in most of the situations of British life, especially for the English. One contemporary critic of this enduring Anglo-centricity (Brown 2005: 197) observed that this British identity was never subsidiary. 'When, each year on Trafalgar Day, Nelson's monument on the Carlton Hill in Edinburgh is dressed with his signal to the fleet as it engaged with the enemy, this is not a result of English predominance.' Or as Kidd succinctly put it (2008: 6–8): 'unionism's grammar of assent did not preclude criticism of England'. Moreover, in Scotland as elsewhere in the UK unionism was compatible with depths of cultural nationalism and in its diverse expressions is a reminder 'that Scots unionists often defined Britain and the Union with a Scots inflection which was incomprehensible or even offensive to English ears'. Equally, it has been argued in the Irish case (Southern 2007: 100) that 'British' is mediated by Ulster experience without either diminishing its meaning or exaggerating its significance. Ulster unionists 'feel that Britishness is something which they have a right to define. They do not conceive of themselves as being helplessly dependent upon the definitions of others', especially of the English. The Welsh legitimately have a grievance about being (at least partially) defined by the English insofar it appeared as a mere appendage in the designation 'England *and* Wales'. Yet Welsh patriotism too was perfectly compatible with a strong British allegiance much to the amazement but also fascination of Gwyn Williams (1991: 141–2). And this interpretation complements a major historical review of British identity (Brockliss and Eastwood 1997) which stressed the cultural diversity of its expression along with the integrative role of common parliamentary representation.

If this should all appear a little fuzzy, a recent study (Brown 2007: 17–18) has argued convincingly that diverse ideas of national identity do not necessarily mean incoherence and division. Rather, 'it is precisely such intertwining of the different ideas of nationhood that promotes and sustains the cohesion of the nation'. That study identified three visions of national identity which are frequently interwoven in the symbolic and political life of a state and in the minds of its citizens: 'the civic vision of ethnically blind citizenship, the ethnocultural vision of assimilation into an ethnic core, and the multicultural vision of the just accommodation of ethnic diversity'. Brown's conclusion is one which corresponds neatly with the thesis of this chapter – that multinational states are cohesive enough insofar as the distinctions between visions 'remain fudged and out of the limelight of public political discourse'. The banal unionism of which Kidd wrote operated at that level of fudge and semi obscurity, especially in England. It allowed the Scots, the Welsh and the Irish to read into the UK their own sense of ownership irrespective of what the English might think, confirming that having 'an elaborated, multi-layered identity is not the same thing as not having one at all' (Cohen 2000: 582). It is that older British fudge which devolution has disturbed and nationhood is no longer out of the limelight but very much in the spotlight. Once notions of national identity become disentwined and compete for attention then the potential for division arises as it has done periodically in British history and does so today. The stage becomes set for 'the noisy, the quarrelsome, the disputatious, the thrusters, the monopolists and the informers who carry books in their pockets and half-remembered quotations in their heads' (Oakeshott 2004: 187), all nationalist disturbers of an ideal British peace.

Nevertheless, the virtues of the old order continue to find new leases of life. Though Gordon Brown (1992) had once claimed that constitutional change would signal 'a decisive shift in the balance of power in Britain, a long overdue transfer of sovereignty from those who are governed, from an ancient and indefensible Crown sovereignty to a modern popular sovereignty', this radical concession to popular sovereignty was qualified by a vision of the UK as 'a community of citizens with common needs, mutual interests, shared objectives, related goals and most of all linked destinies'. One truth – the light of progressive reform based on popular sovereignty (which potentially raised disturbing questions about *which* people and *whose* sovereignty) – would be combined with another – the heart-warming and enduring solidarity of the British constitutional people. In this regard, faith in devolution had conservative intent even if it was sometimes wrapped up in a radical-sounding form. This was a view some had of the historical narrative of Colley's *Britons* which helped shape New Labour thinking on the British question. Colley's book, it was argued (Harvie 2006: 441), seemed 'more attuned to the 1990s than to 1680–1837', its historical research delivering the 'comforting thesis' that 'devolution within a revamped constitution' was a heart-warming substitute for the sort Britain which *Britons* otherwise declared had now passed away. By the time of changing political conditions in the late 1990s, Vernon Bogdanor (1996: 196–7) could write that though the principle of parliamentary sovereignty – Westminster as the supreme legal authority in the UK – implied a uniform and homogeneous state, 'we have, fortunately, rarely taken our ideological presuppositions to their logical conclusion'. He felt that this tradition was a factor of British national self-confidence, a claim that would probably not be made with such conviction today (by academics at least). 'So it is that the United Kingdom has been able to accommodate a considerable diversity of relationships' throughout the twentieth century, relationships 'which have proved perfectly compatible with the unity of the state'. After 1997, the New Labour government's exercise in Britishness was also informed by that tradition, concerned as it was with multinational cohesion, where the objective was to make of Britishness 'a good house to accommodate various identities of minorities as well as majorities' (Kim 2005: 75). The early theme of 'Cool Britannia' was most clearly expressed in *Britain TM* (Leonard 1997: 72) which tried to galvanise 'excitement around Britain's core values – as a democratic and free society in an interconnected world – and finding a better way of linking pride in the past with confidence in the future'. This exercise in providing a new narrative – expressed as 'rebranding' – was treated with widespread scepticism, not least because of its very metropolitan and Anglo-centric perspective, the very thing that was increasingly identified as being part of the problem. Adapting to new devolutionary circumstances the older trope of Barker's, a more intelligent and sympathetic version defined the purpose of the British debate to be about not assimilation to a 'mono-culture' but about the development of 'a stronger sense of why we live in a common place and have a shared future' (Kelly and Byrne 2007: 11). And in the final years of the Brown government heart-warming language still dominated in an intelligent collection of essays seeking the values which bound the nation. The editor, Matthew d'Ancona (2009: 20–3) claimed that the 'debate on twenty-first-century Britishness should be, first and foremost, a celebration, rather than a defensive operation'. This was because the confidence to adapt to new historic settings was thought to be one of the defining characteristics of the British personality. Indeed, and almost directly repeating Barker's view, d'Ancona stressed his 'long-standing belief that Britain's cultural diversity is a national strength and true to a long history of porousness and heterogeneity'. Moreover, this Barker-esque 'belief' was also acknowledged by one of the most perceptive modern thinkers on 'being British' (Parekh 2008a). Here the multi-cultural character of modern Britain seemed to complement the older one of multinationalism. Or at least – since this was an ideal as much as a practice – the virtues of the one could be employed ideologically to sustain the other.

Whigs alive

If providence associated faith with purposive history, its narrative of the ever onwards and upwards of liberal progress conveniently put British experience at the centre of world history. Reviewing that historical presumption, David Cannadine (1987: 174) thought there was once good reason for this Whiggish belief that 'Britain's past always seemed to be anticipating the future'. The key proposition here was the distinction between change and revolution, a distinction sharpened by hindsight. Reform was essential for continuity because it moderated change and controlled its tempo. 'That was the prudent, even the conservative view. But liberals and radicals too came to see how lucky they had been to adopt legislative rather than revolutionary methods' (Watson 1973: 43). Barker (1927: 157) had also called this the 'habit of compromise which the process of our history has infused into our political temper' and he believed that when there was failure to adapt there was also no prospect of success. This was a very powerful myth which invested faith in the institutions of the UK and in the tactically astute wisdom of the country's political elite. It was also adept at drawing a veil of oblivion over the historical incompetence of government whose connection with providence seemed very tenuous indeed. Except the veil has a habit of falling off, compelling periodic recourse to humble re-statements of faith and re-commitment, as David Cameron professed (Winnett 2011), to institutions that are beyond reproach, in which the powerful serve the people not themselves and which sustain 'a country – and a people – which has our confidence back'.

It is tempting to assume that the Whiggish narrative no longer resonates and that the rhetoric is unpersuasive. In one sense that is self-evident since contemporary intellectual discourse can no longer accept co-operation with providence. The country, according to G. R. Elton (1991: 115), used to be ruled by two anchor-points of moderate certainty in a dangerous world. 'These instruments were religion (reassurance in the hereafter) and law (reassurance down here).' Both of these anchor-points have lost their grip and the story itself no longer has the claim it once had upon the popular imagination. The Whigs, Elton thought, 'have had their day' along with their serviceable myth of the beneficent evolution of British political institutions. Much of this is true, especially for the professional historian, but a certain caution is required since British history is not completely free from the ghosts of the Whig past (Stapleton 2008). Indeed, it was the contemporary commercialisation on television of the Whiggish 'recycling of the old stories of Anglo-Britain' that provoked the righteous anger of Harvie (2006). And if Whiggish myth lingers in professional history it certainly does in popular history. In his political testament *The Progressive Patriot* (2006), Billy Bragg attacked the Whig interpretation of history which he associated with the deluded or disingenuous 'traditionally correct brigade'. Lord Macauley's idea of history as one of physical, moral and intellectual improvement he dismissed only to celebrate its re-expression as a story charting the road to popular liberty from Magna Carta to the Welfare State. Bragg thought that his story of political improvement and historical progress did not rely on 'foreign philosophies or imported ideas' but was 'part of the core fabric of our nation', about which he was 'immensely proud'. By way of this narrative he found that he could identify with 'British values of fairness, tolerance and decency'. As Robin Cohen (2000: 579) observed, the characteristics upon which national self-regard are based (that the British are tolerant and freedom-loving, for example) are generally 'sociologically illiterate' (scientifically unenlightened) but they can also have practical effect (warm the heart to positive action) for 'what is real in the mind can be real in its consequences'. Which is to say: people are not always in the habit of distinguishing fact from imagination, or science from art, and are motivated politically when creative imagination interprets fact persuasively (as Chandler knew very well).

Whiggishness is still evident in a certain style of reflection on British institutions. Writing a few years before the constitutional reforms of the New Labour government, Rodney Barker (1996: 13) argued that although the history of the British constitution could be distinguished by more or less distinctive phases it 'has rarely been marked by sharp transitions of a kind which bring institutions sharply to the attention of those who are involved in or subordinate to them'. What this interpretation conveys is what in more traditional discourse would be called the 'genius' of British constitutionalism, for it suggests that change is a product of continuity and that continuity is the consequence of necessary change. Or, to put that slightly differently and in terms of the very

British tradition which it shares, revolutionary transformations indicate a failure to reform and radical discontinuity is the enemy of improvement. That there *is* a lineage of constitutional thought here can be traced once more to reflection on the hard case of Irish Home Rule, where sharp transitions were certainly in evidence and institutions were brought sharply into focus. Rooted in the conviction that the politics of the Irish Question were very *un*-British in their revolutionary posturing, the great Whig regret is that the failure of Home Rule meant the impossibility of preserving the whole of Ireland within the UK, the source of all subsequent rancour and bloodshed. That liberal opinion should harbour resentment towards Ulster unionism for the great sin of being unaccommodating is understandable if only because it illustrated the limits of liberal constitutionalism and its own ideological assumptions. This is constitutional practice as faith, where policy science meets political art and becomes British pragmatism. In this light, then, devolution can be understood as the modification of the UK better to reflect changing political circumstances. This too warms the heart of traditional political self-regard, confirming the accommodative genius of muddling through (inevitably, naturally and perhaps providentially?) to stability. Adjustment not resistance and accommodation not confrontation represent the wisdom of British constitutionalism and this can be read as a historical vocation.

A representative exposition of this wisdom can be found in Elizabeth Wicks's *The Evolution of a Constitution: Eight Key Moments in British Constitutional History* (2006). For Wicks, the constitution has evolved in both substance and form through eight key constitutional moments from the Bill of Rights in 1688 to the devolutionary changes of 1998. Each of these key moments, she believes in good Whiggish fashion, elucidates (198) 'the general movement towards democratisation of the constitution', the consequences of which – for the territorial politics of the UK – has involved two tendencies which affect its *substance*. The first tendency is 'towards decentralisation as a means of achieving greater democratic legitimacy within the component parts of the union state'. The second is the development and entrenchment 'of a right to self-determination within the UK constitution' which can be seen as 'a modern reconciliation of the need to pay regard to the wishes of the people (as a group as well as individually)'. The Whiggish flavour of the complementary character of these two tendencies is even more pronounced in Wick's reflection on the corresponding *form* of the constitution. Here, she notes, the constitution 'bends but does not break when encountering a radical event'. Therefore 'it is flexible enough to evolve in line with the changing priorities of society without endangering the core principles' and those principles are familiar: democracy, individual liberties, limited government and the union state. 'This view of the constitution means that, although it is an evolving constitution, sufficiently flexible to incorporate, and elevate to core status, new principles, laws and practices, it is not without strength and standards.' In sum, any change to the constitution which would violate its core principles would fail and the constitutional would be broken. The result would be revolution and, according to Wicks, 'we have seen only constitutional evolution not constitutional revolution' because the constraints of British political practice have fostered a valuable rule of thumb: 'prevention is always better than cure' (200). For Wicks, then, devolution is an evolutionary move which prevents disintegration and one which secures the core values of the British system.

She is aware (167) of the significance of what devolution calls into question, namely 'the very nature of the United Kingdom, a state founded by unions between England and the now devolved territories and nations'. This new condition of the multinational union is described with reasonable optimism, expecting that devolution would disturb neither the constitution's ability to adapt nor the citizen's, especially the English citizen's, capacity to accommodate. In other words, devolution represents another evolutionary and necessary shift from the bureaucratic arena (former Scottish, Welsh and Northern Ireland Offices) to the democratic arena (Parliament and assemblies). What is at issue here is the recognition of popular sovereignty in a constitution formerly and exclusively conceived in terms of parliamentary sovereignty. Popular sovereignty is attenuated in the case of Wales though not entirely absent because 'devolution has involved a process of demarking Wales from the UK and from England' (Trench 2006: 120). It is expressed in terms of 'consent' in Northern Ireland but in a uniquely international agreement (see Aughey 2005). But it is most self-conscious in Scotland where the idea of popular sovereignty has a historical lineage. Wicks accepted that there is a distinction between the legal and the political conceptions of sovereignty such that, while the Scotland Act 1998 retains the principle of parliamentary sovereignty, there is a sense of unreality about Westminster's legislative supremacy when confronted with Scottish popular expectations (Bechhofer and McCrone 2007). Though this is a profound contradiction in theory it is compatible with creative British practice where the political can be reconciled with the legal in the manner of traditional pragmatism. In sum, the challenge of devolution is one 'that the evolving constitution is well suited to meet, given centuries of development in response to the needs of contemporary society' (Wicks 2006: 201). Such faith in the capacity for adjustment is neither unusual nor unrepresentative in British public life even if the suspicion is that it is as much heart warming as enlightening.

In sum, devolution was another example of evolution because (193) the 'fundamentals of the constitutional structure remain, but are modified to incorporate new principles and constitutional ideas'. There is complexity, asymmetry and untidiness, certainly, but complexity and untidiness indicate the flexibility of British constitutionalism. The retention of parliamentary sovereignty at Westminster (continuity) but within a reformed set of territorial relations (change) requires (194) 'a subtle evolution of its place and priority within a constitution with competing and potentially conflicting principles'. As one eminent legal authority observed, here is an example of that very British way of thinking about the constitution in which authoritative judgement apparently emerges through an account of evolving customs (Fried 2004: 724). If this seems a little too academic, consider Sir Malcolm Rifkind's assessment. Each generation, he argued (1998), likes to believe that it has a unique solution to its problems. However, it was ironic that devolution was not an outworking of a novel thesis but could be traced to ideas pre-dating even Gladstone. The Union of the Crowns in 1603 provided 104 years where 'Scotland had its own Parliament but ultimate power remained with a Government in London'. For territorial politics after 1997, 'the future is not what it used to be' but the 'whole history of the British constitution has been of a gradual evolution of Constitutional change to meet new requirements'. Like Wicks, Rifkind believed that devolution 'is simply a further stage in that evolution and while it may be difficult for the constitutional theorist to categorise it, the crucial question will be whether it works'. On balance, he thought it would because devolution merely formalised a new democratic association which had been implicit all along. Here was an echo of that old providential faith in the evolutionary capacity of British politics.

In his brilliant survey of the recent history of British constitutional politics, Vernon Bogdanor (2004: 733) remarked (in Chandler style) that facts do not always destroy myths and that there is a popular mentality which takes relatively brief historical periods to constitute the norm or truth from which everything else is a deviation. This way of thinking was not entirely misconceived for it was based partly on fact and experience but it frequently sacrificed insight into the course of current events by cleaving to heart-warming legends. This was especially true, he thought, of the 'view as to how the British constitution works and how it ought to work'. There are those like Marquand (2009: 16) who would argue that such received wisdom about the UK merely distorts reality, preventing people coming to terms with the state they are in.

However, as this chapter has tried to show things are not so simple if only because in the course of disposing of myth we tend to recreate it. The conclusion is that it is not the idea of being bound up with the fate of the country, of belonging together, of being 'differently' British, of constitutional adaptation and political pragmatism which are distorting but ideas of exceptional genius, special favour and historical providence. That the former can be retained without the latter is the subject of Chapter 3. The next chapter considers the nationalist challenge to these ancient pieties of British political history.

2

Endism

The British past as it was outlined in the previous chapter stressed historical continuity, institutional adaptation, progressive achievement of a more inclusive culture of democracy, with providentialism lingering in the inheritance of pride in its distinctive character. Whenever critics challenged the recent iteration of British 'values' as being universal and not particular to the historical experience of the United Kingdom their objection was correct but also misconceived. As Lord Parekh answered in a powerful contribution to a House of Lords debate on Britishness (2008b), the objection involved a logical fallacy. 'These are uniquely British values because we fought for them, internalised them and we also define and relate them differently from the way other countries define and relate them.' And this interpretation confirms Clark's point that relating these contemporary values to the past is not (mainly) about historical truth but about delineating the sort of society worthy of one's patriotism. Speaking in the same debate as Parekh, the Bishop of Norwich (2008) cited the philosopher Alasdair MacIntyre's proposition that answers to questions about what one is to do presuppose answers to questions about what sort of story one finds oneself a part. And the story of the modern UK, as one historian (Cullen 2000: 240) wrote of the Irish Union, is always being 'written from the future into the past'. The sort of history described in Chapter 1 assumes that the future will exhibit great continuities with the past because of the inevitability of benign reform and this is conservative only in wishing to preserve the UK. There is another sort of history which writes a very different and radical story from the future into the past. In Pocock's words (2009: 208), the radical, like the conservative, 'reconstructs the past in order to authorize the future' but unlike the conservative 'historicizes the present in order to deprive it of authority'. This alternative story attempts to delineate a society worthy of patriotic attachment, but one in which the future will show little continuity with the past. It also exhibits the Chandleresque combination of truths which light the way and truths which warm the heart, where scholarly interpretation engages with explicit or implicit wished-for outcomes.

In the late 1950s and early 1960s the debate about 'the state of the nation' was summed up in Michael Shanks's point (cited in Grant 2003: 29) that there needed to be a choice about 'What sort of island (sic) do we want to be?' The choice, Shanks believed, was between the cosy glow of imperial sunset with its attendant genteel poverty and a dynamic society given over to the pursuit of economic growth. This sort of thinking English and Kenny (2000: 279–80) later called 'declinism', an inversion of traditional Whiggism, where historically observable phenomena 'which can be neatly defined, measured and demonstrated' confirmed a 'traceable process whereby Britain diminished as a world power'. If the history of British decline had a basis in historical fact, 'declinism' – its ideological alter ego – was rather different. It revealed 'a series of mentalities which position their respective possessors in relation to modern British experience' and English and Kenny set out three broad and inter-related aspects of these mentalities. There was, first, a cultural critique, locating poor economic performance in an archaic, almost anti-modern, social structure. Second, there was a critique of entrepreneurial failure and industrial conservatism linked to an imperial and complacently providential heritage. Here the old story of the inevitability of British success was a fatal gift, one which induced inevitable failure. Third, there was an institutional critique of government and its misdirection of resources which highlighted continuing illusions of British power in the world. As English and Kenny (293) demonstrated, the ideological attraction of declinism had less to do with the precision of scholarly detail and more to do with visions of the sort of society Britain should become. They recommended that attention should be directed 'less at decline than at declinism: a state of mind relatively autonomous of the actual, historical decline of Britain as a world power'. Their final reflection, reminiscent of Butterfield's remark on Whiggism, was that though one might be sceptical about the ultimate value of its claims 'that should not rule out the possibility that influential figures and a wider public audience might continue to think within declinist parameters into the next century' (295).

One tendency in contemporary literature about the fate of the UK shares much common ground with the older literature on decline, in particular an 'obsession with Britain as a kind of museum piece of insular decay' (Morgan 1990: 199; see also Hewison 1987), an obsession which also reveals a similar relationship between fact and ideology. Like 'declinism' this sort of discourse expresses – unsurprisingly – a normative and judgemental perspective and its effect relies on the persuasiveness of its affect (Tomlinson 2009: 249). The term given here to this ideology is 'endism'. It has persuasive force because it reflects real historical trends and traces a changing political context, especially the loss of popular belief in a providential role for the UK along with its diminished place in the world. And it conforms to a style of thinking which assumes that 'modification must mean liquidation' (Pocock 2000a: 46). The 'endism' considered here is a radical reconstruction of the past in order to authorise a different future, one which historicises the UK's present in order to deprive it of continuing authority.

This endist discourse may be traced specifically to that inventive and influential melodist of the UK's break-up, Tom Nairn. The purpose of Nairn's seminal *The Break-up of Britain*, first published in 1977, was not only to describe but also to hasten the end and it proved to be an endist *tour de force*. *The Break-up of Britain* has influenced a whole generation of reflection on the politics of identity and it could be said that Nairn not only anticipated but also helped to establish the link between declinism and endism. He transferred analysis of British economic 'backwardness' in the early 1960s (developed with Perry Anderson in the *New Left Review*) to British constitutional 'backwardness', charting the 'transition from the management of decline into the management of disintegration, leading eventually to a suitable testament and funeral arrangements' (2000: 58). Nairn's political agenda corresponds to a widespread belief in a historical trajectory towards the end of the UK as a consequence of 'devolution, the disappearance of Empire, the problems of the monarchy, the death of Protestantism as a signifier of Britishness, a distrust of parliamentary democracy' or whatever other measures of political change happen to capture the historian's attention (Kineally 2004: 217). This reverses neatly Edward Cooke's recommendation that the Union be 'written-up, spoken-up, intrigued up, drunk-up, sung-up and bribed up'. One could be forgiven for thinking that, in recent times, the UK has been written-down, spoken-down, intrigued down, drunk-down, sung-down if perhaps not yet bribed down. Or as one critic summarised the trend in this radical re-working (Sturm 2003), the old British story has 'passed from being one of the soundest properties on the international ideas market (liberal, trustworthy, decent, first among equals, "Mother-of" this-and-that, Progressive, haven, etc.) to being a down-market left-over'. A millennial subtext of all this could be found in the title of an introductory commentary in the *Political Quarterly* (Wright and Gamble 2000: 1): 'The end of Britain' where it was argued that the 'twentieth century ends, and the twenty-first begins, with the idea of Britain in big trouble'. There are a number of elements to this trope of endism which replicate declinist thinking. The first identifies the dissolution of the UK with the undoing of colonialism and the programme of constitutional reform dedicated to removing what remains of the archaic, anti-modern, UK political structure. The second retails a mood of frustrated national possibility in large part the result of self-imposed cultural and political limits infected by residual imperial thinking. The third not only links this colonial experience and national frustration to a critique of the enduring illusions of British world power, sustained by the vanity and self-interest of the elites in Westminster and Whitehall, but also outlines the alternative which a new *Zeitgeist* brings.

Internal colonialism

In a masterly survey of the recent role of imperial discourse in framing how British politics has been interpreted, Stephen Howe observed that the history of empire was frequently the measure of all the country's ills. From the nineteenth century when Liberals worried about its corrupting influence on both the ancient and prospective liberties of domestic society, to the twentieth century when Old Labour feared that it would distract from social and economic transformation, arguments about empire were not so much about the facts of history as they were about the question, as Clark (1990) thought, to what sort of country could people be legitimately patriotic? This has remained the case into the twenty-first century even though empire has long gone. For Howe (2003: 296) 'the languages of decolonization increasingly pervaded British domestic debate through the 1980s and beyond, from argument over the futures of Scotland, Wales and Northern Ireland, through a dramatically renewed and often febrile attention to the nature of English and/or British patriotism and the future of national identity, to analyses of Britain's economic performance, governing institutions, and constitutional future'. Mostly, this engagement led to imaginative and intelligent contributions to the debate about the character of British politics but at one extreme, the anti-colonial paradigm disposed some on the left to dally with Provisional Irish republicanism, as if the campaign of the IRA was some ultimate measure of the reactionary nature of the imperialistic British state. If Northern Ireland's experience can be said to have proved anything, it proved the insufficiency of the anti-colonial paradigm in UK politics.

One of the most influential books in this tradition was Michael Hechter's *Internal Colonialism: The Celtic Fringe in British National Development* first published in 1975 and a text which, by trying to provide an economic explanation for nationalism, helped to link together the concerns of declinism and endism. Hechter (1999: 350) thought that internal colonialism could be 'the *modal* form of national development in industrial societies' and he proposed that the UK had never been a benignly accommodative 'floating commonwealth' but a state of uneven, exploitative, economic development favouring the English core against the Celtic periphery of Scotland, Wales and Ireland. Hechter acknowledged (1983: 32) that as 'one of the few attempts to offer a positive theory of nationalism', his book tended to be dismissed by historians, by Celtic specialists and by 'anti-nationalists' (quite a damning constituency, one supposes). And one can add to that list most political scientists. For example, though A. H. Birch (1976: 232) acknowledged that *Internal Colonialism* was 'a distinguished contribution to historical and political sociology' and though he accepted that the book contained much to illuminate 'the way in which the United Kingdom was established as a centralized state', he was sceptical of both the thesis and its pretensions ('Hechter is interested in the British Isles only as a case study to verify a model of national development'). Equally, Ed Page (1978: 301–3) pointed out the theoretical flimsiness of the concept and thought that the presentation of the data – the book's real claim to novelty – made 'what Hechter *sets out to prove* into one of the *assumptions* of his whole analysis'. Hechter's general theory of the development and maintenance of ethnic boundaries – one which favoured the core region of England – was also challenged (Orridge 1981) and a detailed analysis of its relevance to Wales concluded that his thesis was extremely loose theoretically, flimsy historically and that the empirical predictions it generated did not accord with contemporary reality (Lovering 1978: 65). The simple designation of British history as 'England versus the rest' (Page 1978: 305) struck most scholars as being excessively crude. Indeed, Howe (2003: 298) wrote that the story of colonialism, when used to explain transformations in British life, may be interesting but that did not make it true. 'Life would be more interesting if there were plesiosaurs in Loch Ness than if there were none; but that is not a good reason for believing in aquatic monsters if there really aren't any.' And because it appeared to explain everything the suspicion was that it explained very little.

Certainly, the internal colonial model never fitted well with Scottish history and, by taking the line of *most* resistance to Englishness, Hechter conveyed a simplistic interpretation of Scottish experience (see Devine 2011). 'Scottish political argument', it has been argued convincingly, 'has long been conducted in the vast yet variegated terrain which constitutes the middle ground between the extremes of anglicising unionism and Anglophobic nationalism' (Kidd 2008: 300). Indeed, Kidd's sparkling revision of the imperialist story concluded that unionism in Scotland – and the argument can be extended to unionism in Wales and certainly to Northern Ireland – emerged as a type of 'anti-imperialism' designed to act as a counterweight to forms of Anglo-centricity. It was a 'community of fate', not hostile to England (141; see also Kidd 2003: 889) but demanding what, after 2010, would be known as the *respect* agenda. As the historian of Ulster attitudes put it (Stewart 1986), there was nothing more annoying to unionists than the assumption that the UK existed only for the convenience of England and the English. That remains the case (in Scotland and Wales too) and if English respect often appeared to be absent that did not mean the relationship was colonial. Intelligent commentators have been either reluctant to subscribe to an internal colonial model or have rejected it entirely (Howe 2003: 300).

Of course, this does not mean that the notion of internal colonialism has no effect for it contributes implicitly and sometimes explicitly to a nationalist culture of dissent against the venerable British story recounted in Chapter 1. Its pretension to light the way may have been abandoned but it lingers as part of the heart-warming truth of nationalist faith in which the position of popular victimhood is secured. According to Hechter (1999: xiv), the argument 'holds that lack of sovereignty characteristic of internal colonies fostered a dependent kind of development which limited their economic welfare and threatened their cultural integrity' but the question which Hechter really asked was one which nationalists still ask: why wasn't nationalism more assertive in British history if the value of sovereignty is so self-evident to the model of internal colonialism? This is a question, of course, which fits neatly into the nationalistic world view. It has been argued that 'Scotland has been important to English ideas of Britishness, but historically no two-way negotiation on this has been possible: any Scottish behaviour perceived to challenge existing arrangements, or even to take perceived advantage of them, is met with an outbreak of negative stereotyping intended to stress English solvency, responsibility, civility, temperance, balance, and generosity by highlighting Scots as possessed of the opposite characteristics' (Pittock 2009: 302). Whatever the substance, and there is some, the argument serves a double purpose, one other-determined and the other self-determined. The first asserts that the marginal influence of Ireland, Scotland and Wales has been the result of English domination under the guise of Britishness. The second asserts that this marginality continues because of the acceptance of English power in the UK. This view is common in literary studies and is widely shared by postcolonial theorists.

Thus Michael Gardiner's *The Cultural Roots of British Devolution* (2004a: xi) traces the movement towards Scottish self-government as the product of a long cultural process in which the old imperial form of Britishness decays, permitting new creative social energies to emerge, a sort of 'Cool Caledonia'. New Labour's domestic 'project' from Blair to Brown, with its ideas of multicultural diversity alongside devolution, merely confirmed the old sense of 'peripheral *national* cultures as *regional* variants on an invisible standard' of English/British culture. This has remained invariably Anglo-centric, imperialistically substituting the part (England, or even London) for the whole and that there is something to this argument, we noted when considering Barker in Chapter 1. Devolution is an intimation of necessary internal de-colonisation and Gardiner's is a sophisticated rendering of its purpose, adding in the required ideological conclusion that it is possible to imagine now that the British 'subject-self will have ceased to have currency'. The proposition is that Scotland has become already (beneath the remaining constraints of the UK system) the post-imperial, multi-cultural, progressive society which radicals have longed to fashion and it is assumed that Wales is embarked on the same journey. Now it is England, once first amongst British nations, which becomes the laggard of history. Indeed, Marquand (2008a) accused the English of being 'entirely reactive' to the 'wonderful growth of national feeling in Scotland and Wales'. There is no 'moral vision of what England and the English stand for' within 'an increasingly threadbare Britain', such that the construction of a progressive democratic culture must take its cue from the Scots and Welsh. The least said about Northern Ireland (an old liberal failing) the better. Gardiner is adamant (2004b: 265) that this development has nothing to do with the 'older, less nation-aware and often misleading "internal colonialism" model' only that the 'open-ended changes beginning to occur in the constitutional form of the British union represent the terminal phase of Anglophone colonialism'. In an interesting inversion of the old Scottish anxiety about English influence, Gardiner's perspective on the dissolution of the historically imperialist UK now puts Scotland at the centre and England at the periphery. Devolution is 'possibly the final instance' of the 'unmaking and remaking of Britishness' as a site of 'post-colonial emergence' and in this era of end time, Scotland's 'centrality to the creation of colonial knowledge' – its willing participation with England in British imperialism – allows the Scots to take the lead in its 'democratic unravelling' (280). And there is a temptation to see this as a sign of the times and that something significant is truly afoot when a former Conservative critic of nationalism (Fry 2010) can write that empire allowed Scotland to act as if it were a big nation with a sense of world mission. 'I doubt if, without all that, Scotland could ever have conceived the aspirations of at least a part of its own people today – that is, to take its place in the world once again as an independent nation with a special contribution to make.' Providence has moved on and settled in Edinburgh.

In Wales too, once almost appropriated entirely into the Anglophone world, the distinctiveness of Welsh 'community' (Wood 2009: 93) is now being complemented, so it is claimed, by a new sense of popular and inclusive sovereignty which together intimate a developing autonomy from the decaying British 'system' (Osmond 2009: 200). National multiplicity and diversity, in other words, have become subversive of the old totality. All this is very heart-warming for after all it suggests *Tiocfaidh ár lá* – our day not only will come but in a sense has come already. The meaning of British political association which was in origins elitist, imperialistic, other-defined, outward-directed and hierarchical is long gone and the intellectual requirement, according to Preston (2008: 722–3) is to 'deal with it'. Therefore 'it is difficult, indeed impossible, to envision its effective deployment to mobilise the population' and any attempt to promote 'an elite-sponsored atavistic official ideology will have little purchase'. In this post-colonial reading, the future of the UK is past, to be replaced by democratic nationalism. The colonial insinuation is also found today amongst English historians, one of whom has described England as the last 'stateless nation' (Weight 2002) and it serves to advance a particular conclusion: that dignity can only be attained by a radical restructuring of the UK (at least) or by independence (at best). There is essentialism in these arguments at odds with its supposed openness to complexity, as if the return to the nation is not only to understand the *fons et origo* of culture but also to know the 'end' of history, a benign secular theography. At its most complacent, it echoes the enlightened self-satisfaction of the old Whig story.

Thwartedness

In a penetrating review of the state of Scottish historiography, Richard Finlay (2001: 384–5) argued that representations of history – in Scotland in particular but also elsewhere in the UK – had become important arenas for current political conflict. Most of the former heart-warming stories of British history had given way to a disposition on the part of historians to explore the multinational character of British politics and to challenge older Anglo-centric perspectives. While illustrating the imaginative possibilities open to post-devolutionary historiography, Finlay identified one tendency. If the *political* nations in Scotland and

Wales have become visible once more in their respective democratic institutions then the loss of nationhood and absorption into the British state can now be presented as a 'mistake' of the past. History can become the search for explanations of that mistake (in the way that Hechter prescribed) and it would reverse the agenda which Pocock had earlier announced. That plea (Pocock 1975) for a new subject, sought to put Scottish, Welsh and Irish history together with England's in order to provide an inclusive British history. From that perspective devolution, insofar as it promotes consciousness of national and regional diversity, should encourage a richer style of historical research, acknowledging the inter-relationship between the peoples of these islands. However, the agenda which Finlay identified points to an alternative course, giving a distinctive twist to Gwyn Williams's mission to put the Welsh back into Welsh history (see Croll 2003: 324) but in this case not only putting the Welsh back in but also taking the Welsh back out of British history. 'The main line of justification for this approach is that with devolution, absorption into Britain has stopped and may even be reversed. Inevitably, political change in the present opens up opportunities for revisionism in the past' and there exists the possibility that Scottish and Welsh historians will 'declare historical UDI' (Finlay 2001: 386–7). Whether this would be enlightening or heart warming was moot.

For example, Page (1978: 319) criticised Hechter's assumption that nationalism was a universal and perennial truth, an example of what modern theorists would call primordialism (Smith 2001). If nationalism is always regarded as having existed but somehow diverted into a British channel, this avoids having to think seriously about why and how nationalism does become a serious political force. In this case, the nation is both 'in time' – formerly sovereign but its sovereignty will come to fulfilment again in the course of history – and also 'outside time' – it is the natural condition of humankind. Conor Cruise O'Brien (1988) once called this sort of thinking 'God Land', encouraging a history that reveals nationalism 'thwarted'. The term here is adapted from Neville Meaney's reflections on Australia (2003: 124–5) where he identified a trend amongst some historians to create a national story opposed to Britain and its supposed betrayals. 'The new teleological history, frequently given a radical slant, has seen Australia's past as a story of "thwarted" nationalism, a thwarting which was the result of British manipulation, Anglo-Australians' subversion and security dependence.' That sounds very familiar. It has informed a consistent lament against the fatal embrace of the Union, though now the expectation is that history is about to be un-thwarted, that today is the springtime of revived nationhood and this is particularly noticeable in Scotland.

Antonia Kearton (2005: 40) traced the use of history in the nationalist story to justify a wished-for, inclusive, self-determined, civic nation in which a continuous sense of the nation is combined with an idea of a constructed one, as modernists demand. 'Time is transcended: the uses of history lead to a continuous understanding of the nation beyond history.' An interesting example here is the work of Murray Pittock who, in *Scottish Nationality* (2001: 12), made positive reference to Hechter's thesis of internal colonialism and presents nationalism as the golden thread of the Scottish experience. In this history, the British thwarting of the nation's full flourishing is coming to an end and one of the reasons for this is that the old self-abasing caricatures of Scottish culture are giving way to new self-confident histories (145). And one assumes that Pittock's own work is a harbinger of this emancipation. He is honest enough (2008) to confront the question of why Scotland? – *the* question which, as Kearton has shown, is neglected by the heart-warming story of civic inclusiveness – and to risk the criticism of academics who are not persuaded by the perennial claims of either nation or nationalism. Pittock is too good a historian to deal exclusively in a heart-warming story of a nation once again and is careful to caution against an optimistic expectation that with only a leap and a bound Scotland will be free. His 'road to independence' is followed by a question mark. However, Pittock has sufficient faith in the potential to achieve it now that he advises – with, one assumes, an ironic poke at New Labour's Britishness – promoting Scotland as 'an independent brand' (178).

In sum, the pessimistic acknowledgement of thwartedness or the rage against it has been replaced by an expectation of national fulfilment. There remains ambiguity, nevertheless. On the one hand, there is a belief that history involves process and transition. Since devolution is (to use Ron Davies's celebrated expression) a process, not an event, it presupposes a transformative process in which the nation throws off political self-denial as the UK comes to an end, for movement is the key to constitutional transcendence. On the other hand, it is also tempting to think that things are much as they ought to be because they are already on their way to becoming what they ought to be. In the meantime the 'ought' (national independence) takes on the temporary shape of the 'is' (a devolutionary settlement) and practical achievement takes priority over the final objective (see Gallagher 2009a). The Scottish debate between independence and 'independence-lite', the Welsh debate about cultural and political autonomy and the Irish nationalist debate about devolution and unity all fit neatly. Of course, these are not entirely antagonistic perspectives. Nationalists in Scotland, Wales, Northern Ireland

and even England (for rather different but related reasons) are not without hope that the 'is' (working devolution) will deliver the 'ought' (the break-up of Britain). This is a very different mood from the 1980s. This mood was captured well in 1981 by Harvie in the pessimistic tone in the first edition of his popular history *No Gods and Precious Few Heroes* – and it was probably even truer of Wales than of the Scotland about which it was written. As Harvie admitted (2000a: vii–viii), the original version was informed by the pessimism of Lampedusa's Sicilian novel, *The Leopard*, provoking the self-defeating thought that although nationalists were generally correct about the failures of the UK, their diagnosis only implied gloom and doom about the potential for salvation. Things change but stay the same and the Scots (and the Welsh) did not have what it takes. Harvie's fatalism seemed to imply the political futility of all schemes for political improvement for history obliged one to believe in unavoidable defeat, a ready excuse for both political failure and for cultural indolence. Moreover, a diet of betrayal and humiliation, real or imaginary, confirmed a vision of history which was beyond one's influence. That was Harvie's summary of national purpose in 1981. But this is not all that can be said. There is another side to the fatalistic coin. Being able to survive in this (British) world has engendered the possibility of securing one's interests in hostile circumstances, making fate possibly bend to one's will and overcoming thwartedness. That is the sense of national opportunity which we find in Harvie's later editions.

In a review of Harvie's original edition and summing up the new nationalist mood, Fry (1998) thought that the spirit of the first edition was teleological, a sort of reverse Whiggism, in which the story was a melancholy record of national failure, with only 'the odd dim beam shining fitfully through this national night, but in the end only as a cruel delusion, showing no way out'. There was a 'perilous tendency' to suppose that while the Scots had a past, they might not have a future. For Wales too, the failure of the 1979 devolution referendum suggested that the country continued to 'indulge in the masochistic luxury of self-inflicted wounds' (Williams 1979: 33). But now it appeared that salvation has finally come and the history of 'continual disaster' would be 'redeemed at the last moment by Nationalism' (Fry 1998). Ironically, Fry (2007) has come to accept the same form of redemption which tells a similar story: the imposition of 'a regime of provincial subordination' (Scotland's devolved Parliament) can only invite a self-respecting nation 'to become its own moral arbiter. It means independence'. And Harvie (2005: 159) can provide not only a (newly) positive Whig explanation for this outcome but also a providential validation. 'Scotland is in a situation, however, where both national self-interest and the good of a stable world order – things that have combined fatefully in earlier epochs – have again coincided, in the shape of a revived balance of power and the promise of a renewed European autonomy.'

The story in Wales is certainly more measured, modest and cautious, though it also seems to be the case that since devolution 'the framing of Welsh public life, whether by politicians or by the media, has appeared like a non-stop journey to discover Welshness, discuss its character and develop its future' (Bradbury and Andrews 2010: 246). Nevertheless, some Welsh nationalists are confident enough to claim that once Wales takes its rightful place among the independent nations of the European Union, it can dispense with 'being tied in to the most centralised and unequal economy in Europe' (Lewis 2003). How this might come about is not directly addressed except with the suggestion that the non-stop journey has enthused a new generation of Welsh people with a distinctly national vocation. This would be the affirming story, according to Adam Price, of Wales's 'independence generation' (BBC News Wales 2009), a generation determined to be thwarted no longer. This is certainly heart-warming stuff and not without hope that it might light the way forward for nationalists.

Times change

Humphrey Lyttleton was once asked where he thought modern jazz was going. Lyttleton replied that if he knew where it was going it would be there already – a sufficiently witty remark from a master of that art. For those disposed to political modesty, the Lyttleton doctrine involves a profound scepticism about the claims of prediction. However, for those disposed to political self-confidence, the Lyttleton doctrine suggests a more radical interpretation – that some certainty is possible because the future is there 'already' in the complex goings on of the present. In this case the complex goings-on all involve endings where the *becoming* of separation already *is* taking place and perhaps best summed up in the words 'the strange death of Unionist Britain'. As Michael Keating (2010: 365) summarised the story, until the 1970s it was difficult to persuade British academics that there was much to say about territorial politics in the UK. A generation later, there was a whole genre of literature on the end of Britain, of Britishness or of the Union, with some willing to proclaim that the 'auld sang' of the UK had finally ended. As one historian (Robbins 2005: 1096) reflected on this new fashion, some writers 'appear to believe that "after Britain" is already with us or, if not, the break-up is advanced and will accelerate. The

"British moment", on such a reading, is already in the past. Such authors as feel the urge turn to writing elegies or, alternatively, liberation anthems'. Another historian (Mandler 2006: 282) detected how the 'steady drumbeat of commentary from journalists and politicians has summoned historians to consider the alleged "crisis" triggered by the "break-up of Britain", mostly to show how and why "Britishness" was so fragile'. This new fashion of attributing a terminal crisis to British politics failed to acknowledge the historian's motto of '*caveat* commonplace' if only because talk of crisis is frequently a way to avoid serious examination of what 'crisis' actually means (Marwick 2005: 808). To speak of politics being 'after Britain' is to advance not only a factual analysis but also to invite heart-warming emancipation from old identity-constraints. Its purpose is not only to light the way but also to keep the faith. To argue that we are 'after Britain' suggests that the fate of the UK has been decided already, if not yet at the polls, then at the bar of history. It assumes that history has an intelligible design, the pattern of which reveals the end unfolding. The response to the question 'where is the UK going?' can be given a reasonably confident response because it is there already. Once again Northern Ireland is no longer the exception but the rule because the supposed inevitability of Irish unity has been a staple of radical imagining for years. This endist expectation has almost become banal, illustrated by the interview with the novelist Ian McEwan in *The Independent*. McEwan remarked that the UK was always an artificial construction of three or four nations and that he was 'waiting for the Northern Irish to unite with the Irish Republic sooner or later and also Scotland could go its own way and become independent', a prospect which left him undisturbed (Popham and Portilho-Shrimpton 2008). This insouciant acceptance by some of the end of the UK is considered again in Chapter 9.

If 'banal unionism' once assumed that things were always thus, that the UK was somehow providential and eternal, this talk of endings provides a historically grounded and factually impressive alternative narrative. If the UK has a beginning then it will also have an end and, like the Owl of Minerva's spreading wings, it is likely that this truth is clearer because it is already dusk for the Union. Only now can one detect the process at work and the transition taking place. Here is a pattern which appears to make sense of events in the manner in which declinism appeared to explain British economic performance. As Paul Ward (2004) has correctly argued, this makes available a new grand narrative of British disintegration, telling a story of a Union already broken up in spirit and awaiting the fact which will inevitably follow. Endist speculation plots the historical trajectory of how and why 'the people of Britain stopped thinking of themselves as British and began to see themselves instead as Scots, Welsh and English' (Weight 2002: 1). Indeed, one of the purposes of Norman Davies's bestseller *The Isles: A History* (1999: 1053) was to put the existing body of knowledge on British history into a firm chronological and analytical setting in order to account for 'the rise and fall of Britishness'. He illustrated the historical contingency of the present UK, its necessarily ephemeral condition, by identifying fifteen preceding states which constituted the Isles over the centuries. What had come into existence only in 1922, the United Kingdom of Great Britain and Northern Ireland, was equally likely to pass away as did the old Union of 1801. Indeed, Davies thought that the end was nigh, the break-up 'imminent', even expressing doubt that the Union would last to 2007, the three-hundredth anniversary of the Anglo-Scottish Union. In his latest book, Davies (2011) suggests 2014.

In the first decade of the new millennium, the mood had become more insistent. McLean and McMillan's *State of the Union* (2006: 256) captured it well and argued that unionism 'always suffered from deep intellectual incoherence', an incoherence only 'masked by its usefulness to politicians and its popular appeal' and now that both had expired they asked: 'can the union state survive without unionism'? Their answer was that it could lumber on 'anomalies and all, for at least a few decades more' but that the writing was on the wall. Krishnan Kumar's wide-ranging and influential sociological history, *The Making of English National Identity* (2003: 239), observed that calls for English independence no longer appeared as outlandish as they once did. 'It might be stretching things too far to say that a true form of English political nationalism has emerged, that "England for the English" has become a rallying cry with which to go to the polls or take to the streets – at least with any realistic chance of success. What is striking though is the fact that such things can be talked about now, and that there are people for whom such an outcome would not be unwelcome.' Even sceptics of British break-up (Jeffery 2009a: 16) were prepared to accept that there would continue to be 'centrifugalism' which could lead in the near future to 'two or more different states' in the territory of the former UK.

The popularity of this narrative may be traced again to Nairn, especially to his book *After Britain* (2000). Vernon Bogdanor (2006: 57) once described Nairn as 'a man of apocalyptic visions' and there is a precise truth in that description, the apocalypse literally being an 'unveiling' of a hidden truth which reveals the end time, in this case the end of the UK. It is the final moment of un-thwarting, a heart-warming prophecy of national fulfilment, and Nairn's great energy in proclaiming this supposed truth has established a significant part of his reputation. It involves a number of elements. There is, firstly, a polemical dismissal of the present state of the UK which is irredeemably in decay and dissolution. It presents an understanding of Britishness in terms of museum-piece monarchy, antiquated political institutions with a defunct imperial class structure. Here is a 'crumbling polity' and any attempt to prop it up is futile (including the current effort of devolution). The 'dwindling zombiedom of Great-Britishness' pathetically feeds off itself because real democratic life is elsewhere, in the nations and in Europe. 'No wonder returns from the grave feature so prominently in British cinematic culture: Brits don't just watch the House of Hammer, they live in it' (Nairn 2007). The gap between the practice of British politics and the *Zeitgeist* – a gap which also fascinates Davies – is unbridgeable and invites only radical rejection.

A second element is a distinctive perspective on internal colonialism. Howe is correct to argue that Nairn does not subscribe to Hechter's thesis but he makes instead a psychological reworking of the theme. Of course the Scots were active imperialists as the historical researches of Tom Devine (2004) have extensively documented. Nor were the Welsh or the Irish laggards in this enterprise either. What Nairn does (2008) is to turn historical experience into psychological submission and 'what one might call the "self-colonization" implicit in such triumphs has proved much harder to recover from than other, cruder forms of imperial hegemony'. If the Scots in particular had been successful in the past they were only successful because (in an inversion of Kidd's history) they accepted 'the broader rules of the new age. This perforce meant adopting British nationalism'. Times have changed and only the deluded or desperate hang on to Britishness, for these new times call for the throwing off of 'self-colonization'. That internalisation of British subordination has always been at the root of national thwartedness, not only in Scotland, but in all the nations of the UK, including England. It was the hidden truth of the imperial experience and today it is all which stands as an obstacle to emancipation, for the nations have nothing to lose except their self-imposed mental chains. This is a heartwarming tale but there is a dangerous truth lurking there and it is Harvie's old suspicion that the people are not up to the task and are serial *self*-thwarters. This aspect of the Nairn style can be called the higher populism, at one and the same time flattering and contemptuous. It is flattering because the style provides intellectual depth and erudite sophistication for a range of national desires and expectations. It is contemptuous because the people may not be sufficiently aware of, or prepared to grasp, the world-historical significance of their present condition and the role it requires them to play. Since he has already discerned that devolution is the harbinger of the end of Britain then surely only parochial limitations of mind – and the imaginative indolence/self-colonisation of the Scots and Welsh – prevent everyone else from discerning it too. If, as Nairn (2002: 250) claimed, the 'Scots really know what has to be done to the Treaty of Union' failing to do so is not only illogical but also despicable because would it not 'be best to anticipate it now, or as soon as possible?'

A third element is a reading of the logical unfolding of (post)modern history and Nairn (2008), as ever, has developed this with accustomed panache. History, he argued, has moved from 'the bigger-and-better epoch' of the nineteenth and twentieth centuries in which states had to conform to the rules of the 'Body-builders Club', one rule of which required the global exercise of independent 'clout'. Britain was the imperial cheer-leader of this club, another rule of which was to exclude or to deny the rights of small nations. Though the end of the Cold War and the spread of globalisation have undermined the exclusiveness of that old club, British governments still believe that 'global history must be frozen in its tracks'. Furthermore, the traditional British elite cannot grasp the new truth that the old maxim of 'bigger is better' was just 'a phase social evolution had to go through'. They want to ensure that the Union's 'bigger and better' integrity remains permanent. But history is wrong-footing these muscle bound states all over the world and the old rules are being re-written. Now is the 'springtime of victorious dwarves' and no more convincing illustration of the new 'sliding scale' of statehood is the experience of how Wales, Scotland and Northern Ireland are 'queuing up to claim their places' in this emerging world order. The old question used to be: 'Are you big enough to survive and develop in an industrialising world?' The new question is: 'Are you small and smart enough to survive, and claim a positive part in the common global culture?' This a view which Nairn also shares with Davies.

A further and politically consequent question is: 'How on earth can anything like that be achieved without "independence"?' The process of history means the 'emergence of new, small communities of will and purpose – the nations of a new and deeply different age'. In 1977, Nairn accused the British state of failing the test of modernity. Today it is accused of failing the test of post- or late-modernity. In both cases the same sort of historicism is at work to the same end. In short, globalisation makes some larger states 'irreversibly "smaller", in the sense of rendering older styles of imperium and domination possible'.

In this new world order 'smaller is, if not better, then at least just as good' and it is no surprise that 'the United Kingdom should be the one prime site' for this to happen (Nairn 2007: 131–2). As English and Kenny (2001: 267) noted in the literature on British decline, this sort of historicism affords opportunities 'to delegitimise some constructions of the nation's development and to encase some others through formulations such as "there is no alternative"'. In this case, those promoting the break-up of Britain suggest that the UK has now become like the old Austro-Hungarian empire (that favourite Nairnite trope), simply a machine for ill-considered external military adventures like those in Iraq and Afghanistan. This has the happy consequence for those expecting the British break-up because it shifts the whole weight of the argument against the narrative discussed in Chapter 1, reversing the older Barker mantra of exclusion and exile, with the consequence that never 'have unionists been under so much pressure to explain the advantages of remaining in the UK' (Thomson 2009: 131). The old scare tactics which frightened people into self-colonisation work no longer.

The four constituent nations 'after Britain' (if we accept that Northern Ireland is a nation) can find a secure association and substitute solidarity in a new Union, the European Union. There is, of course, a large academic literature looking at the ways in which states mediate national and regional interests in the European Union (Cavallero 2003: 197–8). The endist perspective is definitive in its judgement that the UK has become the dispensable political middle, retailing a history where globalisation, Europeanisation and nationalism co-exist harmoniously and authentically. Britishness either becomes dispensable insofar as people are persuaded to support independent expression in sovereign national institutions or it becomes an empty catch-all term disconnected from popular sentiment and irrelevant to the new Europe (see Squires 2007). Davies ended *The Isles* by arguing that in the 'old European jungle of sovereign states' independent nations like Scotland, Wales or even England would have lived precariously. Fortunately, in the European Union 'the jungle has been banished' and there is no reason for small nations to feel precarious. They have every chance of doing as well as 'Ireland-in-Europe', the 'arc of small, prosperous member states' in the European Union offering nationalists a set of good examples (Davies 1999: 1054). No one should fear giving up the British nurse if only because there is no reason to fear of worse.

This is an influential and interesting historical narrative but (to repeat Howe) being influential and interesting narrative does not thereby make it true. Critics have pointed out the uncritical looseness of the idea of Europe and the naivety of the benign European future which is expected

(Colley 2000). As Pocock suggested (2000a: 50), what Nairn's narrative supposes is 'the capacity of a people to say now and then, and to possess the means of saying effectively, "This is who we are, what we have been, where we are now, and this is what we are, or are not, going to do."' Is this the sort of European future which beckons? Is this new globalised Europe interested in such assertions of national sovereignty? Pocock certainly thought not. Others (Open Europe 2011) hold that this historicism generally borders on 'thought-terminating cliché' – using phrases which are meaningless without precise definition but which discourage further reflection from the reader or the listener; and specifically in the case of European Union it involves an 'appeal to process', circular reasoning in which the process of integration and liberation is defined by the virtue of being the wave of the future and the inevitable outcome. Moreover, it is claimed that what is often missing from these grand theories of globalisation is indeed a sense of history, a sense that there are continuities as well as innovations in the relations between states, cultures and economies, and that it should be a vocation of historians to 'eradicate the *telos* from processes ultimately subject to agency and political choice' (Bell 2003: 813).

The European prospect has been alluring, if often contentious, to a generation of nationalists though the reality has never been so fulfilling (Keating 2004). In 1988 Plaid Cymru's President Dafydd Elis-Thomas (cited in Wyn Jones 2009: 138) linked together in a European vocation the themes of national thwartedness, recovery and revival when he proclaimed that the shift must be from containment within the British constitutional form to openness to Europe. 'If we succeed in replacing the British dimension with a European dimension in our thinking, then we will have become the Welsh European internationalists we always were in our hearts.' As Wyn Jones concluded (144), for Plaid as for the Scottish National Party (SNP), European integration created new opportunities to challenge the old British dominance and to instigate a process of change favourable to nationalist or regionalist aspirations such that 'banal Europeanism' became the common stock-in-trade of debate. Here was a trinity of expectation along the lines enunciated by Nairn and his less-gifted acolytes. Firstly, globalisation has changed the structural demands of states and economies; secondly, this structural change favours the rise of small nations; and thirdly, the European Union provides a congenial, protective and nurturing association for these small nations to flourish in the global market. This expectation that cutting loose from the UK would be painless and positive is reminiscent of Kant's dove which, feeling the resistance of the air in flight, imagined it would fly easier in empty space. In this case the wider European space gives flight to ideas of greater national freedom and prosperity. Almost like Julian of Norwich, the message seems to be: 'All shall be well, and all shall be well, and all manner of things shall be well' and that all one needs is the self-confidence to replace self-colonisation (see Nairn and Kerevan 2005).

Here Ireland, once one of the 'good examples' for Scottish and Welsh futures, provides a cautionary tale. In a concise digest of the political economy of independence, Keating (2011) noted the Irish effect, highlighted by opponents of nationalism and side-stepped by proponents. The precise details of the Irish financial crisis are not central but its recent economic crash questions the plausibility of, even if it does not undermine, the trinity of expectation. The Irish economy had become open, fulfilling Nairn's requirement to be small and smart enough to play a part in the global culture and it appeared to be sustained by its position at the high table of European power-brokerage. However on 18 November 2010, the editor of *The Irish Times* could ask 'whether this is what the men of 1916 died for: a bailout from the German chancellor with a few shillings of sympathy from the British chancellor on the side. There is the shame of it all. Having obtained our political independence from Britain to be the masters of our own affairs, we have now surrendered our sovereignty to the European Commission, the European Central Bank, and the International Monetary Fund'. This may seem too self-pitying but even the normally restrained journalist Fintan O'Toole (2010) described the 'rescue plan' for the failing Irish banks as a 'Versailles Treaty', claiming that there *is* no European solidarity only the 'sadistic pleasures of punishment'. There was certainly a widespread view throughout Ireland that the EU was less than friendly to small nations but, in this crisis, revealed itself to be the arena of big state power. Of course, a hard case does not make for good law. It can be argued that this is an exception to the European rule and that economics is not the main consideration anyway for those who are seeking to emancipate Scotland and Wales from the UK's clutches. Nationalists expect that independence will bring prosperity but economic patriotism would surely be just as demeaning as ninety-minute patriotism. It simply indicates potential problems for the flight of the nationalist dove, the 'Wales has nothing to lose but its chains' sort of argument (Lewis 2003). Forecasting the future from the past is deeply fraught with danger (Grant 2009) and the nationalist *telos* – even the European one – is just as uncertainly heart-warming as the old Whiggish one.

It is plausible, of course, and it has what Kenneth Minogue (1992: 27) once called the 'charm of potentiality', the charm lying in its present plausibility and in its appealing suggestion of inevitability. It proposes that a new global, European and state dispensation is unfolding as a series of inter-related trends and it predicts that these trends mean the end of the UK. Like arguments about British decline, endism captures real changes in British politics and national self-understanding(s). These changes and the prospect of independence have been the subject of serious academic analysis, especially in Scotland, and are thus not exclusively in the realm of fond speculation (Keating 2009). Endism would not be such a persuasive and vital element in contemporary debate if it did not express certain truths. Despite its charm of potentiality, there is also good reason to distinguish between the extravagant heart-warming 'truth' (Nairn 2008) and the cautiously academic truth (Devine 2006). One is reminded of Pascal's aphorism (cited in Pieper 1954: 34–5): 'Could anyone enjoying the friendship of the King of England, the King of Poland and the Queen of Sweden have believed that he might be without refuge and without asylum in the whole world?' – written in 1656, the year of the King of Poland's deposition, two years after the Queen of Sweden's abdication and seven years after the execution of the King of England. In short, Pascal's moral is that grand predictions (like endism) are often poor at reading historical and political events. There are more questions than answers. 'As the empire has ended, what is left of Britain? Is it simply a memory trace? Time will tell' (McCrone 1997: 595). It certainly will but this brings us back to the beginning, not the end. 'Questions about when things ended – or may yet end – and perhaps more importantly questions about what persists and remains formative of national experience, cannot be resolved while we remain so uncertain about what the most important things are, or how best to characterize the twentieth century UK polity' (Howe 2003: 301). Endism, one can say, is discursively inventive, historically debatable and (as yet) politically unproven. This is not to argue that its political attractiveness for the potential 'independence generation' may not outweigh the questionable history and dubious predictions, especially as older British narratives wane. The next chapter proposes a more satisfactory way of understanding historical change and the ambiguities of modern British politics.

3
Dry wall

An era of constitutional change such as the UK is undergoing opens up all sorts of speculation. One is reminded of Stendhal's despairing question in *Lucien Leuwin*, where the hero feared that he would be doomed to spend his life between mad, selfish and polite legitimists in love with the past, and mad, generous and boring republicans in love with the future. The political debate about Britishness has mainly avoided these excesses of ideological polarisation and, in recent times at least, it is rarely given over to despair, though Timothy Garton-Ash (2001: 26) has written of an 'almost German-style debate about British identity' which has alerted people to the 'fragility' of the Union. Those matters once thought to be settled in the certainty of the old British story – national identity, statehood and political legitimacy – have now become questionable again, suggesting that the contemporary *Angst* of unionists is matched by a corresponding *Schadenfreude* on the part of nationalists, surely a sign that things are amiss. Nevertheless, it is wise to be cautious. Barker (1947: 558) once argued that German-style debates are a distinctly un-British, specifically un-English, thing because people are not given to an 'indulgence in *Weltschmerz*'. Their solid and pragmatic virtues do not lend themselves to such soulful self-torment. Except, one should add, in the recent history of Northern Ireland where politics appeared to be dominated by either mad legitimists or by mad republicans. But things have changed even there, at least for the moment, and who should be anxious and who taking pleasure at the other's discomfort is not so obvious. Stendhal's point was that an obsession with the past or with the future was really a *present* madness. It calls to mind once more Butterfield's criticism (1931: 31) of the Whig interpretation of British history: 'The study of the past with one eye, so to speak, upon the present is the source of all sins and sophistries in history.' But is it possible to avoid those sins and sophistries? Can one tread a fine Chandleresque line and keep one's historical and political balance, avoiding both uselessness and emotional quackery? As the first two chapters tried to show, there are historical interpretations which are far from being mad, selfish and boring but which read current complexities either with an eye on past evolution or with an eye on future unfolding. These may be unavoidable temptations but perhaps sin and sophistry can be mitigated.

Old designs and new

In the late 1950s, the conservative journalist Peregrine Worsthorne (cited in Gamble 1974) wrote that not only would the dignified parts of the British constitution like the Monarchy and the House of Lords come to seem tacky and ridiculous once the country had lost its global power but also the whole system would lose its former magical ability to command respect. Of course, Worsthorne was writing about class rather than about nation and there was a deeply nostalgic tone to his reflection but nevertheless his message has been quite prophetic. This can be mainly attributed to loss of faith in the sustaining Whig myth of progressive purpose which was discussed in the first chapter. As one would expect, there has been a political dimension to this diminished historical sense, one which has called into question the natural, exceptional and even exemplary virtues of what was called until recently the British story. As David Cannadine (2008: 181) argued, this was bound to have important consequences for British identity because that identity, by contrast with ethnic nations elsewhere (and especially those held responsible for wars in Europe in the twentieth century), was associated with the uniqueness of its institutional life. The historic path of the UK was to trace a middle way between the European experience of revolution and reaction and the evolutionary wisdom of that middle way was confirmed by the stability of the country's institutional life (see Pocock 1999). Unfortunately according to Cannadine, in the 1960s and 1970s 'many once-great British institutions which had seemed for so long the embodiment of national identity, national values and national success lost much of their sense of purpose and the confidence of the public'. Contrast this with the view of Wicks in Chapter 1. Cannadine linked together the declining persuasiveness of the old British narrative with more recent predictions about the break-up of Britain. It seemed that having lost its story, the UK had not yet found another one, with one leading analyst going so far as to ask: what is the UK for? (Trench 2008a; see also Chapter 5). And it was this same mood which John Gray (2009: 115–16) thought now informed not only the interest to reformulate what it means to be British but also to dismember it altogether. Such a thoroughly old-fashioned polity like the UK, he thought, was bound to look inadequate to those who either wanted their brands neatly packaged or their identities clearly defined. 'What could be more obviously in need of radical reform than a state grounded on a succession of accidents?' For Gray, there was obviously a peculiar philosophical irony at work. The home-grown principle of utility, which Dicey (2008: 329) believed had protected the UK from all that dangerously romantic European nationalism, had been transformed by false usage into a clear and present danger for the country. 'No one any longer believes the British state functions well, but its current malfunctions are mostly the result of treating institutions as instruments used by the government of the day.' Loss of faith in the old way had made faddishness into a public philosophy, almost confirming the old saw of G. K. Chesterton that the danger for those who lose their faith is not that they will believe in nothing but that they will believe anything. Gray thought that the current dispensation ran as follows. 'If any institution does not deliver whatever goals government has set, it must be "re-engineered" – a process that, given the ephemeral nature of these goals, is unending.' As a consequence there had been 'a hollowing out of ethos' which had gone so far that it might never be reversed. J. C. D. Clark (2003: 213) also thought that this hollowing out of ethos was profoundly subversive of former self-regard and that it has had an effect beyond the boundaries of the UK itself. If British history lost its Whiggish spirit and became 'instead only a story of material decline, political fragmentation and the dissolution of identity' then it was hard to see what relevance it had to anyone, anywhere. Philosophical and historical Jeremiads one may think, but there were other important voices which associated changing historical self-understanding with the significance of the institutional changes taking place in British politics.

In his highly accomplished work which sets out to define precisely what is 'new' in modern British constitutional practice, Vernon Bogdanor (2009a: 276) observed pointedly: 'Little is heard today of the "evolutionary", "historic" or "adaptable" nature of the British constitution.' However, as Chapter 1 showed, much of it *is* still heard and what Wicks's study, for example, states academically others have stated politically. Thus Lord Irvine (1998) could Whiggishly defend devolution as an incremental policy response reconciling demands for reform with the status quo. The result of this wise evolutionary approach meant that the 'continued harmony' of the UK was secured. This remained the consistent view of government and almost a decade later Lord Falconer (2006) could repeat that constitutional reform, and in particular devolution, was not concerned with the question of 'constitutional symmetry' but with the practical accommodation of 'difference and rough edges'. There is some truth, then, in the remark that the concern shown after 1997 both to justify devolution in traditional language and to recover a sense of Britishness had elements of a 'Whiggish rehash' (Andrews and Mycock 2008: 150). The real force of Bogdanor's argument, however, is that if this rehashed understanding of UK constitutional practice continues to warm the heart it no longer properly lights the way. Because Whiggish language is hard-wired into the political psyche after generations of repetition, it may encourage both people and politicians to make false assumptions. This is what Pierre Bayard (2007: 10–12) called a matter of orientation, 'a command of relations', in which people feel part of the political system even if they are ignorant of much of 'their' history or 'their' politics – as most of us are. Many of the old texts on British politics form part of a popular 'virtual library' of political understanding and though Dicey or Bagehot may be hardly read outside the academy, and even infrequently within it, many of their ideas continue to be accepted as truth. And so long as not only politicians and civil servants but also the people acknowledge the living force of the references – nostalgic, idealistic, emotional, traditional, historical, conventional, mythological – then it can be said that the system continues to have some vigour. Those Whiggish certainties of the 'ancient constitution' may not be a good guide to how things are, or should be, done but their traditional influence continues to confine debate about possibilities for they provide a narrative of inheritance, expedience, legitimatisation, association and efficiency (Rhodes, Wanna and Weller 2009: 229).

For Bogdanor there is now a profound gap between that Whiggish romance of the UK and the country's institutional reality, and the situation today has reached a definite 'Worsthorne moment'. Like arguments according to providence – which may strike a patriotic chord but which few take seriously any longer – so one cannot any longer believe the old Whiggish message that the UK is the best possible of all political worlds and that everything in it is a necessary evil. Bogdanor's point here is that ideological forces determine constitutional and political forms, a proposition recalling Oakeshott's (1991: 36) account of votes for women in which women's suffrage was achieved not by claiming abstract rights but by identifying a new social fact: that the status of women had already changed substantially. Therefore their continued exclusion from the franchise looked anomalous in terms of British public expectations and that this incoherence in the status of women 'intimated' the necessary political reform. Similarly, one could argue that the accumulated changes in British institutional arrangements intimate a new political order which is already emerging, pragmatically and without self-conscious planning. The story that Bogdanor tells is how the major measures enacted since 1997 (2009a: 4–5) have contributed to Britain's transformation into a constitutional state in which the old sovereignty of Parliament is slowly but surely being replaced by the 'sovereignty of a constitution'. That indefinite article is quite explicit because Bogdanor believed that the shape of that constitution remains uncertain. 'Formally, the doctrine of the sovereignty of Parliament has been maintained, and no explicit attack has been made upon it; but, nevertheless, all of the reforms have served to limit the power of what had hitherto been an omnicompetent government' (Bogdanor 2009a: 40). Certainly, the old heart-warming histories would not do any longer and though Bogdanor was convinced that things had changed, he was also certain that the constitutional future had yet to be written. Equally Catterall (2000: 33–4) thought that the tradition of 'studied ambiguity', which had for so long secured 'efficiency and freedom', had been steadily if not entirely squeezed out the British constitution. Hence the new arguments, mainly but not entirely as a consequence of devolution, that remedying present uncertainties requires further constitutional reform. Others of course believe that the future can be known with greater certainty and the character of this greater certainty was described in Chapter 2 as endism.

As that chapter tried to show, endism is history according to the *Zeitgeist* and the attraction of arguments according to the *Zeitgeist* is that it supposedly recruits the course of history to one's side. Roger Scruton (2010: 129) called this the 'moving spirit' fallacy, an idea which has become a rhetorical weapon not only to justify radical change in the UK but also to deny the UK any future at all. Argument according to the spirit of the times proclaims a necessary course of action, the logic of which neatly coincides with one's own political objectives. For Scruton, the fallacy involved two major characteristics: applying a method for making sense of the past to understanding the present and future; and applying to the complexity of human affairs a notion of progress only appropriate to science. In the first instance, the sort of interpretative abstraction which is necessary to make sense of a period of history is only available to those who understand what they study as being 'past'. 'To suppose that you can look at your own times in this frame of mind, that you can explore what "the *Zeitgeist*" now requires', or even to project that exploration forwards into an unknown future', involves the fallacy of 'seeing what is wholly accidental under the aspect of necessity' (132). In the second instance, it actually repeats the old myth of Whiggish history, only this time progress demands rejecting the present rather than celebrating it. For Scruton, the moving spirit fallacy became the 'reigning superstition' of the nineteenth century and it has lingered into the present. This is providentialism in radical form and it is perhaps even smugger than its conservative counterpart. To deny the *Zeitgeist*, then, invites being condemned as a reactionary, having misunderstood the laws of historical development and refusing to recognise the new dawn 'breaking before our eyes' (136). For example, these are often the criticisms which Scottish National Party supporters make of their opponents. This spirit is not really historical at all but identifies historic moments, especially the one momentous transformation presently unfolding. It can be described as certainty mixed with two anxieties. To anticipate rapid progress towards the new dawn but finding only obstacles in the way fosters the first anxiety, the anxiety of impatience; and to assume that the UK has only a past and not a future but to come up against the fact of its continued existence creates the second anxiety, the anxiety of frustration. People must be encouraged to think that their historical destiny is being thwarted either by others, by Westminster or by themselves (self-colonisation).

It is important to make clear the substance of the criticism of endism, with its moving spirit fallacy. The point is not to deny that changes have taken place and are taking place in British politics; or that these changes intimate a significant re-ordering of political practice. Neither is it to suggest that the Scots, Welsh or the English are incapable of either self-government or independent statehood (Northern Ireland is a special case). Both suggestions would be absurd. Nor is it to imply that the nations of the UK lack the resources, intellectual and material, to organise and improve their condition. It could very well be that the UK will break up, that its independent parts will prosper better in the global market and that they will find their respective niches in the EU and the UN. Indeed, endist logic may help to bring about these outcomes by persuading people that they have the blessing of history. Rather, the criticism is that the politics of the inexorable deflects meaningful reflection firstly about how the territorial parts and the whole of the UK could be better governed today and secondly about satisfactory alternatives to independence in the 'shifting politics' of the UK (see Keating 2009). In sum, it ignores that vast yet variegated terrain which, as Kidd (2008: 300) observed, has constituted that middling ground on which territorial politics has been generally conducted. And even in the Irish case, recent historical scholarship has pointed out how the supposedly 'illegitimate' Union lasted 120 years, longer indeed than the history of the independent Irish state. 'Throughout that period, British governments showed a willingness to respond to Irish grievances with far reaching concessions' and the movement for self-government often competed with parliamentary alliances for reform. One must avoid, then, the temptation 'to reinterpret a relative as an absolute', cutting across historical complexities on a flight path of political necessity (Connolly 2008: 408). For that sort of historical logic has been well described (Rifkind 1998) as the art of going wrong with confidence. Scruton (2010: 152) concluded his attack on the moving spirit fallacy with reference to Heidegger's remark that we attain to dwelling only by means of building. However, he suggested that with equal truth Heidegger could have reversed the proposition: 'only by learning how to build do we attain to dwelling'. This is an idea which usefully introduces the argument of the next section: that there is an idea of historical change which is more adequate to understanding the condition of the UK than either the old Whiggish narrative of integration or the fashionable endist narrative of disintegration. For both of these narratives actually have much in common and their common problem is that they make change harder to explain mainly because in both cases it is inevitable. The proposition is that a better account of historical change can be found in Oakeshott's idea of the dry wall and it is worth taking a short intellectual detour to consider the usefulness of this idea for understanding changing political relationships after devolution.

Dry wall

There is an interesting connection here with the Whig interpretation of history. Butterfield's first published work *The Historical Novel* made the distinction between historians who love the past 'for its own sake' and those who have their own practical uses for it (1924: 7–8). Butterfield was a contemporary of Oakeshott's at Cambridge and as one critic has suggested (Sanderson 1966: 218), Oakeshott's understanding of history may not be wholly unconnected with the ideas outlined in *The Historical Novel*. Throughout his life, Oakeshott devoted sustained attention to the question of historical understanding and, like Butterfield, distinguished between the practical past and the historical past. The practical past, he argued, was concerned with the use to be made of history for political purposes and 'the dogma it can be made to prove' (cited in Sanderson, 219). As he defined it in *On History* (1983: 44), the practical past is 'an accumulation of symbolic persons, actions, utterances, situations and artefacts, the products of the practical imagination, and their only significant relationship to the past is not to the past which they ambiguously and inconsequentially refer but to the time and circumstances in which they achieved currency in a vocabulary of discourse'. Both Whiggish history *and* the claims of endism would fall under that designation. By contrast, the historical past is not concerned to prove the rights or wrongs of any political ideology or to infer any practical policy at all. For Oakeshott, historical enquiry was concerned to identify a past composed of events 'understood as outcomes of antecedent happenings similarly understood and assembled as themselves answers to questions about the past formulated by an historian' (32). What the historian recognised in the past was 'a continuity of heterogeneous and divergent tensions', even 'a continuity of change', for which terms that we find in the old British story and the new nationalist one – like 'evolution', 'providence', 'unionism', 'nationalism', 'imperialism' or 'globalisation' – would be merely convenient abridgements of complex experience. If it is impossible to avoid the use of such abridgements (and here Oakeshott appeared to write like a postmodern theorist), these 'tentative, multiform historical identities' must not be confused 'with the stark, monolithic products of practical and mythological understandings which these expressions may also identify (117).' Certainly, one can recognise the limitations of the sort of history in which moral and political opinions are exercised 'like whippets in a meadow on a Sunday afternoon' (1962: 159).

The ambition, then, must be to avoid as much as possible those historical abstractions which give (1962: 13) 'the new shape a too early or too late and too precise a definition, and to avoid the false emphasis which springs from being over-impressed by the moment of unmistakable emergence'. This is not to neglect the interest of such moments, merely a warning not to pitch the ambition of interpretation too high, like endism, or too complacently, like Whiggism. Moreover, Oakeshott's (1996: 26) thought that if you posit a single path 'no matter how slowly you are prepared to move along it or how great the harvest you expect to gather as you go, you are a perfectionist, not because you know in detail what is at the end, but because you have excluded every other road and are content with the certainty that perfection lies wherever it leads'. It is not that one cannot tell a story about political society but story transgresses easily into fabrication when history is given an 'overall meaning' in order to make a case about the necessity of a direction or a destiny (Oakeshott 1975: 105). And myth, like Scruton's moving spirit fallacy, is 'a drama from which all that is casual, secondary and unresolved is excluded; it has a clear outline, a unity of feeling and in it everything is exact except place and time' (Oakeshott 1962: 166). It is impossible not to put words into the mouth of history but one should always be reflective about what one is making history 'say'.

Scepticism about such historical narratives returns us to 'the unavoidably contingent and circumstantial character of political life, and the recognition that this character is part of the very stuff of politics, not something that can sensibly be wished away' (Horton 2005: 34). Since there is no general law of historical change, unintended consequences in politics are what one would expect and Oakeshott expressed this insight in the following manner: 'The idea of change is a holding together of two apparently opposed but in fact complementary ideas: that of alteration and that of sameness; that of difference and that of identity' (Oakeshott 1983: 98). He used the image of a feature of the countryside, the dry wall, to suggest how historical change might be explained. Historical events 'are not themselves contingent, they are related to one another contingently'. The relationship is one of proximity and 'touch' and is 'composed conceptually of contiguous historical events' but with no place for 'the cement of general causes'. Rather the stones '(that is, the antecedent events) which compose the wall (that is, the subsequent event) are joined and held together not by mortar, but in terms of their shapes. And the wall, here, has no premeditated design: It is what its components, in touching, constitute'. The image of the dry wall, then, conjures change in terms of continuity. But this continuity is not the continuity of Whiggish evolution or improvement. Neither is it the history of unfolding purpose which we find in the endist formula. It is a history of contiguity, a contiguity which can unsettle and disturb much of what went before. It is an understanding in which it will be rare that certain moments are of such revolutionary significance that all is changed and changed utterly. The relations between antecedent and subsequent events in a reasonably stable political order like the UK open up new possibilities but they also deny others. Some things come on to the agenda but some things also go off. Some things come up for debate but yet others appear to be settled, at least for the moment. Some things may improve but others may get worse. The wall changes shape, as does the relationship between its parts. The eccentricities, irregularities, inconsistencies and (some might think) absurdities in the history of the UK are not irrationalities, therefore, but constitutive characteristics of its politics and this would be true of all states. Then again, these things are not 'set in stone'. They are not 'natural' but 'artificial' in the sense that they are always open to amendment. And the further one gets from an event the more it appears – in the course of change – a modification of specific circumstances. However, to understand devolution in this manner still leaves open the questions: how significant an adjustment was it to British political practice and to what extent has it modified the shape of things?

If the word contingent is usually taken to mean the fortuitous or the merely accidental, as it is used here 'the term designates an intelligible connection between related circumstances' (Minogue 2004: 244). These intelligibly related circumstances compose in different periods what Oakeshott calls a 'character', formed by human choices but recognisable according to certain recurrences. 'It is not to be expected that this activity will not at some future time reach out towards something new, that it will not add to its stock' but 'what is already there' at any one time may become regarded as its current 'character' (Oakeshott, 1993: 31). These recent related circumstances – devolution – may be also understood to compose a political 'character'. This character will itself likely become modified and may at some future point reach out towards something new (which could, of course, be independence and the break-up of Britain) but what is already there provides some analytical purchase in order to speak intelligently about it. The situation may be said to resemble Oakeshott's remark (1962: 124) that the arrangements of any political society, its customs, institutions and laws, are at once 'coherent and incoherent; they compose a pattern and at the same time they intimate a sympathy for what does not fully appear'. This cannot mean the inevitable working out of a premeditated end, rather it implies the shifting arrangement of parties, policy-makers and opinion, their manoeuvres and dispositions. The image of the dry wall is employed not only to indicate the erratic sequence of events and the rough interconnection of political purposes but also to emphasise the fragility of all arrangements, their mutability and the potential for events to disturb expectations. That is the truth of the point Davies makes about political transience. From this perspective, the old heart-warming notion in which providential continuity knitted the British past to the devolved present in 'an organic whole which confronts the future with the resources of a thoroughly mastered and assimilated history' loses much of its former imaginative hold (Kumar 2006: 414). So too does the notion that a deconstructed British past provides a historically correct reference point from which the trajectory of break-up can be predicted (Clark 2003: 60). If there is no story of unbroken progress there is no necessity to assume a story of decline and fall. What are the implications of this understanding?

Standing in relation

The first concerns how the institutional inheritance of British history is to be conceived. There has always been a temptation to think of it architecturally like a great arch or building and it is a small imaginative step to consider such an arch to have a definite coping stone like the principle of parliamentary sovereignty. This is a popular way of conceiving

British politics which appeals to the legend of stability and durability of the sort which may give a false impression of long continuities in British life. It also contributes to the problem that the institutional shape of a relatively short period of British institutional history – such as the first three decades after 1945 – can come to be thought of as natural and fixed. It also encourages the thought that tampering with the design will bring the whole edifice crashing down, a position ironically shared by both conservative die-hards and radical ditchers. Of course all analogies are inexact and even a non-architectural image may invoke an impending apocalypse. As Virginia Woolf wrote of the abdication of Edward VII in 1936, 'this one little insignificant man had moved a pebble which dislodges an avalanche' (cited in Cannadine 2001: 153). The problem with this sort of thinking is that things never are the same again but only because things never were quite like that in the first place. The dry wall suggests neither architectural grandeur nor structural catastrophe but something messier, more ramshackle but, ironically, probably more enduring. As Benjamin Arditi (2004: 138–9) perceptively argued, the mean point of institutional order is not a central point of repose but a 'middle region of movement' (echoing Kidd's view of the variegated middle terrain of Anglo-Scottish relations). This implies that institutional settings 'have nothing to do with the static beauty of geometric forms and refer instead to contingent arrangements' which result from the unpredictable mix of politics. For Oakeshott, the political dry wall may be said to be 'neither fixed nor finished; it has no changeless centre to which understanding can anchor itself; there is no sovereign purpose to be perceived or invariable direction to be detected; there is no model to be copied, idea to be realized, or rule to be followed. Some parts of it may change more slowly than others, but none is immune from change. Everything is temporary' (1991: 61). However 'flimsy and elusive' this may appear, it is not without identity. Everything is temporary, yes, but the crucial qualification is that 'nothing is arbitrary' – in other words, change is never quite a bolt from the blue (though some may not see it coming) and it is a recognisable product of the debates going on at any one time (though some may not even be aware of them). Each modification, rearrangement and addition has consequences for the whole, even if they are not immediately apparent.

Secondly, the dry wall image at least has a place for the history of unintended consequences. It is also much more accommodating of the very practical demands with which politicians and administrators must deal and with the cloud of unknowing which usually envelops those demands, haunted always by the spectre of Harold Macmillan's celebrated phrase: 'events, dear boy, events'. This may give the impression that within the confines of what went before, key actors and commentators 'often make it up as they go along' (Rhodes, Wanna and Weller 2009: 69). It has to be admitted that not only is there a good deal of truth in that observation but also there *must* be if only because constitutional reform is the product of contested meanings. Some find this intolerably vague and with some justification have argued that British politics has become increasingly confused and unprincipled (perhaps a view which reflects the collapse of faith in Whiggish institutional virtue), arguing that there is an obvious need for a greater degree of clarity and consistency. To take one example, Philip Norton (2007: 269–70) wrote of Tony Blair's approach to constitutional reform:

> It has been said of Christopher Columbus that when he set sail, he did not know where he was going; that when he got there, he did not know where he was; and when he got back, he did not know where he had been. Tony Blair appeared to adopt Columbus' approach, though without the benefit of finding a new world. He set off with an agenda in which he had little interest, he generated a set of constitutional changes that do not hang together, and he bequeaths to his successor an absence of any coherent view of what type of constitution is appropriate for the United Kingdom.'

One can acknowledge the force of these criticisms, accept the enormity of personal indifference and lament the failure 'to think critically and holistically about our constitutional arrangements' (280). Indeed, this lack of logical thought is what Matthew Finders (2008: 128) has imaginatively generalized into the thesis of 'walking without order', a sustained critique of the 'incoherent arbitrariness' of British governance in the twenty-first century. Nevertheless, one needs to be cautious about assuming that one can know the destination before one sets out since most politics involves journeys to unknown destinations, something which is considered further in Chapter 7.

Pocock's (1975: 602–3) famous plea for a 'new subject' of British history had acknowledged both the possibility of British history coming to an end. It did not seem beyond the bounds of possibility that the UK would one day become 'annihilated' such that in the future 'historians may find themselves writing of a "Unionist" or even a "British" period in the history of the peoples' of the UK and 'locating it between a date in the thirteenth, the seventeenth, or the nineteenth century and a date in the twentieth or the twenty-first'. This was not 'endism' for there was neither nationalistic intent nor predictive claim (indeed the lack of clear categorisation of the 'British' period of history indicates a concern to avoid stark, monolithic products of practical and mythological understandings). It did, however, acknowledge the eclipse of Whiggish faith in the providential and exemplary nature of British history. Since the

British cultural star 'no longer emits those radiations we felt bound to convert into paradigms, we are free and indeed necessitated to construct cosmologies of our own' (621). His concern was to reinvest British history with meaning and to understand it as the history of contacts, interactions and penetrations, a pluralist approach rather than a simple Anglo-centric one. This was to be a post-providential history for a Britishness which had diminished in imaginative scope. He 'did not propose that each star should consider itself the center of its own universe – though this is within limits a legitimate perspective – so much as it should seek new and interesting ways of defining its tangential identity by remapping the various systems within which it moves' (621). The bias was towards relations and connections of history within the islands (and beyond) rather than self-contained or integral histories of the nations in the islands, 'histories both as they have been shaped by interacting with one another, and as they appear when contextualised by one another. There must be tensions between such a history of interaction and the several "national" histories that have come to claim autonomy, and it is probable that these tensions must be re-stated each time a "British history" is to be presented' (Pocock 2000b: 165). This is the sort of history which fits well with the idea of a dry wall, a history (Clark 2000: 275) of the resilience of diverse identities standing in changing relationships with one another 'rather than the rigidity but final shattering' of a simple unitary identity.

In sum, the polity of the UK was one of weaknesses and strengths. It could not be mobilised along the lines of a homogenous people but it did have the strength of being able to accommodate regional and national differences. And as Clark was also to argue (2010: xxvi) this shared history of the diverse parts of the UK is 'not a share of an unchanging asset'. A multinational state, then, remains stable (or not) by virtue of the touching shapes of its component parts rather than by the mortar of national purpose or collective destiny (which is not to deny that some people *do* see being British in that way). The territorial parts of the UK 'stand-in-relation' to one another and the term may be taken to designate an intelligible connection between circumstances and dispositions. It was Barker (1961: 76), a close friend of Oakeshott, who described a state as one 'united by the primary fact of contiguity', its members being led by such contiguity to develop forms of 'mental sympathy'. These forms of mental sympathy constituted a common capital of thoughts and a common will to live together. Barker made it clear that 'common' did not mean 'one-idea' and he proposed that 'social thought proceeds by the way of a plurality of ideas, by the way of debate and discussion between the different ideas, "when they meet together" and come into contact with one another, and by the way of a composition of ideas attained through such debate and discussion'. In short, a state is 'some composition of the different threads of thought' but a composition that is neither finished nor completed. In a UK more plural than Barker could have imagined, this seems a remarkably apt reflection and it was this mental sympathy, Barker thought, which constituted the will to live together. None of this means that the UK will continue to find stability in multinational contiguity and it may be that annihilation is closer today than ever. This may seem too tentative and conditional given the supposed grand continuity of constitutional history which some politicians, with heart-warming reassurance, assume to have stretched unbroken for one thousand years. But it is a more enlightening account.

But surely this is too thin to sustain political cohesion? Surely there must be more to the UK than historical association and experience of contiguity? This anxiety is not exclusive to a quest for British identity but is also familiar in a certain kind of literature about all the nations of the UK, one which mixes travelogue, social investigation and state of the nation commentary, attracting writers from A. V. Morton to Jan Morris, J. B. Priestley to Neal Ascherson. However, there is a distinctive edge to concerns about the integrity of the UK and there has certainly been disquiet about the absence of collective ideological mortar. Firstly, it has prompted the thought that there was such cohesion in the past and that it must have been the result of having an external 'Other' – be that 'Other' France, Catholicism, continental Europe or the Orient – a view popularised by Colley's influential *Britons* (1992). Once those 'Others' no longer function to hold the UK together, disintegration beckons. This is the assumption we find also in 'endism' which links together post-British nationhood with a 'reaching out' to a new European and global condition friendly to small statehood. Secondly, it has encouraged the related idea, prompted in part – but only in part – by devolution, that the term British is merely a formal, perhaps empty, category of convenience for the real and substantial identities of Irish, Scottish, Welsh, English as well as the so-called 'ethnic minorities'. A good example of this style of thinking was Vron Ware's *Who Cares about Britishness?* (2007: 1) a study commissioned by the British Council's think tank *Counterpoint* to capture the 'modern sense of identity' in the UK. Ware wrote that 'Britain may be a country but it is not really a place. When you emerge from the Channel Tunnel by train the steward welcomes you to England, not to some abstract notion of the United Kingdom or Grande Bretagne.' Moreover, few people expect to be told 'they have arrived in Britain when they disembark in Glasgow or

Cardiff'. It is only when you pass through immigration that 'your relationship to Britain defines who you are or what right you have, or don't have, to be there at all'. This interpretation assumes that globalisation has now undermined 'the very idea of national borders surrounding separate spaces that demand special allegiance' (3). This claim, if it were true, would relegate 'British' to no special status whatsoever, simply designating it as an empty political space which just happens to have the functional label the 'UK'. Of course it is easy to spot the inconsistency here, for if globalisation has indeed undermined the idea of the national borders why would Glasgow or Cardiff have any special significance as separate national spaces? Only the supposedly 'forged', 'functional' or 'abstract' entity of the UK is required to justify its 'special status'. The well-meaning concern to challenge the claims of 'ethnic' nationalism ends up by justifying ethnic naturalness at the expense of the UK's political artifice.

Fears about an identity crisis and the lack of civic 'glue' stimulated the recent debate about what being British actually means. Gordon Brown (2004), for example, frequently gave the impression of a metaphysical quest for an enduring Britishness, a quest to 'rediscover and to build from our history' the shared values 'that bind us together and give us common purpose'. His questions: 'what is our equivalent for a national celebration of who we are and what we stand for?' and 'what is our equivalent of the national symbolism of a flag in every garden?' conveyed deep unease about fragility and instability. And there was a strange addiction to corporate marketing of national identity, understanding Britishness as some sort of mission statement. 'Most other countries have a national mission embodied in their constitution' (Wills 2006). Unfortunately, there appeared to be a sort of identity Catch-22 which meant that attempts to clarify the meaning of British would provoke the very nationalisation of opinion such clarification was designed to prevent. 'This view that there is a "crisis" of Britishness has been fuelled, indirectly, by recent government attempts to foreground Britishness' and emphasis on its distinctive virtues risked encouraging the rise of nationalist sentiment in Scotland and Wales (Bechhofer and McCrone 2007: 251). That was a view which chimed well with Gray's observation that the loss of the old Whiggish certainties could be a disorientating experience but that the last thing the country needed was the conversion of Britishness into an ideology. Being British, Gray (2009: 120) argued, required the decencies of a *modus vivendi*, the acceptance 'of the shared practice of peaceful coexistence' and if it had any distinctive merit, it was the 'way of life in which people with different views of things have learnt to rub along'. In a classic rendering of a dry wall perspective, Gray concluded that it is 'true that the future of the British makeshift is not assured. Still, it has muddled through before and may do so again'.

If this all appears rather elitist, consider Julian Baggini's journey to England's *Everytown*. Though the book was concerned with Englishness in particular, his findings can be generalised to the UK as Baggini acknowledged. He addressed the question (2007: 72–3): could national identity function properly as an integrative force if people were living differently? Did the country not require deeper emotional attachments? Baggini thought that worries about insufficient national glue (or mortar) holding society together were misplaced and that 'the shared values we all need to sign up to are actually pretty minimal and civic'. If people differed in their strength of feeling about national identity this was to be expected and not to be deplored because it reflected strength, not weakness. The country had been – and continued to be – reasonably good at providing people with often 'incompatible ideals about how society should be run' the space to rub along together, precisely the point made by Gray. In short, Baggini's experience led him to conclude that those who 'wring their hands over the question of national identity' were missing the point. They mistook the need for people to feel they belonged with the need for everyone to feel the *same kind* of belonging. There was no need for that sort of intense commonality and banging on about it could actually threaten political solidarity since not everyone was likely to feel that way, precisely the point made by Bechhofer and McCrone. In a telling phrase, Baggini realised (251) that what he had thought of as a single group of people was really a loose coalition of overlapping alliances and this 'is surely what any apparent community is: a series of networks'. And so long as those diverse networks stay in mental sympathy and so long as sympathy flows sufficiently then contiguity of historical association, articulated in shared institutions, is probably sufficient. In an age like our own which has dispensed with the certainties of providential history, this may have the quality of a modest recommendation, a sort of 'dry wall' patriotism. This appears to correspond with Lindsay Paterson's (2002: 40) point about the multinational character of the UK: changes in attitudes throughout the UK may suggest break-up but 'there is really no reason to believe that Britain as a set of relationships among people is anywhere close to disintegrating'. In that sentence, Paterson intelligently holds together both the continuity of the UK's historical association and the ever-changing relation between its parts. And even if the political Union might end, it is unlikely that relationships among people would.

A further observation can be made. It may be said that the notion of the dry wall looks like another example of path dependence theory and therefore a social scientific perspective rather than a historical one (Kay 2005: 562). There are some superficial similarities if only because for path dependent theorists 'history matters' in that 'formations put in place in the earlier stages of an institutional or policy life effectively come to constrain activity after that point' (Greener 2005: 62). Moreover, the notion of 'punctuated equilibria' – that is, historical change being the transition through disruption from one stable formation to another – has political as well as academic persuasiveness. According to Deputy Prime Minister Nick Clegg (2010), who had obviously read his path dependency brief, 'Britain's proudest political tradition is our capacity to modernise and our constitution's history is punctuated by distinct periods of swift and dramatic change. These moments allow for the radical updating of political practice and this generation is in the middle of such a constitutional moment.' Clegg's historical perspective was sequential (and evolutionary), envisaging an institutional pattern of long continuity, a moment of radical change and a return to long continuity. At first sight that may seem to make a good deal of sense about the British political tradition but it is a heart-warming truth rather than an enlightening one, ignoring as much in British history as it reveals. The limits of the approach can be seen in an otherwise very perceptive article by Andrew Gamble (2006: 20) when he asked how far devolution had changed the historical pattern of British governance: 'Do the changes introduced by the devolution measures enacted after 1997 mark a shift in this pattern, a deviation from the historical path of development, with wider implications for the nature of the UK state, or are they merely an alteration of form without substance?' And he concluded that though the new system had yet to be fully tested 'it may well prove to have established a new equilibrium in Britain's constitutional affairs' (30). The dry wall perspective suggests something rather different, namely that change is already in the equilibrium, that there is change in continuity and continuity in change. The pattern is never fully set, the path can be deviated from because there is no path *as such* and it is sometimes difficult to distinguish form from substance. This is not to deny that there are important questions to be asked about the consequences of devolution. It is only to stress that we should be alert to the distractions of historical paths, be they Whiggish or endist. And an insight into this comes from a surprising source. The Democratic Unionist politician Sammy Wilson (2010) used the dry wall metaphor to describe not only the specific challenges of sustaining relations in the devolved Assembly at Stormont – 'it is not hard to see the parallels between what we are trying to do in Northern Ireland and drystone walling' – but also to illustrate a general principle of constitutional politics – 'drystone walls by their nature required constant attention' – a phrase calling to mind Oakeshott's description of politics being 'the activity of attending to the general arrangements of a set of people whom chance or choice have brought together' (1991: 44). And if recent Northern Ireland history shows anything to good effect (even when the so-called 'hand of history' is involved), it is that for all the perceived fixity of principle and values the stones of destiny have a habit of being arranged to convenience and of being made to fit the circumstances.

Devolution can be understood as a modification of how the UK's component nations stand in relation to one another. The democratic institutions in Scotland, Wales and Northern Ireland provide new – but not exclusive – locations for expressing patriotic citizenship: participation in elections, lobbying representatives, identifying with new public symbolism and so on, such that the arrangements within the UK between central and devolved institutions take on a more transparently contractual character in the sense that bargains have to be arranged between administrations rather than exclusively within central government. James Mitchell and Graham Leicester (1999) argued that devolution meant strengthening the democratic credentials of the nations in UK affairs rather than creating 'out of nothing of an additional tier of government'. Understood in this light (and in language of the dry wall), devolution 'does not break with tradition but simply recognises the "less than perfect" integration within the state in a new and pragmatic way'. It seeks to repair common citizenship within the shared space of the UK, where national identity need not conflict with the achievement of multinational purpose. To put that otherwise, if the UK can no longer be governed *bureaucratically* – or by what Nevil Johnson (2000: 121) once called 'self-administration' – it can only be secured *politically*, that is within the democratic arena of assemblies and parliaments and adjusted on the basis of democratic politics. This new standing in relation of the territorial parts requires a more open process of public and institutional negotiation. It suggests that a more formal relationship between the devolved institutions and central government is now required. If change is recorded in traditional language, the tradition is now adjusted to the new political arrangements. The fit of the political stones may not be entirely secure and this is always work in progress.

Phillip Larkin thought that most things are never meant. This chapter is not suggesting that thought as a general political principle merely proposing that it might be a useful rule of historical thumb when considering the intentions of politicians. What it has tried to do is suggest a way of conceiving the historical modifications, meant and not-meant, which devolution has made and continues to make to the UK. The purpose has not been either to rule out the break-up of Britain which endism predicts or to claim that Whiggish thinking has no further place in British political discourse. There is nothing in the idea of the dry wall which implies that the first is any more or less likely or that the second will cease to be the language of choice for British political elites when discussing constitutional affairs. It has only questioned the teleological bias in both views and if there is a moral to the chapter it is this. Detecting meaning in history is attractive as a way to mitigate mystery and it is hard to avoid for those who have political objectives to achieve if only because it usually provides heart-warming conviction. As Isaiah Berlin (1981: 353) pointed out, what the Whig interpretation and its radical alternatives share is the conviction that they are the completion of the present and the wave of the future. Perhaps instead of this quasi-religious sense of time it would be better to adopt a 'pagan' sense of time, replacing the certainty of providence with the uncertainty of 'fortune'. The advantage is that it allows us better to render unto politics those things which are political and unto history those things which are historical. It puts the emphasis on calculations and wagers, making the stuff of politics much more interesting. We can rely neither on evolution nor *Zeitgeist* but are faced with the burden of judgement and choice. It calls on the skill of politicians because things don't evolve nor are they inevitable. What it excludes are hopes that are false in the first place and guides, reputed to be of superhuman wisdom, which turn out to be human, all too human, a realisation which 'should depress only those who have lost their nerve' (Oakeshott 1962: 127).

Part II
Themes

4

Identity and allegiance

In his article 'Devolution: decentralisation or disintegration?' (1999a: 194) Bogdanor explored the question of how political societies are held together. The traditional British response had been to concentrate responsibility and sovereignty in Parliament. But he thought that an alternative answer was now being offered – 'that a society may be held together through what Gladstone once called, in a speech given in Swansea in 1887, a "recognition of the distinctive qualities of the separate parts of great countries"'. Bogdanor concluded that if there was truth in Gladstone's answer, then devolution would strengthen the UK and not weaken it, holding together in the dry wall of the UK the two truths of a multinational people and distinctive national peoples. In Chandleresque terms, the political science of administration would be complemented by the national art of accommodation. There were those who either feared or hoped that these two truths would not hold together but were contradictions which must lead inevitably to separation. There are as many, if not more, who think that way today and one reason has been the increasing significance accorded to identity politics, not only in the UK.

James Tully, in the introduction to *Multinational Democracies* (2001: 1), reflected on a decade of constitutional transformation in Europe and observed that multinational democracy appeared to run against the prevailing norms of national legitimacy. However those 'norms', he argued, were only the particular norms of single nationhood and not the general norms of constitutional democracy. Tully identified implicitly the key political questions in the contemporary debate about the future of the UK – which nation? which democracy? and which constitution? For it is now commonly argued, and not only by 'endists', that the UK's multinationalism is running against the historical tide and it has become a struggle to defend not only the values but also the normality – as in the 'taken-for-granted-ness' – of UK institutions. Interestingly, the tension here was spotted very early in the study of territorial politics.

Peter Madgwick and Richard Rose (1982: 1–2) argued that, on the one hand, it has been the UK's capacity to act as a unitary state despite its multinational composition which has distinguished it internationally (and this distinctiveness was to become even clearer with the break-up of former communist states in the 1990s). On the other hand, they noted that the very act of describing the UK as a multinational state 'is to call attention to those things which differentiate its parts' and this possibly risked undermining its capacity to see itself as a whole. Devolution, of course, has institutionalised and politicised that differentiation of parts and has done so on the Gladstonian principle of accommodating national identity. It is possible to say of British politics: 'We are all Gladstonians now.' One consequence of the current concern with 'identity', as Madgwick and Rose suspected, is that it can skew understanding towards the national (or sub-national) and away from the multinational, where the fixing of identity in potentially antagonistic forms seems to be a by-product of identity politics itself (Hekman 1999: 10). In principle, greater autonomy for the parts need not affect the integrity of the whole but in practice comparative studies show that the possibility of mobilising support for the national at the expense of the multinational may be increased as in a 'zero-sum' game (Martinez-Herrera 2002: 447). This is the nub of the difficulty when trying to hold together the two truths of British and national peoples under the simple category of identity. In short, it is possible that the politics of national identity may bring about the politics of multinational fragmentation by promoting *one* truth of differentiation – unless, that is, a countervailing truth of commonality can be persuasively asserted. This requires an intelligent statecraft by the 'centre' to avoid encouraging such a nationalistic 'zero-sum' game. If all identities are spatially 'nested' (Herb and Kaplan 1999), there is no iron law which determines that they should fly the multinational nest. In this chapter the challenge to the UK is re-expressed as holding together the two truths of national identity and multinational allegiance.

While the concept of identity has been generally deployed when discussing devolution, the concept of allegiance has been relatively neglected, and it is that absence which appears to give substance to the notion which Tully identified: that multinational democracy appears to infringe national legitimacy. And if it is true (Elkins and Sides 2007: 694) that effective democracy depends on allegiance to the state but that the democratic state may have difficulty sustaining such allegiance, then the difficulty for the multinational UK is that much greater. After devolution, *which* identity should be expressed in sovereign pitch – the multinational or the national – can become critical. If this differentiation between allegiance and identity may appear a very academic concern with the niceties of words, it can be argued that the absence of serious reflection on the idea of allegiance has led to some confused and incoherent reflection about the future of the UK (Andrews and Mycock 2008: 41). Perhaps a useful principle in this case is the Calvinist one of *distinctio sed non separatio* (MacCulloch 2010: 635): it is possible to distinguish allegiance and identity in the UK but hitherto it has not been possible to separate them. To put this very briefly, to be British has involved primary allegiance to the multinational political community of the UK complemented by profound sentiments of particular national identification. There has always been tension in that relationship and the history of Ireland shows just how threatening that tension could become but the distinction – not separation – between constitutional allegiance and national sentiment has always been vital for the UK's survival. Identity politics, on the other hand, sometimes suggest that this is no distinction at all but a *contradiction*, that these two truths cannot hold together and that allegiance should be consonant with national identity for otherwise it runs against Tully's designated norms of democratic legitimacy. This has been a common nationalist claim but its elements require some further explanation.

The matter of identity

The first thing to be considered can be loosely described as cultural. It has been argued (Resnick 2008: 803–4) that identity in multinational states is characterised by hubris and melancholy. In the UK case, hubris defines the mentality of the majority nation, England, and melancholy the mentality of Scotland, Wales and Northern Ireland. Four implications appear to follow from this characterisation. Firstly, the hubris of the English has fostered resentment on the part of the other nations in the UK 'over their weaker power position coupled with a perception that their concerns have usually been swept aside by the majority'. Secondly, hubris and melancholy promote conflicting 'visions of history' and in particular (as the first section of the book explored) a complaint that 'British' history should be much more than merely 'English' history. Thirdly, there is a tension between institutional allegiance and identity insofar as England's allegiance to the UK has been relatively unproblematic if only because the English assume 'a single *demos* that underlies the common state' while the other nations 'retain a distinctive sense of their own often marginalised national identity within the larger ensemble'. These factors combine finally in a tug-of-war between 'majority nationalities with their tendency to centralised state-building and minority nationalities with their quest for significant political autonomy'. Resnick's is an imaginative and ingenious examination of these familiar matters. His definitions, of course, are strict separations rather than fine distinctions but the thesis has some plausibility when applied in the UK's case. Identity politics challenges cultural and political relations that assume an English core and a 'Celtic' periphery. Englishness-as-Britishness asserts not only its significance against the provincialism of the other nations but it also appears to confuse Englishness with the world (a substantial factor in the distinctively English understanding of historical providence). As a consequence, the strength of English influence has promoted two anxieties in the other parts of the UK: the anxiety of parochialism, in which acknowledgement by English cultural elites is thought necessary to validate local achievement, and the corresponding anxiety of influence, in which such validation runs the risk of appropriation by English culture. Much of the discontent that informed and continues to inform grievances against Britishness as surrogate Englishness may be traced to those two related anxieties, what Nairn has called 'self-colonisation'. It was perhaps representatively expressed in 1983 by the Irish poet Seamus Heaney's open letter to the editors of *The Penguin Book of Contemporary British Poetry* where he objected to being described as British and, in the (very English) guilty words of one of those editors (Morrison 1995), 'gently biting the hands that had colonised and anthologised him'. As Chapter 8 illustrates the hubris/melancholy relationship has been reversed in some recent English reflections on the operation of devolution and today those anxieties are far from being uniquely 'Celtic'. And that goes some way to confirm Liah Greenfeld's view (1993: 487) that questions of national identity are fundamentally about dignity.

The second matter concerns the nature of belonging. If identity is concerned mainly with selfhood – what one feels oneself to be – allegiance involves something rather different, a sense of authoritative political obligation. In a very suggestive article, Benner (2001: 162–4) explored the changing relation of identity and allegiance in terms of the older doctrine of 'patriotic unity'. This once meant loyalty, allegiance or duty to one's country or ruler especially in times of crisis and presupposed a hierarchical or *vertical* connection between classes and orders in society. The call for a common, modern national identity meant something different. It implied that 'national consciousness should last beyond periods of crisis, such as war or invasion'. The relationship here must be *horizontal* rather than vertical, requiring a bond which transcends class and intimates a fundamental popular equality. 'Such wider and deeper identifications were seen as a more reliable source of support than abstract allegiance to a sovereign or his dynasty.' There is an important truth here because, as Hegel argued, there is a certain banality to patriotism and if extraordinary sacrifices are an ultimate test of a people, it is the everyday of common trust which secures continuity in the state (see Fine 2007: 33–6). In short, national identity is more likely to secure such patriotism in an enduring way that older forms of allegiance could not. This was also the general thesis of Nairn' *Break-up of Britain* (1977) and of all those who followed him. To put this differently, the argument is that the horizontal relationship of national identity involves a sense of community and solidarity necessary for a modern democratic state. Allegiance, on the other hand, maintains a vertical relationship between un-equals and underpins a conception of a monarchical order ill-equipped to meet the needs of modernity. The measure of this transformation traditionally has been the fate of the multinational Habsburg monarchy, a familiar trope in the literature of endism which also owes much to Nairn's inventiveness. It constitutes part of a family of arguments about the nation and modernisation which has its roots in the academic work of Ernest Gellner (1983).

Therefore, so this argument goes, in order to modernise British politics and in order to sweep away the so-called 'deformations' of the old order, what is needed is an idea of the people that permits popular political – horizontal – mobilisation. Without such popular legitimisation and participation the political system will be fated to endure permanent crisis, not the stability precious to Whig constitutionalism. In Nairn's view, the British state has experienced a form of arrested development precisely because of its frustration of the egalitarian idea of the people victorious in America and France in the eighteenth century and it has remained trapped in the old order of vertical allegiance. Unfortunately, dedication to this archaic monarchical constitution is not the 'secret of England's greatness' but the condition of its long-term decline. And so long as its component nations remain confined by the vertical limitations of the UK polity, their prospects are also diminished. Nairn here neatly reversed the old Whig nostrum that had become part of British political self-understanding in Leo Amery's formulation of the virtue of 'government of the people, for the people, with but not by the people' (cited in Marquand 1993: 218). According to the new politics of identity, allegiance – with its associated code of deference – can no longer be good enough. It is as relevant to modern political consciousness as the Great Chain of Being is to modern scientific consciousness. Popular nationalism, with its thick web of horizontal solidarity, will finally undermine the vertical 'patrician' state of the UK. Nairn was certainly ahead of most of his contemporaries in arguing that the primary challenge for radicals was not to modernise the economy but to modernise the *constitution*, an idea which only began to agitate the radical imagination a decade later with the emergence of Charter 88 (Flinders 2009). Pocock (2000a: 46) once unkindly compared Nairn's certainty to being hectored by a member of the Kirk and criticised the impoverished nature of its reasoning. But this is actually un-Calvinist thinking because it tries to make an absolute distinction between the horizontal (identity) and the vertical (allegiance). Recent research has shown that even in Austria-Hungary, taken as the touchstone of failure, the relationship between national consciousness and multinational allegiance was 'not necessarily a zero-sum game' and that there was a more creative synthesis between the two (Cole and Unowsky 2007: 9).

The third matter concerns empirical evidence of changing public attitudes. National identity (Curtice and Seyd 2009: 117) 'is often thought to provide the emotional "glue" that helps keep a country together' (though, as Chapter 3 suggests, 'glue' is often a metaphor for historical contiguity and networks of sympathy rather than a description of tight political community). In the first flush of devolution, it was argued (Heath, Taylor, Brook and Park 1999: 173) that 'British nationalism' could have reached its apogee and was destined for inexorable decline. This was not a 'trendless fluctuation'. The judgement was based on a generational assessment of British 'national sentiment' which 'might have a limited life span as older generations gradually leave the electorate'. The one qualification the authors made was that this judgement applied to British identity 'in its current form', leaving open the possibility that there was scope for adaptation and modification. A decade later that qualification was more tentative, the scope much narrower and it was thought that the 'glue holding the different parts of the UK together is likely to become weaker' as the generations with stronger British identities die out, allowing those arguing for the break-up of Britain to make headway. 'Of course, the success of such movements will depend on political contingencies that cannot be predicted' but it appeared from the evidence 'that affective attachments to Britain will provide a weaker defence against separatism than they have done in the past' (Tilly and Heath 2007: 675). What these authors had detected was a decline in 'British national pride' which they explained according to the main themes of endism (end of empire, decline of Protestantism, loss of 'Other'). Therefore, the identity question and certainly the application of the Moreno scale – to what extent a respondent feels 'more Scottish/English/Welsh/Irish than British' – have been taken as key measures of the weakness of the UK. Changes in national self-perception seem to deliver hard empirical evidence of belonging from which a separatist politics potentially develops, disrupting the multinational 'flow of sympathy' and dissolving the allegiance formerly given to British institutions. For example, the *British Social Attitudes 23rd Report* found further evidence of fewer people willing to volunteer 'British' as the best way of describing themselves. Between 1996 and 2006 the proportion describing themselves as British had become a demographic minority, declining from 52 per cent to 44 per cent. (Heath, Martin and Elgenius 2007: 11–13). In Northern Ireland, of course, the demographics of identity have always been at the heart of politics and, though the Belfast Agreement of 1998 has quarantined the issue somewhat, trends elsewhere could well threaten its place within the UK (if only because the UK *in its current form* might at some point no longer exist). Moreover, even a reasonably optimistic survey of citizenship in Britain (Pattie, Seyd and Whiteley 2004: 263) discovered that people increasingly identified themselves with their own nation rather than with the UK as a whole.

The wager of devolution as Bogdanor defined it – on sustained support for the UK – seems at first glance to have been a dubious bet. The old Irish Question had been formulated thus (Boyce 1988: 8–9): 'was the United Kingdom inhabited by a single nation, however much regional or even patriotic differences might distinguish its component parts'; or was it 'one whose national distinctions made it essential that they should be given some constitutional recognition?' Contemporary devolution suggests that the latter is the right answer to the British Question but the evidence is less than convincing. What distinguishes varieties of nationalism is that they all aspire to the correspondence of allegiance and identity in separate statehood. It is possible to argue that the Scottish Parliament (certainly) and the Welsh Assembly (possibly) provide the institutional framework for this correspondence to be achieved. Bernard Crick (1998: 109) was fond of referring to what the philosopher Gilbert Ryle, using Oxford as his intimate example, used to call a 'category mistake': 'I have seen the colleges, but where is the university?' The category mistake is that the colleges are the university but that the university, whatever the strength of collegial loyalty, has an identity through the colleges but larger than them and recognisably 'Oxford'. The example can also be taken to illustrate a relationship between identity and allegiance or the relationship between national and multinational, a metaphor perhaps for the traditional state of the UK which (in the Whig tradition of Macauley) thought nothing of symmetry and much of convenience, one that could see no point in removing an anomaly simply because it *was* an anomaly, disposed to 'fudge issues of purpose in favour of registering political pressures' and to maintain 'an unending faith in the virtues of "muddling through"' (Dyson 1980: 280). Indeed according to McCrone (2002: 310), in post-devolution Britain identities are increasingly fluid but though McCrone's reading of this fluidity is subtle and nuanced, there is a political reading of identity politics which thinks that the flow is all one way. It contrasts the decadence of the UK (a bloodless Oxford, empty of identity) with the vitality of the nations (colleges of self-determination, full of creative potential) with allegiance and identity devolving together as the value of national independence waxes and the old British order wanes. These emerging patriotisms involve emancipation not only from the old political and cultural system of the UK but also from the 'melancholy' of old anxieties and resentments (and the English too will be emancipated from their old 'hubris'). Emancipation is to be found in a separation which is really a re-connection with the world, announcing nationalism unblemished by the inwardness of parochialism, xenophobia and certainly free of the imperial hangover of the UK. Rodney Barker (1995: 209) considered that there is a widespread belief that we are witnessing a movement of the (national) peoples against the (British) state. Though he was sceptical of this assumption he also acknowledged the attraction of the 'populist phenomenon' of immediate national community by contrast with the messy mediation of the multinational state, apparently held together only in 'artificial uniformity'. It could appear that defending the UK is to mortgage one's future on an Oxford-type lost cause.

In sum, it is possible to argue that the nations of the UK have now become more authentic democratic expressions of identity than the artifice of the UK; that political identity increasingly finds satisfactory expression in devolved, not British, institutions; and that these national institutions are more effective at delivering policy and protecting interests in the new multi-level – not multinational – governance of the European – not British – Union, a Union which, it is claimed, provides security of association for small nations. That has been the message of the leader of the SNP, Alex Salmond (2007), who argues that the British Union 'is past its sell-by date'. It no longer serves any political function except to promote resentment between nations, a view held by many in Plaid Cymru as well – though the historical irony of endism could well be that this vision of the EU is now 'past its sell-by date' (Salmon 2011). The existential question of identity is an appeal to have self-confidence in the vibrancy of national culture and an invitation to people to take responsibility for their own political destiny (to abandon 'self-colonisation'). According to a Plaid report on the economics of independence (Price and Levinger 2011: 65) small is definitely beautiful and all it requires is the courage to be a 'Kant's dove' where 'Wales could even expect, like Ireland and Denmark, to catch and surpass a now non-existent "United Kingdom" and become a prosperous, smart, successful nation'. It is a political vision which complements the post-colonial turn in the academy (see Gardiner 2004a) and recent academic interest in liberal nationalism (Moore 2001), where the identity-based conception of nationality is thought essential to achieve the civic openness which modern societies require. That emphasis upon the centrality of national identity in the contemporary world; the empirical evidence that Scottish, Welsh, English and even 'Northern Irish' identities (Todd, O'Keete, Rougier and Canas Bottos 2006: 334) are waxing while British identity is waning; and the decline of pride in British institutions all suggest that the devolved parts of the UK are becoming more important in the lives of citizens than the former British sum of those parts. Arguments in favour of traditional allegiance may become as quaint and archaic as Royce's (1995: 57) formulation of the principle of loyalty: 'In choosing and in serving the cause to which you are to be loyal, be, in any case, loyal to loyalty.' To remain allegiant to British allegiance may be magnificent but it is not the politics of the *Zeitgeist*, this newly nationalising age where 'focused on the needs and aspirations of smaller nations, there are many compelling reasons to believe that being a small, independent nation is more desirable than being a small, dependent region' (Evans 2011). The Owl of Minerva does not hover over nationalism, as Eric Hobsbawm (1992) rashly suggested but over the UK itself – or it would do if the growing separation of allegiance and identity was as clear-cut as this narrative suggests. This is questionable, however.

The matter of allegiance

By qualifying the over-exposure or weighting of identity, this chapter follows the lead of Brubaker and Cooper (2000: 1) who argued that identity can often 'mean too much (when understood in a strong sense), too little (when understood in a weak sense), or nothing at all (because of its sheer ambiguity)'. When spoken or written of politically, the term 'identity' frequently has a practical purpose and they issued a warning to scholars about a category of practice becoming a category of analysis. The language of identity almost pre-disposes the user to take the existence of identity as axiomatic and the rhetoric of identity can also have a 'performative dimension, contributing, when it is successful, to the making of the groups it invokes' (33). The qualification being entered here is not that the term national identity is meaningless (it clearly is not) but that its use may often imply less of political or cultural significance than is sometimes thought, especially 'about the *depth, resonance*, or *power* of such categories in the lived experience of the persons so categorized' (27). In other words, it was once thought that 'character' could best capture meaning of nation, a thought which today seems highly dubious and it may well be that in the future the weight now put on 'identity' will be similarly questioned (Romani 2002). The other matter which it is important to examine in order to get a fuller picture of British experience is the matter of allegiance.

Firstly, it may be useful to distinguish between identity and identification. Identity is shaped by the emotional and sentimental education of nationhood and, though it is likely that these formative influences are important for both the individual and the collective, it does not necessarily mean identification with the objectives of political nationalism (Charney 2003: 303). In short, the political science of identity may not always clearly light the way. Mandler (2006: 275–6), in a subtle historical assessment of the matter, thought that identity could be a blunt instrument of analysis. Opinion polls often relied too much on forced choices and even open-ended interviews may not entirely capture the complexity of experience. The 'identity' of the nation may appear stable but perhaps at the expense of becoming a caricature. On the other hand, ideas about what that identity means can be highly variable. Certainly one 'cannot assume that "national identity" trumps other identities, or indeed that one "national identity" must trump others' (297). Mandler's reflections, of course, cannot be cited in support of the continuing integrity of the UK and neither do they rule out its demise. They simply enter a note of interpretative caution. Reviewing the evidence in Scotland a decade ago, W. L. Miller had already addressed the reservations of Brubaker and Cooper and the qualifications of Mandler by arguing that admitting one's identity to be more Scottish than British did not necessarily have political consequences. To say that someone feels more Scottish than British 'is not to say *how much* more Scottish than British they feel' nor to indicate the political implication of that identification (Miller 1998: 191–3). And the same goes for the English, Welsh and Northern Irish. A simple reading from opinion polls or focus groups often underexposes how national identity stands in relation to the multinational UK as well as the depth of political allegiance to the UK.

Secondly, empirical evidence that a fundamental shift is taking place in the UK and that the tectonic plates of national identity are pulling apart also requires further qualification. On the one hand, according to Curtice and Seyd (2009: 118) there is some truth in the claim that devolution has weakened British attachments. Three-quarters of Scots choose Scottish over British, in Wales 56 per cent choose Welsh and

British identity has declined most in England. On the other hand, the more apocalyptic claims about devolution's impact on the UK have not been borne out. Why, then, are the Welsh, the Scots and the English (Northern Ireland was not surveyed) relatively content to remain in the UK? For Curtice and Seyd the answer is reasonably straightforward. 'People's constitutional preferences are not tied to their national identity as strongly as is sometimes supposed.' And their conclusion is that for those who feel Welsh or Scottish, devolution appears to be sufficient recognition of their identity; while those who feel British do not see devolution as an affront to theirs (125–6). In their assessment of the situation in Scotland, one which they admitted was 'somewhat charged', Bechhofer and McCrone (2007: 258; 2009: 201) endorsed this view, finding that (for the moment at least) national identity was only loosely associated with constitutional preferences, especially support for independence. They thought that their survey evidence 'weakens the already severely damaged argument that we are seeing a decline in "Britishness"' because it was difficult to mobilise national identity either in any simplistic political fashion or according to any single nationalist agenda. Such mobilisation cannot be ruled out in the future but it is not an inevitable by-product of national identification. What these academic analyses of identity show is that one needs to be careful about reading political events through the media headlines for those headlines frequently overlook attitudinal complexity.

For example, a BBC *Newsnight* poll of January 2007 dramatically headlined that about 50 per cent of respondents in Great Britain thought the Union 'had less than a century to go' (which is about as vague as one can get). However, the same poll also found that a majority – 73 per cent of the English and 56 per cent of the Scots – wanted 'things to remain as they were' and only 14 per cent of Welsh respondents thought that separation was a good idea (BBC News 2007). Despite devolution, with its different configurations of party support and even nationalist parties in government, the evidence still points to continuity in British 'mental sympathies', a sense of a common public life, allegiance to the institutions which sustain it – in short, that most citizens, irrespective of nationality, continue to attach importance to their place in the UK. In a general survey of opinion polls two researchers discovered that 'in all three territories [again they excluded Northern Ireland] a majority of residents have dual identities and there does not appear from these data to be a continuing decline in British identity or a continuous rise in exclusive national identities' (Heath and Roberts 2008: 8). Even in the hard case of Northern Ireland, nationalist desire for eventual unification of the island does not in the meantime displace practical involvement with mainstream British politics. Remarkably, a Northern Ireland Life and Times Survey (2010), conducted using a sample of 1,205 interviewees, found that only 33 per cent of Catholics want a united Ireland, with 52 per cent content for Northern Ireland to remain part of the UK. Nearly three-quarters of all respondents, including the overwhelming majority of Protestants, approved of the devolved status quo. The politics of national identity, it can be argued, has not displaced – though it has modified – continued allegiance to the UK. Equally, though Pattie, Seyd and Whiteley (2004: 205–6) had found evidence of scepticism and mistrust towards traditional UK institutions, they also concluded that citizenship in Britain was not in 'deep crisis' (283) and the reason for this may be that identity is not as politically salient as nationalists would like.

Thirdly, there has developed a habit when speaking of the UK to argue that its legitimacy is problematic precisely because there is no uniform British cultural identity. 'British' is artificial, invented, forged, and so is assumed to lack real substance. Yet Clark has argued consistently that this is a questionable thesis (2010: xx). The use of allegiance may help to augment the 'thick' and 'thin', 'civic' and 'ethnic' configurations of identity, what Brubaker (1998) has elsewhere called 'pernicious postulates', ones which frequently bedevil understanding of national and – especially – multinational politics (see Ignatieff 1999). At first sight this appears counter intuitive since allegiance suggests an external relationship between citizen and government and would almost by definition be the thinnest of thin associations. And this condition of 'externality' appears to weaken the appropriateness of allegiance as a modern concept of political loyalty, especially when the state calls upon the citizen to make substantial patriotic sacrifices for the common good, today in treasure more than in blood. This is where the 'artifice' of the multinational state can lead to semantic confusion where 'artificiality' is often taken to mean 'inauthentic'. Yet if it is true that 'demonstrating the constructedness of group identity does nothing to decrease the importance of identity' (Orlie 1999: 145), surely the artifice of multinational allegiance does nothing to decrease its significance? The assumption of the recovery of a fixed national identity once the tide of Britishness has receded is not one which historians would readily acknowledge (Finlay 2001: 245; Kidd 2008: 134). For example, contemporary Wales is very self-consciously forging a new political identity and with a sense of self-worth which older (often melancholic) forms struggled to assert (Aughey, Bort and Osmond 2011). This does not necessarily displace Britishness but it does represent a new standing in relation of the territories of the UK. As one scholar observed of Scottish nationalists, their 'contingent, ideological construct' of Scotland 'to the exclusion of Britishness' is a political myth (Sutherland 2005: 199). Furthermore, it begs the question of nationalists who claim that their brand of nationalism is exclusively civic: if national identity is exclusively civic, how does that civility – once you reject the core of distinctive 'ethnicity' – differ in substance from the 'artificiality' of multinational allegiance?

Because it does not require an indiscriminate love of one's country, right or wrong, and because it does not demand any deep affection for all of one's fellow citizens, allegiance may appear too patriotically and civically 'cold-blooded' for modern purposes (Thompson 2007: 158). On the other hand, allegiance does suppose loyalties, duties, responsibilities and belonging which can involve personal sacrifices for country and for fellow citizens. This (one might say) is the Harry Palmer factor. In the film version of Len Deighton's book *Funeral in Berlin*, the British secret agent is asked by Colonel Ross's wife how he can work for such a horrible boss. Palmer (Michael Caine) replies: 'Loyalty.' It is clear that Palmer has neither 'thick' patriotic loyalty for his country nor any great affection for his fellow citizens, especially not for members of the governing class like Ross, and yet allegiance to country leads to acts of commitment and heroism. The point is that allegiance does not present itself as choice at all. Though Palmer's loyalty exists at the cynical end of an allegiant spectrum, it is allegiant nonetheless and it helps to illustrate the common person's patriotism, a 'quiet patriotism', an obligation often based on what allegiance requires rather than what national devotion proclaims, the sort of mood which Orwell's war writings capture so well. Being 'allegiant' allows different meanings to be read into being British. Keating (2010: 379–81) put this well. The English could think they were part of a unitary state governed by parliamentary sovereignty and the Scots could believe that they had a contractual relationship with Westminster. What a 'traditional unionist' always understood was that 'Britishness itself is constructed differently in the various parts of the UK' and that there was no simple formula of identity. Perhaps the 'hard case' of Ulster unionism may again help to illustrate this point.

In the course of the recent Troubles, unionists in Northern Ireland came increasingly to describe themselves as 'British' even though, as Kaufmann (2008: 454–5) has argued, they also saw themselves as increasingly distinct. Furthermore, unionists have been suspicious of the political intentions of successive governments, fearing that their allegiance would be betrayed. 'In short, the ideology is British, but the referent and many resources most certainly are not'. This does capture something of the way in which difference can be sustained within a common allegiance. For some (Walker 1998) devolution is beginning to clarify again the relationship between national identity and allegiance, such that in Northern Ireland it has become possible once more (especially following the Belfast Agreement of 1998) for unionists to acknowledge they are Irish but 'part of the Irish nation which is unionist, which still wants British citizenship and which is loyal to the Crown'. Reflecting on the Census form question on nationality, the journalist Gail Walker (2011) thought that ticking the box for British confirmed a truth about her identity but that it was not the whole truth. 'Ireland win Eurovision, I'm happy in a fleeting kind of way. England beat Australia for the Ashes, great. Someone from Northern Ireland hits No. 1 – ecstatic. These may be trivial emotions but they are not meaningless.' This expression of the interaction between closeness and distance is perceptive and captures well the experience of everyday 'identity'. This is often called 'duality' or 'nesting' – one can be Scottish, Welsh, English and British – but Walker's references show another truth which can be called multiplicity. Or perhaps Susan Condor's term (2010: 540) 'the complex, laminated, character' of national dispositions captures this best. And while the Northern Ireland unionist may shift in feeling and sentiment depending on the moment, it does not mean that allegiance to the UK is thereby diminished. Membership of the UK is experienced as, in that Delphic expression, a 'community of fate'. This can be approximately defined as more than a *modus vivendi* – it goes beyond the mere 'rubbing along together' of which Gray has written (see Chapter 1) – but less than a single national *identity*. Rather, it exists where 'a widely accepted sense of shared fate may generate strongly shared identities, loyalties, and mutual affection among citizens' (Benhabib, Shapiro and Petranovic 2007: 9). In his subtle exploration of the politics of identity, Parekh makes a similar point, differentiating between Britishness and being British. Britishness, Parekh argues (2003: 309), refers to 'national character', to 'the kind of *people* we are' and to the qualities a people is supposed to share, involving psychological dispositions and temperaments. Being British, on the other hand, refers 'to the kind of political *community* we are', to citizens collectively, has an institutional focus and is 'a matter of collective self-definition'. That distinction properly complements Parekh's further point that one can 'question parts of the current view of British political identity without inviting the charge of disloyalty or being un-British'. The re-expression here would be that questioning what it means to be British requires allegiance to the UK and a sense of what Parekh calls the 'well-being of the wider political community'.

The UK's political order may be 'artificial' (which order is not?) but to arrest understanding at that point is to misconceive the emotional significance of allegiance because its members have feelings of shame, pride and dignity about its sovereign actions (Canovan 2003: 144). What constitutes the community of fate is (Canovan 1996: 71–2) 'less the characteristics they possess as individuals than the inheritance they share as members' and so 'we are British not in virtue of conforming to some particularly British way of thinking but because (either by inheritance or adoption) we jointly own the complex legacy' of the UK. Canovan emphasised that what unites in allegiance is 'shared ownership of something *outside* us', not necessarily 'similarities *inside* us' (1996: 71–2). Her distinction has been repeated in recent official attempts to define what it means to be British. According to the Life in the United Kingdom Advisory Group (2003: 14, emphasis added): 'To be British seems to us to mean that we respect the laws, the democratic political structures, and give our *allegiance* to the state (as commonly symbolised in the Crown) in return for its protection. To be British is to respect those over-arching specific institutions, values and beliefs that bind us all, the different nations and cultures together in peace and in a legal order.' However, it is important to enter a note of caution here.

The Life in the United Kingdom Advisory Group was chaired by Sir Bernard Crick and Canovan, with some justice, had already taken issue with what she thought to be the limitations of his perspective. She dissented (1996: 78–9) from the brisk clarity of Crick's attempt to resolve the British question by arguing that there is no such thing as a British nation but only a British polity. In her view the 'claim that the UK consists of four nations and one state is too simple'. It was also a criticism of the over-emphasis by those, such as Viroli (1997) who have tried to separate 'patriotism' (good) from 'nationalism' (bad). Both perspectives ignored the complex inter-relation of national identity and constitutional allegiance. They also missed Barker's insight (1927: 17) that the UK combined 'separate national funds with a common national substance', where no line had been artificially drawn between the 'social fact' of nationality and the 'political scheme' of the state. It may be, as opinion surveys show, that the common 'substance' (as Barker called it) of the UK is less prominent and that the 'separate national funds', in Wales and Scotland especially, are more so but devolution has not firmly separated these two truths, only modified their relationship. Canovan is surely correct to argue that this is a fine example of *distinctio sed non separatio*. If it is important to avoid confusing nationality with citizenship, as Parekh rightly points out, it is equally important not to ignore their connection in 'collective self-definition'. That people do 'rub along' implies a sense of belonging 'together' in the first place. This was well expressed not by an 'old' but by a 'new' citizen of the UK. Being of Bosnian origin, Miroslav Jancic (2007: 147–8) felt that by taking on British citizenship he could be bringing bad luck. What if his politics were contagious? His Yugoslavia, after all, had broken up and would not the UK risk such a fate through the process of devolution? He thought that it would not. Taking tea with his neighbour, he was asked: would he not feel better becoming an *English* citizen? Jancic felt superior to his neighbour in being able to make the distinction between ethnic and territorial nations. However, he was willing to admit that the start of the war in Iraq had made him feel ashamed of being British, as it did his neighbour. Here they shared a common identification with the fate of the country. This confirms two truths: Parekh's truth that it is possible to feel allegiance without having to agree with Britain right or wrong and Canovan's truth that political allegiance can be every bit as emotional and self-defining as national identity.

To present that British relationship in terms of allegiance, however, is often assumed to pre-dispose one to conservatism. According to Miller (1995: 127–9), at the core of 'conservative nationalism stands the idea that national identity integrally involves allegiance to authority'. In short, conservatism subsumes national identity within 'allegiance to customary institutions and practices' and that sort of allegiance – by definition – is hostile to multiple identities which require horizontal equality between citizens. Some conservatives may very well think these things but 'these things' do not exhaust the concept of allegiance. Miller also argued that nationality should involve a process of change along the lines of 'a collective conversation in which many voices can join'. As Benner (1997: 199) wryly observed, this is a 'very British way of thinking about nationality' because few countries have enjoyed the allegiant stability and security to think with that 'easy assumption' about identity. What made Northern Ireland different for most of recent history is that Miller's easy assumption could *not* be made, something which Rose (1982b) had pointed out a decade earlier. Moreover, the association of allegiance with constitutional monarchy in the UK as opposed to popular sovereignty has tended to put it outside the pale of reflection for those interested in Miller's type of 'republican citizenship' and certainly for those following in Nairn's footsteps. That position seems misconceived. It was said of the nineteenth-century historian John Horace Round that he defined 'national identity as a sense of liberty tempered by a habit of authority to legitimate government' (Cosgrove 2008: 42). Perhaps it can be said of the UK's multinational ideal, if it survives, that it involves distinctive national identities tempered by the habit of allegiance to legitimate government, where peace and order in the civil sense of the word requires not only horizontal relations but vertical ones as well. In both cases the (constitutional) monarchy does have a role to play and it can be taken here as emblematic, though not exclusive, of the principle of allegiance.

Bogdanor's (1995: 301) magisterial study of the British monarchy observed that: 'Constitutional monarchy is a form of government that ensures not conservatism, but legitimacy.' It does so by settling the question of who is head of state and putting it beyond politics. In doing so, it represents the whole of the country and helps to represent the country to itself. It is these two inter-related functions which draw the considerable ire of its critics because they do think of it as ensuring a conservative, hierarchical social order, preserving an unhealthy obsession with a unitary conception of sovereignty (for an intelligent examination see Everson 2003). This argument, however, is more often claimed than fully justified. In the first of his lectures on the *Relation between Law and Public Opinion in England during the Nineteenth Century*, Dicey (2008: 421) had already noted an apparent paradox. 'France is the land of revolution, England is renowned for conservatism, but a glance at the legal history of each country suggests the existence of some error in the popular contrast between French mutability and English unchangeableness.' And though he used 'England' Dicey meant 'Britain'. In France and the United States republican constitutionalism told against the 'promotion of that constant legislative activity' which characterised the UK. In a similar vein Keating (2009: 174) argued that the archaic British institutions so frequently denounced by radicals had 'managed the transition to a "postmodern" order of diffused authority, mixed sovereignty, and diversity better than states that have become stuck in a nineteenth-century form of modernity marked by Jacobin uniformity or constitutional rigidity'. And monarchy has been the constant factor between the re-structuring going on now and the transformations of the last two centuries. Bogdanor (1995: 305–9) concluded that allegiance to the monarchy remains difficult to explain in rationalistic terms and that in a more critical and less deferential age that old 'magical' loyalty has been difficult to sustain. However, he thought that it continued to be of inestimable value that the Crown remains free of party ties and 'uncontaminated by political controversy'. It is not merely a piece of constitutional machinery but is an important symbol of political unity. Far from undermining democratic institutions, British monarchy – revealing another peculiar paradox – now serves to support them. Of course there is a history here too. In the eighteenth century, Montesquieu thought that

Britain was already a republic in practice if not in name (see Jacob 1996); and in the nineteenth century Bagehot, following Montesquieu, believed that a republic had insinuated itself 'beneath the folds' of monarchy, what Tennyson called a 'crown'd republic' (cited in Bell 2006: 12).

Despite what is often claimed, modernisation of the state need not entail the abolition of the monarchy but it is likely that debates about the monarchy are really debates about the character of the state (Craig 2003), a judgement confirmed in a survey of elite opinion in the *New Statesman* (2009). One further advantage in a multinational state is that the Crown is not only above politics but above nation. There are those who believe it has a more important role today than hitherto not only as a focus of allegiance in a multi-cultural UK but also in a UK where national identity, before and after devolution, has become a matter of politcal debate (Whittle 2011). And if this does appear to be incorrigibly conservative, consider Tristram Hunt's view (2011: 170) that the British monarchy 'has long offered a far more open, flexible and inclusive idea of nationhood' than many European and republican states. As Canovan pointed out (1996: 79) it is often forgotten that the monarchy has played an important role in sustaining the multinational character of the UK 'while soothing the sensibilities of the Scots and Welsh and allowing their own national traditions to be honoured'. Even the SNP has accepted that if independence were achieved the Crown should remain head of state in Scotland, returning the association between the countries to that 'forged in 1603 by the Union of the Crowns' (Scottish Executive 2007: 24). Of course, affection for monarchy is not evenly spread throughout the UK – as the street parties for the wedding of William and Kate proved, it is not only a case of the monarchy being more popular in England than in Scotland and Wales but of their being different degrees of sympathy within England itself (Raynor 2011) – and it is completely absent in large parts of Northern Ireland. Like all institutions it cannot claim universal esteem. However, acquiescence (if not affection) is another form of allegiance. As David Hume believed (cited in Buckle and Castiglione 1991: 480) people 'imagine not, that their consent gives their prince a title: But they willingly consent, because they think, that, from long possession, he has acquired a title, independent of their choice or inclination'. And like all institutions, and like the UK itself, the monarchy's ultimate foundation (as Hume also believed) lies in public opinion. That opinion may change, at which point it is hard to predict what will become of the UK if only because the two truths of constitutional and national peoples may no longer hold together.

Henderson and McEwen (2005: 187) have shown how after 1997 the Labour government stressed 'national values' rather than 'national identity' as a way to strengthen allegiance and to promote solidarity as the bedrock of commitment to the UK. In this way the presence of shared national values would be deemed more important than the weakness which polls revealed in collective British identity. That weakness, as this chapter has tried to show, may not be as fundamental as some have thought and diverse ideas of national identity do not necessarily mean incoherence and division. Indeed 'it is precisely such intertwining of the different ideas of nationhood that promotes and sustains the cohesion of the nation' (Brown 2007: 17–18). Brown's study identified three visions of national identity which are frequently interwoven in the symbolic and political life of a state and in the minds of its citizens: 'the civic vision of ethnically blind citizenship, the ethnocultural vision of assimilation into an ethnic core, and the multicultural vision of the just accommodation of ethnic diversity'. His conclusion is one which corresponds neatly with the thesis of this chapter: that states remain strong insofar as the distinctions between these visions 'remain fudged and out of the limelight of public political discourse'. The British question today is one consequence of devolution bringing these distinctions more obviously into the open. Though this chapter began with the thought that the UK's multinational democracy now seemed to run against the prevailing norms of national legitimacy, it concludes with the proposition that it is possible to hold together distinctive national identities in allegiance to an all-embracing political association (for survey evidence see Bond and Rosie 2010: 100). Allegiance and identity – so long as the UK endures – are distinctions *within* a union and *not* contesting ideas. However, there is a further critical question which has to be addressed. It has been suggested that at a functional level the role of the UK is no longer self-evident. This functional aspect of the British question is considered in the next chapter.

5

Instrumental politics

In 2001 (Aughey 2001: 38–9) it was proposed that the UK exhibited a distinctive relationship between two principles of association: the principle of contract and the principle of solidarity. Contract was defined as a sort of bargain of interdependency but one which did not entail any obligations other than those entered into by arrangement or by treaty. Solidarity supposed a sense of common belonging and a duty to a larger common good. The extent to which the 'good' was not commonly shared required action on the part of the whole to redress inequalities between the parts. While nationalists naturally stressed the importance of contract, if only because it implied the right to dissolve the UK when necessary and while unionists obviously stressed the value of solidarity, if only because it implied the enduring priority of the whole, the UK remains an ambiguous political association in which both principles are at work. It continues to involve utilitarian calculations of self-interest by its component territories but these are also practically bound up with requirements of British solidarity. In this sense it complements the distinction between identity and allegiance. 'The debate over the sharing community', according to Scott Greer (2010: 182) 'is one conducted in public, often with high stakes. Welfare states are a key element of nation-building and social citizenship is a major part of citizenship itself.' Traditionally, the UK appeared to be what Hegel had once thought of as marriage: a contract which transcended contract, involving (to use that resonant, if ambiguous Scottish phrase) a partnership for good and went under the collective term of either 'welfare state' or 'social democracy'. Devolution has made the relationship between contract and solidarity much more transparent especially, one can say, for the English such that the idea of universal policies and entitlements appears questionable today. Hence, as Greer also points out (182), 'one's preferred form of solidarity' – nationalist or unionist – involves 'arguments about the welfare state and arguments about regional autonomy or secession are arguments about the desirable size and nature of the state, and it is unsurprising that governments seek to gain control over, and credit from, their welfare spending'. Yet the contract/solidarity distinction fits neatly with Michael Freeden's proposition (1996: 4) that such concepts are constructs reflecting social and historical usage and which acquire meaning 'not only through accumulative traditions of discourse, and not only through diverse cultural contexts, but also by means of their particular structural position within a configuration of other political concepts'. Freeden usefully identified the complexity but also the raw material of political understanding: to use the 'dry wall' image, how ideas stand in relation to other ideas and how all are open to change. As Chapter 3 suggested, devolution means that the nations of the UK do stand now in a different relationship to each other and to the whole and that these institutional changes have affected the way the public thinks about contract and solidarity (even if they would not use those terms).

Recently there has developed a way of thinking about the UK which assumes a trend from solidarity to contract, a way of thinking about the UK in exclusively instrumental terms and it is a trend which has alarmed those intimately involved in the politics of devolution. For example this worried Lord Sewel (2007: 79) who recalled that the UK is 'founded on solidarity' and the notion that 'fiscal contractualism' between its national parts should take precedence flies in the face of its core value. 'A fragmented territorial approach would simply condemn disadvantaged areas to become more disadvantaged, while tax-rich areas would be in the selfishly advantageous position of retaining all their tax income.' What informs that warning is a distinction as venerable as Ernest Renan's. He observed that a community of interests is sufficient for commercial treaties but a *Zollverein* is not a country which needed shared memories and a present will to live together (cited in Abizadeh 2004: 292). Sewel's concern was that shared memories and the will to live together, the basis of British solidarity between the nations, could atrophy and be displaced entirely by the idea of a mere contract of instrumental (and temporary) purpose. His was a powerful defence of the enduring value of the whole but it is precisely this value which is presently being questioned and it is a material British 'question' indeed. The unthinking 'wholeness' of the UK has long been the object of nationalist (but not only nationalist) criticism, a view in which the self-interest of British politicians frustrates a true neighbourly solidarity. Considering relations between England, Scotland and Wales (Northern Ireland again being conveniently excluded), Mike Parker (2009: 182) took the opposite position to Lord Sewel and argued that there are 'deep wells of mutual affection between the three countries of this island, but they can and will be poisoned if only allowed to continue under the auspices of the lop-sided anachronism that is the UK nation-state'. When the separate nations 'work out their own way of defining and managing themselves, there is untold possibility for healthy neighbourliness'. This is not an ignoble perspective, albeit based on essentially untested assumptions, but it radically reverses Sewel's priorities. In Alan Trench's indispensable series of studies on devolution it is possible to track the emergence – rather, the re-emergence – of this fundamental question of state function. In the introduction to *State of the Nations* (2008a), Trench asked: 'What is the United Kingdom *for* in the 21st century?' Certainly Trench is no 'endist' of the Nairn variety and since he does believe that there is an enduring role for the UK, his question requires serious examination. This chapter considers the force and application of the instrumental view of the UK (its contractual nature) and suggests how one can better explain and, if one wished, better defend its continuing resources of solidarity. The substance of the argument is that it is insufficient to interpret the Union in mainly *instrumental* terms – which is not to argue, of course, that instrumental considerations such as welfare benefits, economic prosperity, standards of health care, and so on are unimportant when considering the state of the UK. More modestly, it is to suggest that instrumental matters are only one part of the question and that a focus on instrumentality is partial in both the academic and the political senses of that term. It begins with an examination of the idea that the UK is now a failed project and how that language of project informs the instrumental or contractual logic of its critics. The chapter then considers how the non-instrumental character of the UK might be identified and re-expressed.

Project discourse

There is an academic narrative which has become familiar to students of British politics, a narrative which integrates historical, political and geo-political perspectives in order to give it a substantial degree of plausibility. That narrative is called here 'project discourse' in order to emphasise its instrumental character and some of its major historical assumptions have been considered already in Chapter 2. Project discourse claims to have explanatory value insofar as its narrative integrates the internal cohesion of the British project, intended to secure the stability of the UK, with the external project, the construction and maintenance of empire. To take one interesting academic example, Andrew Gamble (2008: 38) adapted Linda Colley's influential idea in *Britons* (1992) of the 'forging' of Britain in the eighteenth century against the 'Other', (mainly) France, and claimed that union through empire 'was always a political project'. On the one hand, the end of empire has 'meant the disappearance of the project' which for so long defined the strategic purpose of the UK. Its external substitute, the American Special Relationship, can do as much to undermine support for the UK as it does to strengthen it, encouraging its leaders to misrecognise the country's strength and to entice them into costly wars. Jim Bulpitt (1983: 101) had already explored this territory, calling the empire Britain's 'external support system', a system which enabled successive governments not only to secure a powerful role internationally but also to secure allegiance domestically. However, Bulpitt was also aware, whatever the external support, that the 'system' was always subject to crisis internationally and that its capacity to secure stability at home was never certain, as an important re-assessment of his work has demonstrated (Bradbury 2006; 2010). This uncertainty and crisis raises doubts about the answer Marquand (1997: 152–3) gave to his question: 'what is the community to which British citizens might be expected to be loyal?' He thought that empire 'was not an optional extra for the British; it was their reason for being British as opposed to English, Scots or Welsh'. After the imperial project, all that has been left are separate nations and the 'bloodless, historyless, affectless' institutions of the UK, a perspective which highlights the separation – rather than distinction – between identity and allegiance considered in Chapter 4. On the other hand, Gamble also thought that internally the welfare state, symbolised by that grandest of British projects the National Health Service, no longer instrumentally sustains internal cohesion in the manner it once did because its operation has now been parcelled out to the devolved institutions. This is the concern to which both academics and politicians have drawn attention (Wincott 2006: 170): that devolution's fragmentation of the centralised state's ability to ensure equality and redistribution could undermine the bedrock of the social contract of the UK, leaving it a bit like Oxford without its colleges (though to think that assumes that the nationalist 'Kant's doves' would fly unproblematically). It should be said that Gamble was not advocating the break-up of Britain but providing an intellectual framework to make sense of changes in contemporary politics, identifying the context of new challenges and possibilities. But he did evoke what others have called a 'crisis' of British *purpose* according to a template of instrumental malfunctioning deriving from a decayed project. The problem is not with the identification of the challenges for the UK which are familiar enough but with the 'project' framework within which they are discussed.

Project discourse necessarily involves intellectual abridgement, aiding reflection on the changes attending the experiences of British people in the last century but there is a shadow line which can easily be crossed into the territory of political advocacy. A concise and influential statement of project discourse-as-ideology can be found in the work of Peter Preston. 'The political project of Britain', he argued (2008: 722–3), 'originates in the late 18th and early 19th century response of the elite to the loss of colonies in North America, the rise of Napoleonic France and the related domestic demands from subaltern classes for democratic reform.' The British 'project', then, was in origins elitist, imperialistic, other-defined, outward-directed and hierarchical. It generated an empire which was in turn destroyed by the Second World War and its aftermath. That project, along with its instrumental justification, is long gone and the intellectual requirement for politicians and people today is just to 'deal with it'. According to Preston (2009: 517) 'it is difficult, indeed impossible, to envision its [British solidarity] effective deployment to mobilise the population' and any attempt to promote 'an elite-sponsored atavistic official ideology will have little purchase.' If the collapse of the external project of empire has removed the UK's *raison d'etre* as a significant independent player in world affairs, the project of internal cohesion which the idea of Britishness once secured has been reversed by the re-emergence of popular nationalism, especially in Scotland. The UK cannot survive this unravelling of project because economic and political crises can only demonstrate both its external and internal dysfunction. It is now in the process of dissolution into unseemly contractual wrangles between the national parts over the limited resources of the whole. Its soul cannot be saved by a flag in every garden. Nor can it be resurrected by the forging of a different British project since the thrust of the argument is to fix the UK forever to one and only one determinate, historical period (as Davies's history and Nairn's polemics imply).

The ideological value of arguing that the history of the UK can only be understood as a project and that its continued existence *demands* a project, modifies again the terms of political debate because it requires those who wish to defend the UK to imagine or define functional projects rather than to require nationalists to justify secession. Indeed, the habit of describing the union as a project has influenced some of those hoping to promote a renewed sense of Britishness but this is a linguistic trap best avoided. Mark Leonard (2002: x) who was influential in official attempts during the New Labour years to 're-brand Britain', openly proclaimed that it was vital for progressives constantly 'to take stock of where the political project of forging a modern and inclusive patriotism has got to'. The use of language like this and its implied references almost formed part of a rhetorical package for the new millennium, most memorably in the case of Cool Britannia. In similar vein Michael Wills MP (2009), the Minister once charged with promoting the 'Britishness agenda', adopted project discourse in defence of the 'benefits' of national belonging. To make this criticism is not to pour scorn on the notion that a positive vision (however defined) is important for that intangible quality of political life, public morale. It is merely to point out, as did Crick (2008: 77), that the idea of a national purpose or a national project is what Goethe called 'a blue rose', an intense and romantic longing for (in this case) a thing of political certainty. Wisely, Crick thought that the search for – or the belief that one was engaged on – a common project could prove damaging as well as frustrating if only because it was unnecessary as well as imaginatively limiting. Nevertheless, it is this blue rose which even some of the best political minds still hankered for (Brown and Straw 2007: 5).

This notion of the state as project is familiar in radical thought and it is not without coincidence that its application to British experience tends to be found in the work of those in that radical tradition, wishing either to sustain the UK or more often wishing to dismantle it. At its most consistent, it is reminiscent of Oakeshott's (1983: 132) rendering of the Tower of Babel myth, the politics of project par excellence, which invites people to devote themselves to – or to expect that their country be dedicated to – completing some great task of world-historical significance. No political association, it is assumed, can maintain its integrity without some grand purpose or without some noble undertaking, its politicians acting as 'priests of an ideal'. Ironically, this bears a lot of resemblance to that old, but now discredited notion of providence, albeit a secularised providence which seeks not those things which are above but those things which are very much down here, in particular material prosperity and a sense of mission. In the opinion of those who subscribe to this view, like Preston, that mission now bestows its world-historical purpose on the UK's formerly thwarted nations. Like Macaulay's New Zealander on Westminster Bridge observing the collapse of civilisation, the ruins of the British project seem all too obvious (though Macaulay was really pointing to the strength of the Roman Catholic Church, despite tales of its inevitable demise, thinking that it 'may still exist in undiminished vigour when some traveller from New Zealand shall, in the midst of a vast solitude, take his stand on a broken arch of London Bridge to sketch the ruins of St. Paul's'. That may be an appropriate metaphor for the UK's strength rather than its weakness, despite all the stories of its demise). According to project discourse, the

UK is now in a hell of a state. In sum, to understand the UK in this manner means that when the common purpose – the project of empire abroad and political unity at home – has terminated, the parties to it, Scotland, Wales and eventually England – are bound to find their own discrete projects. Project discourse leads smoothly into the logic of instrumental politics. There are two considerations here. Firstly, the UK dimension of territorial politics should be used instrumentally by devolved administrations in order to secure particular national, and not common, purposes. Secondly, for nationalists the UK is a dispensable instrument which, insofar as it does not deliver instrumentally, illustrates the necessity of moving to independence. And the potential is huge for making political capital in the space between these two positions.

Instrumental logic

For Trench (2008a: 20), the 'big long-term issue arising from devolution is not so much about Scotland, Wales or Northern Ireland, but about the UK as a whole, and England's relationship to the whole and the other constituent parts'. (England is addressed in Chapter 8.) This instrumental question can sometimes lead to a strictly instrumentalist answer which makes it possible to claim that the UK is no longer 'for' anything nor fit for any purpose. This is not Trench's position but even he worried that possibly the UK today has 'reached the point where the instrumental underpinning of the Union has started to dissipate, and to the extent that it remains it does not attract support for the UK'. The problem he identifies is a simple but potentially subversive one: how to explain not only *what* the UK does but also *why* it should do it. Trench (2008a: 21) is convinced that there is confusion about these questions and 'in circumstances where Scotland and Wales are developing in increasingly different ways and there is no clear rationale for the Union that explains what it does and what other levels of government do, whether in ideological, policy or financial terms, the challenges that the long-term survival of the UK faces are serious'. As the Commission on Scottish Devolution (Calman) put it succinctly (2008), 'if we are to consider developing devolution further within the Union, we need a better understanding of the nature of that Union', an implicit acknowledgement that its nature continues to remain obscure.

It should be acknowledged that membership of any state, of course, does involve instrumental and functional concerns. Crick (2008: 73), as we have observed, was sceptical of the idea of a common purpose, but he did acknowledge that even in the hard case of Northern Ireland, instrumental considerations were not absent. He noted how opinion surveys showed that a large number of nationalist voters appeared to favour remaining in the UK. 'They may favour, in principle, the unity of Ireland, if that is the only question asked; but they sensibly want to know what is in the package for themselves and their families; how will it affect their day to day interests – welfare, unemployment, schools, health benefits, employment rights and so on'. For Crick this was not a contemptible concern except to the diehard republican or to the incorrigibly romantic who were often one and the same. 'Interest, or the theory of utilitarianism, is not to be scorned or ignored.' Even Edmund Burke, no republican though often romantic, described the state as a contrivance for the satisfaction of human wants but if that were *all* that was involved then the state would be no more than Burke's (1973: 194) description of 'a partnership agreement in a trade of pepper and coffee, calico, or tobacco, or some other low concern, to be taken up for a little temporary interest, and to be dissolved by the fancy of the partners'. That is the sort of partnership implied by project discourse and instrumental logic, a distinctly functional relationship where, if the expected benefits are not delivered, allegiance wanes and the capacity to rule decreases. Nationalists – but not only nationalists – do think that the UK no longer delivers (sufficient) benefits, lacks political authority, is a partnership long in the process of liquidation and history may prove them right. Such thinking would call to mind Albert Einstein's famous remark (cited in Heath-Wellman 2001: 223): 'I regard allegiance to a government as a business matter, somewhat like the relationship with a life assurance company'; or Alistair McIntyre's observation (cited in Canovan 2000: 276) that to give one's life for such a state would be like dying for one's telephone company. Indeed, nationalists think that the UK now reveals itself clearly to be – in its wars in Afghanistan, Iraq and Libya – how A. J. P. Taylor (cited in Sked 1989: 4) once described Austria Hungary: 'not a device for enabling a number of nationalities to live together' but a machine for conducting foreign policy.

Those whose attachment to the state is entirely instrumental may make some minimal contractual sacrifices in return for the benefits of citizenship but such 'fair-weather' – or 90 minute patriots – would not make for political stability. They would only be loyal to the half-crown and not to the Crown, as Ulster unionists used to be fond of saying about nationalists even if they say it less often today. 'Even though a modern state can afford a purely instrumental allegiance on the part of some citizens, it may struggle to sustain itself should such an attitude become widespread' (Baumeister 2007: 496). In any state that is a difficult political problem but in a multinational state it could be fatal. Of course, there are those who believe that such a crisis exists in British politics which is also why they think the UK itself is under threat. That is how nationalists understand the fate of the British project and devolution simply makes it more visible (see Hekman 1999). However, this is surely not how most people continue to think of the UK. Is it possible to imagine it as something more than a trade in calico or pepper, more than an insurance or telephone company and if so, how might one describe it? A recent and very powerful statement of instrumental logic provides an intimation of what that something more might be.

Ian McLean and Alistair McMillan (2006: 10) distinguished primordial unionism – 'British' as an end in itself – from instrumental unionism – 'British' as a means to an end such as welfare, prosperity and security. A primordial attachment to the UK, they argued, 'always suffered from deep intellectual incoherence'. That incoherence for most of recent British history had been 'masked by its usefulness to politicians and its popular appeal' but now both its utility and its popularity are rapidly becoming exhausted. Specifically, McLean and MacMillan thought that primordial unionism was now dead. British primordialism could be only of historical significance today with the one exception of Northern Ireland with its atavistic form of unionism, one which has little or no resonance elsewhere in the UK. If by 'primordial' one means Orange Order marches, sashes, flute bands, Lambeg drums and bowler hats or if one thinks that it can only be expressed in an Ulster accent, then McLean and McMillan certainly have a point. If one means the assertion of a British identity to the exclusion of all other identities – as many Ulster unionists, though not all, sometimes assert – then the evidence, as Chapter 4 outlined, also speaks against it in England, Scotland and Wales. Hence their deadly question: 'can the union state survive without unionism?' Their answer (256) was that it would probably survive for some time, lumbering on 'anomalies and all, for at least a few decades more'. However, the fertile principles of political life had moved on. The decaying body of project UK, now bloodless and affectless as Marquand suggested, has more or less given up the ghost of solidarity.

By contrast, instrumental unionism has only utilitarian and contractual objectives to satisfy. From this point of view, the UK is good only if it has good consequences. It may have had good consequences in the past, such as the benefits which flowed from the imperial project, but McLean and McMillan assumed that it is increasingly difficult now to sell the UK instrumentally to a sceptical devolutionary citizenry. Their instrumental unionism is contract Britain *par excellence*, based upon strict calculations of benefit and loss. To be British means to share a set of entitlements, expectations and opportunities, a business-like estimate of individual and collective welfare. What that bargain involves at any one time is always open to re-negotiation but, according to McLean and McMillan, those assets have now diminished and no longer deliver the returns they once did. If states do not have friends but only interests then this applies equally to the territorial parts of a multinational state. Devolution, then, represents a new bargain between the nations but that very bargain makes it evident that independence for the component nations is no longer unimaginable. The likely trend McLean and McMillan outline is the steady decline of the UK's political capital to such an extent that its break-up becomes instrumentally attractive. This, they predict, is where even that grand project of solidarity, the welfare state, will cause increasing friction as it painfully 'pinches' on finance and expenditure (250–1).

McLean and McMillan do argue persuasively and they marshal significant evidence to support their case. It should be noted, however, that despite their fundamental distinction, McLean and McMillan find it difficult to attribute any substance to the term British beyond the category of utility or Benthamite want-satisfaction. When they assert that the incoherence of unionism in the past was only 'masked by its usefulness to politicians and its popular appeal' 'primordial' unionism is effectively collapsed into 'instrumental' unionism. This is the framework of classical political economy, with the state concerned entirely with outcomes and future calculations. It is the state understood 'externally' as it were, as if citizens could only ask what the state can do for them rather than what they can do for the state. What it recalls is Oakeshott's (1975: 315) description of 'enterprise association', a term for a 'relationship in terms of the pursuit of some common purpose, some substantive condition of things to be jointly procured, or some common interest to be continuously satisfied'. The government of an enterprise association is instrumental to this overall purpose or project which could be described as the politics of cooperative 'doing'. If one is to ask what the UK is for, then, the answer would be that it is 'to specify and to interpret this sovereign common purpose and to manage its pursuit; that is, to determine how it shall be pursued in contingent circumstances and to direct the substantive actions of the associates so that the performances of each shall contribute to its achievement, or to settle disputes about what actions do or do not contribute'. According to Oakeshott, it is sometimes erroneously thought 'that all durable human relationship must be enterprise association' and it is frequently difficult to imagine any arrangement without such a common purpose. That is 'project' politics pre-eminently.

One scholar (Shulman 2003: 46) concluded a study of the economic underpinnings of nationalism by remarking that the results 'cast doubt on the merits of a materialistic instrumentalism in the study of nationalism'. Real nationalism cannot be described in exclusively materialistic and instrumental terms. The not so hidden assumption of McLean and McMillan, of course, is that the UK cannot muster such a *real* national allegiance, its identity must be *artificial* and this artificiality is a fatal gift now that it is challenged by real nationalism in Scotland, Wales and possibly even England. Devolution has raised the prospect of the relational 'degrees' of British multinationalism crumbling before the 'absolute' claims of national separation. The weaknesses of that assumption have been exposed by Graham Walker and Christopher Farrington (2009: 137) who point out that 'the rigid division of categories insisted upon by McLean and McMillan tends to obscure overlaps and interactions between different kinds of belief'. As they go on to argue (and as the rest of this chapter hopes to demonstrate) the 'practical benefits of Union could be said to flow from the essential nature of the United Kingdom as an entity defined by negotiation, compromise and the balancing of different variables', a formulation which reminds one of Barker's view (1927) that the UK exhibited degrees of negotiation between the national and the multinational. If declining primordial identification with the UK appears most obviously in Scotland, then even the Scottish experience shows clear evidence of a willingness to maintain a strong degree of British solidarity. 'The question might be asked if the valuing of the Union – and Britishness – for their portmanteau qualities is not a species of fundamentalist Unionism' (Walker and Farrington 2009: 139). If traditional unionism was a form of nationalism, aspects of Scottish nationalism may also be unionism in another form too. And the answer still appears to be: yes. Nonetheless, there is in McLean and McMillan's notion of primordialism some recognition at least of a dimension other than mere utility. If their instrumental understanding of the UK is partial and their concept of primordial is unsatisfactory, what is required to give a fuller account? The instrumental description of the state captures one aspect of its character, namely the enterprise of government (policy-making). What it fails to describe is the sovereign character of government (which Chapter 4 tried to capture by the term 'allegiance'). The latter may be more difficult to grasp and the main criticism of McLean and McMillan is not the integrity of their scholarship but their failure to explore its significance in any depth. It was in response to the intellectual fashion to concentrate on instrumental intimations of British dissolution that the historian Paul Ward (2004: 9) argued 'that equal, if not more, attention needs to be given to agreement and consent in understanding the formation and resilience of Britishness over a century of rapid and radical change'. For Ward, 'people have been actively engaged in the construction of British national identity, and that this too has made Britishness a resilient force'. There are two aspects of a non-instrumental perspective which need to be considered in the British case, the official and the affective. The first is concerned with the question of authority and the second with the question of legitimacy. It is 'non-project' politics.

Non-instrumental association

Oakeshott (1975: 127) attempted to capture the first aspect with his term 'civil association' which he described as a 'rule-articulated association'. People acknowledge one another 'in the recognition of a practice composed of rules' and are 'related solely in terms of their common recognition of the rules which constitute a practice of civility'. Furthermore (148–9), 'the civil condition is not only relationship in respect of a system of rules; it is a relationship in terms of the recognition of rules as rules' such that civil authority and civil obligation sustain the association and are two sides of the same coin. The civil condition is based on consent but consent here means acknowledgement of the authority of law and its scope and not (necessarily) approval of any particular law or policy of government. This cannot be understood instrumentally because the civil condition is not a project or a common purpose, neither is it a set of managerial decisions. It 'contains rules in terms of which the authority of other rules may be recognized, and the recognition of its authority begins in what may be called the recognition of the validity of its prescriptions' (150). This entails a relationship to the state which 'is at once acquiescent and critical. The acquiescence is assent to its authority. Without this there can be no politics'. That is Parekh's view which was mentioned in Chapter 4. In sum, what distinguishes civil association from enterprise association is that persons are related to one another 'not in terms of a substantive undertaking, but in terms of the common acknowledgement of the authority of civil (not instrumental) laws' and a state so understood can be identified as 'a system of law and its jurisdiction' (117). To understand the UK as a civil association, then, means that it is not concerned with any particular project, is not dissolved by any particular project's ending, is not dependent on any substantive outcome but is sustained by the common acknowledgement of its legitimacy. The authority of the association continues so long as there is public consent to its procedures. Of course, Oakeshott (312) is describing 'analogies' of political arrangements since all modern states have an 'equivocal character' (instrumental and non-instrumental aspects), and it is appropriate to specify civil association if only because, as we have noted, project discourse either tends to neglect it or has already discounted it. And what is often neglected or discounted when speaking of the UK is the continuing assent to its authority. This is not primordial in the sense of that unionist fundamentalism which McLean and McMillan suggest, even though some people in Northern Ireland may think and behave accordingly. It is an allegiance which is not necessarily undermined (though that *may* happen) by changes in geo-politics or by changes of identity amongst its citizens. It is that 'dry wall' patriotism which assumes the authority of multinational association.

If this seems rather abstract, consider, by way of contrast, the attempt by Van Kersbergen (2000: 1) to describe the possible emergence of an integrated European political association. He thought that allegiance involved a double expectation 'because both parties in the relation anticipate a reward or a benefit: protection, security and prosperity in return for submission and support, and submission and support in return for protection, security and prosperity'. In this formulation, the relationship means that if or when the expected benefits are not delivered, the capacity to rule decreases. In short: 'Allegiance presupposes a trade-off.' When this understanding is applied to the experience of European integration, the construction is as follows. 'European integration depends on a *double allegiance*, consisting of a primary allegiance to the nation-state and its political elite and a secondary or derived allegiance to the EC or EU.' If that primary allegiance 'emerges via a reciprocal, advantageous transaction relationship between governments and publics within the nation state' then a secondary allegiance may be said to exist 'to the extent that European integration facilitates nation-states in providing the resources upon which primary allegiance hinges' (2000: 9; see also 2003). For van Kersbergen, that formulation discloses the crucial 'exchange relationship between ruler and ruled'. If that reading makes some sense for the EU, it has limited relevance for the UK. The institutions of the EU have their origin in a partnership agreement, albeit in coal and steel rather than pepper and coffee, calico or tobacco. Of course the EU aspires to become other than that and may well do so. As the previous chapter argued, the relationship between political allegiance and national identity in the UK has been and remains the opposite of this European model. In practice the approach of states to the EU, and especially the UK, has involved 'utilitarian supranationalism' (Bulmer 2008: 597). As the work of Chris Shore (2004) has shown, the idea of European allegiance as van Kerksbergen describes it assumes the detachment of 'rights' from 'identity' and that a new form of 'supranational' belonging can be based exclusively on instrumental rather than 'primordial' attachments. In his view this was not only undesirable but also impossible since citizenship without some emotional grounding was merely an abstract conception. The apparent contradiction (Gallagher 2009a: 189–90) of nationalists finding the idea of European Union attractive is partially resolved because it is defined as another project or enterprise. Supra-nationalism becomes a common enterprise for mutual advantage and the value of the European project is functional to nationalism insofar as it substitutes for 'project UK' and displaces its authority. However, the practice of non-instrumental authority, as Oakeshott put it (1975: 121) 'may be modified in use, but in being used it is not used up' and if one searches for enduring solidarity one will find it in that continuing recognition of the UK to act with sovereign effect. This may best be shown at time of crisis, economic or military, but this only confirms Hegel's point that there is a certain banality even to patriotism for it is the everyday of convention which secures continuity in the state (see Kidd 2008: 31). Devolution, in this perspective, took place within a state possessing authority which the new arrangements (non-instrumentally) continue to acknowledge. Again, it is that authority which nationalism seeks to contest, posing an 'existential' challenge as it does elsewhere, for instance in Canada, where the questions are familiar: 'whether a multinational polity should exist at all as a unified, national political community comprising the various nations (majority and minority) and if so, on what terms' (Choudry 2007: 634).

The government of the UK needs to be judged by what it does, certainly, but instrumentality also involves legitimacy. Political institutions, as Richard Rose (1982b: 2–3) wrote in 1982, make the UK what it is and whatever the diversity of local institutions and the character of national distinctiveness, it is the principle of continuing authority which Rose – rather like Oakeshott – identified as the unifying factor. This is only true because people have been socialised to think of the UK in this way and to acknowledge its legitimacy, a point made also by Bogdanor (2007b: 733) who thought that constitutional forms depend upon political forces. The UK requires 'an equilibrium of disparate forces within nations as well as between national parts' and Rose's pithy summary (1982b: 210) of this non-instrumental authority reads:

'Historical anomalies do not deny constitutional fundamentals. Multiform institutions are consistent with the maintenance of the Union so long as all partners to the Union continue to accept the authority of the Crown in Parliament.' In other words, it is implied in all instrumental practice whether successful or unsuccessful, popular or unpopular. Since the publication of Rose's book, as the next chapter discusses in greater detail, the UK has undergone substantial constitutional reform such that Rose's definition today sounds much more metaphysical than it once did. Devolution has raised the prestige of specifically national institutions as well as giving them distinctive authority, which in turn partly accounts for the tendency to speak more instrumentally of the UK. In other words, the authority of the centre may be leaching downwards to the devolved institutions, making the practical problems of UK governance more acute, and that was certainly not the intention of devolution's supporters.

However, it is possible to invert the instrumentalist thesis in order to make a very different case and we find this in Bogdanor's claim (2009a: 114–15) that the 'Scots who favoured devolution did so for instrumental reasons – that it was likely to make Scotland richer, improve public services, etc. – rather than because they favoured self-government'. They 'saw constitutional reform as a means rather than an end' and are likely to view the global financial crisis after 2008 as a reason to be even more sceptical of proposals for the break-up of Britain. This is a view which can be extended to cover Wales as well which accounts for some of the defensiveness in the otherwise self-confident vision of Price and Levinger (2011: 62 emphasis added): 'in turbulent times, small countries can be said to behave more like the woodchip – tossed about on the waves – but difficult to sink. *When good times return*, Europe's flotilla of small boats may once again prove quicker and more adept at charting a new economic course than the Super-tankers that are all too often "too big to sail" '. For Bogdanor, this instrumentality is the key distinction between the history of Home Rule in Ireland (and later, Northern Ireland) and the history of devolution in the rest of the UK. It is upon instrumental grounds – as means to better ends – that the effectiveness of devolution will be judged and not as primordial assertion of identity – as an end in itself. This underestimates the strength of nationalism, especially in Scotland, but at least it calls to mind the continuing British political context within which devolution exists. But what is this British context? Bogdanor challenges the fashionable notion of the artificiality of British multinationality, especially all the 'agonizing about the nature of Britishness', and restates with simplicity the civic core of British 'primordialism'. 'It consists in wishing to be represented in the United Kingdom Parliament at Westminster and voting for parties which favour such continued representation' (2009a: 118). From this point of view 'a substantial majority of the population in Scotland and Wales as well as in Northern Ireland remain firmly British and unionist' and, with a nod towards McLean and McMillan, Bogdanor claims (97) that 'Britain is less of an artificial or imagined construct and British loyalty is more organic and primordial than many commentators have suggested'. However, if the instrumental understanding alone is insufficient to explain support for the UK then it is also insufficient alone to explain support for devolution. It is believed not only to have desirable effects but also to be intrinsically valuable (Kay 2003). Nationalists, of course, are instrumentalists in both cases. If the UK has no desirable effects, devolution is only desirable insofar as it is instrumental in creating the conditions for independence – or at least that is what the logic of nationalism obliges them to believe even if the politics of nationalism are more complex.

The second, affective, sense can be otherwise called patriotism which is a more appropriate term for the UK than the term 'nationalism'. It suggests, to complement what has been said above, that patriotism does not mean associating together as in a business corporation but living in a manner which ensures common dignity (Boucher 2005: 86–7; 94). It presupposes a sense of history and inheritance which, like the meaning of British itself, allows individuals, groups and nations to read into it their own distinctive experiences (Keating 2010: 379). This is a very different conception of primordial, then, from the one proposed by McLean and McMillan and implies a notion of elective affinity. Holding together society, especially a society like the multinational and multi-ethnic UK, requires that dry wall patriotism discussed in Chapter 3. What defines 'primordial' in the case of the UK is the belief that this contiguity is worth preserving; and willingness to participate in a common public life is the measure of being British. It is also purposeless, sustaining nothing other than itself. Like culture, as T. S. Eliot remarked (1972: 94), it 'can never be wholly conscious – there is always more to it than we are conscious of; and it cannot be planned because it is also the unconscious background of all our planning'. The same can be said of the relationship between the instrumental and the non-instrumental aspects of the UK – that the background condition of all instrumental policy is the popular willingness to accept its non-instrumental authority. As Rose already noted, this depends on the socialisation of acceptance, or consensual legitimacy. The wager of devolution was that this legitimacy would not be shaken by institutional changes in Wales, Scotland and Northern Ireland. Consider Oakeshott's (2004: 187) description of conversation as a juggling act with many artefacts in the air at the same time. 'The art of conversation is not to let them fall' and in post-devolution UK that could well describe the negotiating art of the new politics. Like the authority of British public institutions, this multinational conversation will be sustained only so long as it accords with how citizens in the UK continue to understand themselves.

The UK's legitimacy rests on continuing popular support for historical 'contiguity' and conversational 'sympathy'. Chris Rojek (2007: 19) has pointed out that the supposedly artificial persona of 'British' has historical substance and this 'shared history makes it pointless to argue that England, Scotland, Wales and Northern Ireland consist of four autonomous elements' if only because the 'values of each nation in the union have been formed largely through their historical, economic, political and cultural relations with the other three'. The enduring resilience of the UK in this very particular 'primordial' sense has remained relatively robust and this, as Trench (2010a: 130) noted, 'may come as a shock to many, like Tom Nairn, who thought the British state fragile and at least on the verge of a terminal decline if not in its death throes'. Here is a delineation of the multicultural, multinational UK, the commonality of which may be understood in a number of ways – a sense of kinship, a sharing of economic burdens and financial resources and a mutual conversation – in short, a 'flow of sympathy' associating together the peoples of the UK. Of course, if people no longer wish to continue the conversation then certainly another sort of instrumental discourse of 'interests' will develop, one between increasingly distinctive political communities and exactly as nationalists would have it. Indeed, nationalists want to displace British authority mainly by expanding the instrumental responsibilities of the devolved institutions and by enhancing the legitimacy of their own 'primordial' attachments. This does not necessarily involve provoking conflict with Westminster but requires convincing people in Scotland, Wales or even England (Northern Ireland remains a special case) that self-determination is a better option than UK instrumentalism. The evidence is ambiguous. On the one hand, the Scottish social attitudes survey (Maddox 2011a) showed that 47 per cent would consider supporting independence if it meant they were £500 a year better off. That could be taken as evidence of the strength of instrumental, and the weakness of primordial, unionism. On the other hand, only 21 per cent would support independence if they thought they would be £500 a year worse off. That is even clearer evidence of the strength of instrumental, and the weakness of primordial, nationalism. Contiguity and mental sympathy are also things which nationalists continue to accept as facts of life in the UK but they do not regard them as having any political significance, except insofar as they restrict the achievement of independence.

As Tom Devine observed (2006: 165–6), those who expect and wish for the break-up of Britain have, on the face of it, a plausible case to make. Nevertheless, 'more than fifty years after the independence of India, the dire predictions of the disintegration of the Union have proven to be false'. Nor has the experience of devolution, so far at least, 'precipitated a headlong rush to full independence'. One reason for this is that the instrumental understanding of the UK – project discourse – omits those vital non-instrumental dimensions of institutional authority and popular legitimacy: multinational solidarity and elective affinity. It is important to stress again that these qualifications do not ignore the significance of instrumental calculations – the bargaining element of territorial politics and the material and social expectations of individuals – but considers those calculations to be made *still* within a framework of broadly British assumptions. In other words, social bargains about the scope of rights and entitlements in each devolved administration presuppose the solidarity of common UK citizenship. Nevertheless, this solidarity is likely to be tested by devolutionary tendencies and two of these are of immediate significance.

Firstly, the institutionalisation of territory and democratic politics in Scotland, Wales and Northern Ireland fosters public expectations that devolution is about championing the part against the whole and this may create fragmenting tensions. It is not only a question of institutional relations – the nations *against* the centre – but also an English question – potentially the Scots, Welsh and Northern Irish *against* the English. As for the first concern, there is intimated a potential 'patriotic drift'. Harvie (2000b), for example, proposed that the era of British nationalism can be accounted for precisely: it lasted from 1939 to 1970. After this brief sabbatical, authentic allegiance is returning home to the constituent nations. As for the second, there is the potential for English people to think that devolution is a case of subsidised self-determination in which the Scots, Welsh and Northern Irish get self-determination while the English get to do the subsidisation. Both of these matters are considered in the final section of the book. Secondly, the increasing diversity of entitlements are already putting strains on the public sense of common rights and expectations, possibly weakening the non-instrumental character of the state. And Greer (2007: 136) observed that we 'scarcely know what devolution has done to the UK as a whole', concluding (159) that devolution had already impacted on the meaning and rights associated with citizenship and 'so long as there is no clear sense of what UK citizenship might mean, divergence in citizenship rights will likely rebound on the whole structure of devolution'. Indeed, that is exactly what Lord Sewel warned against. His warning implied that the tendency to think exclusively in terms of four nations and to ignore the UK was to commit a category error, rather like Crick's analogy of the colleges and Oxford (see Chapter 4). However, this does raise a key question: what is 'left over after account has been taken of the enumerated, distinctive traits of the four nations' (Rojek 2007: 19)? The following chapter suggests one answer to Rojek's question by examining what remains to *British* politics after devolution.

6

Fifth nation

This chapter concludes the second part of the book by trying to bring together into a persuasive synthesis the conceptual themes of the previous chapters on allegiance, identity, instrumental and non-instrumental politics. It addresses more directly Canovan's point (1996: 78–9), mentioned in passing in Chapter 4, that the fashionable notion of the UK consisting of four nations and one state is too simple a proposition and fails to convey the subtlety of the relationship. That UK relationship is discussed here in terms of the idea of 'fifth nation', an idea used to illustrate the insight derived from the survey evidence of John Curtice and Ben Seyd (2009: 125) who found that people's 'constitutional preferences are not tied to their national identity as strongly as is sometimes supposed'. This suggests that there is indeed something more to the UK than four nations and a state. As the first part of this book claimed, the meaning of being British has changed throughout its history and its meaning has certainly changed in the decade of devolution. Bogdanor (2009a: 118) has expressed this change in the following way. He argued that if the unitary British state expressed the belief that all parts of the UK composed a single British nation, by contrast devolution expresses the belief that there are separate nations which, nevertheless, choose to remain within the larger multinational constitutional framework of the UK, a formulation of devolution's relevance as venerable as Gladstone's position on Irish Home Rule (Boyce 1988). This contrast may exaggerate the change somewhat because, as Chapter 1 showed, that contrast is part of the partisan passions of politics rather than an entirely accurate description of the middle ground of UK experience. For example, Bogdanor used resistance to Irish Home Rule as the defining example of the present invalidity of the politics of singular nationhood but this charge overlooks the wording of Ulster Covenant of 1912. Certainly, fidelity to the UK was most dramatically stated there but the wording of the Covenant was not concerned to define an integral national identity at all but spoke instead of the importance of the Union for the material well-being of the whole of Ireland (instrumental value), loyalty to the Crown (political allegiance), civil and religious freedom (historical identity), unity of the empire (strategic significance) and the 'cherished position of equal citizenship' in the UK (non-instrumental statehood). It was a very *Irish* document and it did not suggest that either Ulster or Ireland was indistinguishable from England, Scotland and Wales and interestingly neither the word 'British' nor the word 'nation' were used at all. If there is a 'nation' evoked in the Covenant it is, to use contemporary jargon, a civic rather than an ethnic one. This was not how everyone who signed understood things, of course, but that use of language outlines a distinctive association. However, Bogdanor's subsequent sentence that devolution 'transforms not only the state but also the nation' is profoundly insightful.

The term 'fifth nation' first appeared in published form in the introduction by Peter Madgwick and Richard Rose to their jointly edited book of 1982, *The Territorial Dimension in United Kingdom Politics*. It was used as a way of explaining how the UK was able to act as a unitary state notwithstanding its multinational composition. Most studies of British politics, they thought, either substituted the politics of England for the politics of the UK or they tended to concentrate on one of its component parts, Scotland, Wales or Northern Ireland, while frequently neglecting the relationship between Westminster and the nations. To capture that relationship and its efficient secret, Madgwick and Rose proposed that the UK should be thought of as '*a* fifth "nation" in Westminster' (emphasis added). Since their book was an edited collection of essays intended to examine 'the ways in which politics differs among the four nations of the United Kingdom, and how the distinctive parts fit together to form a United Kingdom', the anatomy of fifth nation was implicit in each of the individual contributions (1982: 3–5). When he came to develop the idea at greater length in his monograph *Understanding the United Kingdom* published in the same year, however, Rose (1982a: 3) provided a different stress. In that book he described it thus: 'To understand the parts, we must also understand the government of the whole. Parliament is more than the sum of representatives from diverse constituencies. It is, as it were, *the* fifth nation of the United Kingdom; it is the first loyalty of some and the last loyalty of others' (again, emphasis added). What the UK is for (to use the instrumental language of the previous chapter) can certainly be calculated in terms of benefits and services, but continued allegiance to it cannot be so defined. This requires a sense of belonging which is *not* instrumental and it is this non-instrumentality which the term fifth nation tries to convey. When considered authoritatively it is sovereign and it is the prior condition for the material benefits which all British citizens share. Is there any significant difference between the use of the indefinite and definite articles in these two cases? Given the complementary unionist tone of the two volumes, there does not appear to be. However, more than a quarter of a century later, it may be that the distinction has become relevant to the contemporary debate. Since it is argued that not only the state but also the nation have changed then the following proposition may be made. *The* fifth nation implies an integral form of UK entitlement, albeit one which acknowledges national diversity; *a* fifth nation implies diverse forms of entitlement, albeit one which still acknowledges equal UK citizenship. Again, there seem to be two truths which together characterise fifth nation – the truth of national divergence and the truth of UK equity. In the first instance, however, it is important to examine Rose's imaginative description of the fifth nation which remains the best account what he called the 'steady state' UK.

Anatomy of *the* fifth nation

Understanding the United Kingdom was prompted by the (failed) nationalist challenge of the mid-1970s and by the Labour government's (failed) policy response of devolution. Anticipating Trench's concern a generation later about how one defined the purpose of the state, Rose admitted that there was confusion about why the UK existed and his book was designed not only to understand it but also to defend it. As its subtitle made clear, how the 'territorial dimension' was factored into government policy required a grasp of the scope but also of the limits of difference in British politics. Those territorial differences – the UK's multinationalism – Rose thought of as a collection of territorial puzzles but puzzles which interlocked (1982a: 123). In addition to Trench's concern about what the UK is for (a question of instrumentality) Rose also considered the prior question of why it is (a question of allegiance). Government must be judged by what it does, certainly, but what it does requires an understanding of what it is and the UK was a product of 'a multiplicity of historical events' (a dry wall), not 'the product of a logical plan' (providential or project). This would seem a banal statement of the obvious were it not for the fact that, as Rose (5) consistently demonstrated, 'unthinking' unionism often assumed the opposite, namely that the institutions of the UK formed a great arch of eternal duration and providential meaning. It should be said that this 'unthinking' unionism was rather different from Kidd's 'banal' unionism since Rose was directing his criticism mainly at the English. Rather, he thought that it is the fact of the national parts being so intimately related over a long period of time which has given the UK its comparative constitutional stability, or what Bogdanor (2009a: 119) has called the strength of 'underlying inter-connections'. In Disraelian language, Rose (2–3) proposed that British people preferred to be governed by Parliament rather than by logic. 'Political institutions make the United Kingdom what it is' and, in particular, the 'Crown in Parliament symbolizes what all parts of the United Kingdom have in common, namely, allegiance and subordination to a common authority.'

Whatever the diversity of local institutions and whatever the necessary administrative accommodation of national distinctiveness, it is this act of continuing consent to authority which Rose identified as the integrating factor, or the living substance, of the fifth nation. The 'abstract doctrine of the supremacy of the Crown in Parliament is authoritative' but only because people have been socialised to think so and to acknowledge it. That is where Ireland proved to be the exception, the original hard case which shows that consent is contingent, not inevitable, and that people can be persuaded to think differently. It is the attempt to persuade people differently which defines the politics of Scottish, Welsh, Irish and now English nationalism, the object being to drain meaning out of fifth nation politics. For Rose (1982a: 87), the UK required 'an equilibrium of disparate forces within nations as well as between national parts' and in the 'maze' of government institutions reflecting the territorial dimension in British politics it was the principle of authority – the Mace – which acted as 'an integrating force'. It was this 'unique authority' which symbolised the integration into the fifth nation of different nationalities on the basis of civic equality. Rose supposed that a new democratic people had been brought into existence by the UK where the history of allegiance to common institutions transcended but did not deny particular national loyalties. Indeed, he was obliged to believe (1982b: 129–30) that so solid had become the fifth nation that 'Westminster is not prepared to admit that Scotland or Wales has the unilateral right to withdraw from the United Kingdom, should a majority there wish to do so'. This is where the territorial politics of Great Britain differed from the territorial politics of the UK because Northern Ireland had been already accorded the right to secede unilaterally. This differential treatment of Northern Ireland led Rose to ask not if the UK was a nation (though he accepted the authenticity of the Ulster unionist profession of being 'British') but if it constituted a 'state', if only because a commitment to the integrity of state territory seemed to be the definition of modern statehood.

The practical, everyday reality of the fifth nation was government policy (1982a: 104): 'Policy unites what geography divides.' This was so because the expectation of British citizens, irrespective of place of residence, was to have common standards of public services. From the perspective of the fifth nation, Rose thought that primary consideration was – and should be – given to functional requirements rather than to territorial distinctiveness. Policy was formulated according to priorities set 'by a particular functional minister' and only then modified where necessary by 'territorial ministers with concurrent responsibilities'. The functional premise of government policy-making was common standards while the territorial offices of state – Scottish, Welsh and Northern Ireland – gave voice to their respective national interests at the centre. They had administrative discretion locally but their key responsibility was to modify the delivery of services appropriate to standards elsewhere in the UK. British government, Hugh Seton-Watson (1979: 272) once complained of the political classes in Whitehall and Westminster, 'think in bureaucratic categories, use bureaucratic language and are on a different wavelength' from the national sentiment of the territories they governed. From the functional perspective of the fifth nation, however, that was a perfectly logical and reasonable wavelength to be on not only because it was the basis for the design of common services but also because the artifice of state was to be not only above particular national sentiments but also to identify collectively what was equally necessary across the UK. The principle of the fifth nation (in its post-war shape at least) was 'that the benefits which the individual derives from the state, and the burdens imposed upon her should depend, not upon geography, but upon need' and this demanded a distinctive governing perspective (Bogdanor 2009a: 110). One contribution to *The Territorial Dimension in United Kingdom Politics* made 'constitutional centralism built around the Crown-in-Parliament and ministerial responsibility' one of the crucial 'invisible bonds or linkages of the union', concluding that, rather than any elaborate, dramatic or imaginative form of devolution, what was needed was 'the development of the modest advantages for the United Kingdom as a whole of territorial administration as represented by the Scottish and Welsh Offices' (Kellas and Madgwick 1982: 32). Like Rose, this proposition assumed a particular form of fifth nationhood, one in which the territorial offices assured central integration more so than they secured distinctive treatment and as James Mitchell's (2009: 116–20) survey of the archives has shown, this concern with uniformity of standards across the UK was shared throughout the 1970s by all ministers and top civil servants (for an exquisite mandarin critique of devolution from the fifth nation viewpoint see Isserlis 1975).

This was a very social democratic understanding, of course, but it was one that had also been adopted by Conservatives and added to an older one which emerged once Lloyd George had apparently conjured the Irish Question out of existence. As *The Spectator* (cited in Evans 1998: 25) had recommended in 1922, defence of the UK now had to mean much more than Ireland and it proposed that such credible defence would involve *inter alia* 'the maintenance of the moral, political and commercial fabric of nation – opposition to that dangerous, fissiparous tendency which tolerates every kind of disruptive action'. And though this editorial was addressed almost exclusively to threats of class division it could be, and was, called into service to define the British case against national separatism. Indeed, its advocacy of 'the union of forces and of hearts at home for the internal welfare of the nation' reads a lot like the defence of the UK advanced 80 years later by the Gordon Brown and Douglas Alexander (2006). In this way the moral and the instrumental aspects of fifth nation have for long been bound together in the language of British politics and deployed by all major parties. Rose (1982a: 62) also believed that a major functionally integrative element in the politics of the United Kingdom was the party system. The major parties of state (with the exception of Northern Ireland where they did not organise) helped to translate regional and national concerns into the common (functional) language of fifth nation politics. The concern of parties was only incidentally with territorial questions or even self-consciously with the maintenance of the UK because to 'give major importance to questions of national identity would distract attention from functional issues' like health, education and economic policy. Whatever the policy disputes between the parties, Rose (210) thought that there was universal agreement about where those disputes should be resolved and that was in the democratic forum of the fifth nation at Westminster. In sum, this idea of *the* fifth nation supposed that the UK was an association in which the whole was greater than the sum of its parts, a distinctive, even paradoxical, union of patriotic citizenship and of popular, because consensual, constitutionalism and Rose (62) wished to illustrate its successful cohesion despite national and regional differences. He believed that Westminster was more than the sum of representatives from its component nations but in its deliberations as a whole expressed the interest of the fifth nation by giving integrative effect to the artifice of the constitutional people which was discussed in Chapter 1.

In an otherwise very positive review of *Understanding the United Kingdom* shortly after its publication, Bogdanor (1984: 76) thought that what was lacking was an indication of the dynamic factors in Scottish and Welsh politics. 'We are given not a moving picture but a snapshot taken at a time when the ties binding Wales and Scotland to the United Kingdom seem remarkably secure; but such a snapshot, as we have seen before, can prove misleading.' This was slightly unfair for Rose did think that the old 'steady state' of the fifth nation was now entering a more 'fluid state' though in the 1980s he still felt that it was sufficiently robust to withstand any threat of decomposition (again the position of Northern Ireland was the exception). Certainly, Rose feared that devolution would present an institutional challenge to that sense of commonality. The biggest uncertainty of devolution was 'whether and how competing claims of representative legitimacy would be resolved' (1982a: 202). Today this is *the* dynamic British question and that it has become an urgent question lies – as Rose thought it would – in the divergent logics of competing representative legitimacies. Devolution provides for the institutional recognition of distinctive national peoples and admits the principle of popular national sovereignty most obviously in Scotland and in the provisions for secession in the Belfast Agreement of 1998 but it cannot be said to be absent in the case of Wales either. After the establishment of devolved administrations in Scotland, Wales and Northern Ireland one can detect an inversion of Rose's argument in public commentary. For instance, Douglas Hurd (cited in Bogdanor 2007a) thought that the UK had now become a 'system of amazing untidiness – a Kingdom of four parts, of three secretaries of state, each with different powers, of two assemblies and one Parliament, each different in composition and powers from the others'. The implication of Hurd's remarks was the opposite of Rose's: that the untidiness and internal illogicality of these particular arrangements are far from robust. There are a number of questions here, political as well as constitutional and together these questions mean that it is difficult to speak of *the* fifth nation in the way in which one could before 1999. How have things changed?

Challenges to fifth nation

Firstly, it can be argued that the process of legitimising devolution through referendums in Northern Ireland, Scotland and Wales has weakened the fifth nation by legitimising national mandates at the expense of the multinational one. This, of course, had been one of A. V. Dicey's central arguments against Irish Home Rule because he believed that leaving this major constitutional issue for the consideration of the Irish alone was a matter of political dereliction rather than a matter of constitutional wisdom. Home Rule was 'a plan for revolutionizing the constitution of the whole of the United Kingdom' and as such, it was proper to insist 'that the proposed change must not take place if it be adverse to the interests of Great Britain'. Home Rule for Ireland implied a new political partnership, a revision of the common 'Articles of Association', and there was nothing denigrating to the principle of nationality in the argument that 'no modification can be made which in the judgement of his associates is fatal to the prosperity of the concern' (Dicey 1973: 17–18). As Mitchell (2006: 469) has noted, the main criticism of devolution since Dicey 'has been concerned with its implications for the state as a whole and, in particular, that part that has not been given devolution [England], not with how it might operate within the components of the state'. In the case of Irish Home Rule the principle invoked by its opponents was that of the 'predominant partner'. Lord Salisbury, for example, claimed that Liberal proposals for Ireland lacked legitimacy because they were dependent on Irish votes alone and that the 'predominant partner' – the British electorate as a whole – should be required to give its imprimatur before constitutional change took place (Chadwick 1999: 368). Ironically of course, it was the unreformed House of Lords which ultimately became the repository of that principle of the 'predominant partner', an irony which discredited the notion though, with possibly greater irony, the present House of Lords has again moved into the frame as a possible 'National Assembly of the United Kingdom' (Lord Strathclyde cited in Hope 2011). The proposition that in the matter of self-government the fate of the part should be decided by the whole was lost then and was only to re-surface in recent history when (some may think, surprisingly) Ian Paisley would call periodically for a UK-wide referendum on the constitutional status of Northern Ireland. The devolution referendums in Scotland and Wales in 1997 and Northern Ireland in 1998 were not UK-wide if only because this would have allowed the predominant demographic partner – England – the decisive voice, even though there was no evidence that English voters would have opposed the proposals for either Scotland or Wales and certainly not in the case of Northern Ireland (Curtice: 2006b). Nonetheless, some political theorists have been concerned at such deliberative exclusion. For instance, David Miller (1995) made a strong case for the rights of the fifth nation (though he did not use that term) and challenged the notion of separate referendums, *inter alia*, as a violation of the larger, constitutional people of the UK. He thought that the absence of universal consultation would deprive citizens of an overarching nationality and diminish the resources of solidarity available to individual nations as well as to the whole.

In his discussion of Isaiah Berlin's own 'liberal nationalism' Miller (2005: 116) intimated one reason for this sympathy with a larger, fifth nation, perspective. Berlin apparently had little sympathy with the claims of minority nations such as the Scots, especially claims for secession, because these claims reminded him 'too much of the original Bent Twig:

these are not the nationalisms of oppressed peoples, but of peoples who resent the fact that their nationhood is not being given equal recognition by their more powerful neighbours' (this is a notion revisited in the final chapter). To some extent this perspective set the real question which Miller was addressing in *Citizenship and National Identity* (2000: 37): 'When we encounter a group or community dissatisfied with current political arrangements the question to ask is not "Does this group now want to secede from the existing state?" but "Does the group have a collective identity which is or has become incompatible with the national identity of the majority in the state?".' For Miller, of course, this was not an argument against devolution – indeed he favoured 'a constitutional arrangement which gives the sub-community rights of self-determination in those areas of decision which are especially central to its own sense of nationhood' – but he believed that the larger community should have a voice when difference threatened to become separation – if only because it is possible for people to misrecognise themselves. 'Just as we might say of an individual who tries not merely to reinterpret but to jettison the identity he has been brought up to have that he probably doesn't understand himself, we can say that for the Scots to renounce their higher-level British identity would in one way be to fail to understand who they are, what makes them the people they are today' (138). Simply to ignore the connections derived from a history of overlapping cultures and experiences would be a betrayal of the complex truth. Equally, 'a unilateral English vote to annul Scottish devolution ought to be given no more weight than a unilateral Scottish vote for independence' and for Miller (139–40) the reason is that the 'British people taken together have established a valid claim to control the whole territory of Britain, and this claim would be infringed by unilateral secession'. This concern is taken up again in the final chapter.

If this argument sounds strange to our ears it is because we have become accustomed to a different refrain, one which is not necessarily nationalistic but which can be pressed into nationalistic purpose. A good example can be found in Brendan O'Leary's (1996: 447) intelligent review of Miller's argument: that it was insufficiently liberal and insufficiently nationalist, limiting the 'national self-determination for peoples who are not part of the *Staatsvolk*'. However, O'Leary's is a nationalist antithesis of a multinational thesis for it ignores the legitimacy of the 'and' in fifth nation (Welsh, Scottish, English, Northern Irish *and* British). It promotes the four nations and one state view but with a significant implication – only one of those nations, England, constitutes a *Staatsvolk* such that the political character of the state is already inherently partial, an echo of the old internal colonial thesis. That is loaded language indeed and confirms Rose's expectation that the battleground of the British question would not be between nationalism and Westminster but between nationalism and people with dual loyalties – a national identity and a British allegiance. However, it is language which has gained in strength since the new millennium. The journalist David Aaronovich, for example, reflected that in everyday discourse the term 'border' between Scotland and England was no longer being used only as a metaphor but increasingly as a real thing. A convention was developing that 'you cannot now be something in Scotland and England simultaneously – now you have to choose' (2007). Of course, if that sense were universalised it would mean the death of fifth nation.

It is clear that if the Scots, the Welsh or the Northern Irish did vote to secede from the UK there would be no attempt by the British government to resist. The principle of national consent – become an act of substantial popular sovereignty – would take priority over any residual claims of fifth nation. Rose's view in 1982 was that Westminster would *not* admit to Scotland and Wales a unilateral right to withdraw from the UK but that Northern Ireland was the exception to that rule. Today, by contrast, Northern Ireland has become the rule such that the contingency of consent, rather than the continuity of consent, is thereby accentuated. This may be explained in the following way, indicating a principle which informs a distinct idea of the UK as *a*, rather than *the*, fifth nation. It is intimated in the work of contemporary theorists who argue that 'vanity secessions' may be legitimately constrained insofar as the value of self-government is respected. In other words (Costa 2003: 84), 'there is some plausibility in the idea that, when a union is perceived as voluntary, secession is in reality less likely to occur' and therefore 'the best way of achieving what just-cause theorists aim at – the prevention of instability or violence caused by secession – might very well be, at least in some cases, the recognition of some sort of (legally regulated) plebiscitary right to secede'. This is the implicit principle – it is far from being explicit – informing post-devolutionary British politics. In other words, insofar as Westminster is no longer *the* fifth nation – the exclusively representative voice of all British people on all matters – but the representative of *a* fifth nation in deliberations about common interests, then its claim cannot be as categorical as Rose understood it to be. This informs Bogdanor's point (2009a: 113–14) that, in the new devolutionary dispensation, Westminster's role cannot be to insist that break-up of the UK must not happen. It must be to ensure that the principle of consent is fully acknowledged and 'that this consent be clearly displayed before accepting the break-up of the kingdom'. That is a measure of changed times and a wise dispensation.

This has most relevance in the case of Scotland. How would a fifth nation interest be expressed in the debate about independence? This is of particular relevance given the referendum on Scottish independence which will be held in 2014. The politics of the referendum will be considered further in Chapter 9 but the function of fifth nation in that deliberation would be the sum of what would be lost by the breaking up of Britain. Debating the instrumentality of relations between the parts of the UK, in other words, might encourage a re-statement of those shared, non-instrumental frames of reference thought to be intrinsically good (Frost 2001: 503). On the other hand, events might highlight only the contractual character of the UK and test to destruction the principle of solidarity, especially in England. It is another indication of the times that the outcome of the referendum is uncertain for the maintenance of the UK but it is also far from obvious that nationalism would win the day. As Haesly's (2005: 81) survey of opinion showed, expectations of the demise of fifth nation as a psychological attachment and of the UK as a political association are very premature. A deeply-rooted sense of British affinity, especially elective affinity, remains. 'In other words, Scottish independence and Welsh autonomy are arguments that must be made rather than simply being the inevitable next step of the devolution project.'

The second challenge to fifth nation is the institutional arrangements of rule in which Rose once had such confidence. Writing after the first year of devolution, Meg Russell and Robert Hazell speculated that one of the long-term effects on Westminster might be changing public perceptions of the significance of the devolved institutions. Devolved institutions could become first order with Westminster relegated to second order significance. 'One of the ultimate effects of devolution' they thought (2000: 221), 'may be that Westminster is increasingly eclipsed by the new institutions.' Indeed at Westminster, MPs from Scotland, Northern Ireland and to a lesser extent Wales have struggled to define their role as specialists on reserved matters like the economy or foreign affairs (Paun 2008: 216–17). In this sense, the more exclusively 'fifth nation' these MPs become the danger is the less representative of their own nations they may appear. If their respective publics come to consider them as marginal to daily concerns then fifth nation loyalty may also decline as local interest, group activity and policy networks shift attention to democratic institutions in Edinburgh, Cardiff and Belfast. For the moment, however, such marginalisation at Westminster is a possibility and not a fact as the prominence of MPs representing Scottish constituencies such as Danny Alexander, Douglas Alexander and Jim Murphy and representing Welsh constituencies such as Peter Hain, Chris Bryant and Paul Murphy shows. Fifth nation solidarity which comes from common deliberation about common predicaments could atrophy and promote the incremental dis-aggregation of the UK into bargains about national and regional self-interest. In a rapier-like criticism of the arguments for devolution in the 1970s, A. R. Isserlis (1975: 182) observed that there was a tremendous danger to the UK's integrity in the division of legislative functions between central government and devolved administrations. 'Policy, whether major or minor, needs information to make it relevant, experience to make it sensible, and power to make it stick.' But central government after devolution would 'be discouraged from knowing British domestic affairs in any detail at all'. Isserlis, of course, was assuming that there would be English regional governance as well but his predictions now seem reasonably apt for what is happening in Scotland, Northern Ireland and now in Wales. The role of those countries' representatives at Westminster, he thought, would be curiously thin and lonely 'brooding like impotent overlords; introducing legislation on other people's business; promulgating policies they cannot enforce; and generally trying to keep up a fiction that they matter'. They would not be allowed to do the things which really matter like spending money or cutting it, agreeing to something or stopping it. The likelihood would be that they become confined to the observation of things which 'are interesting topics for academics but not real tasks for politicians responsible to an electorate' (184). Fifth nation, or UK matters, could seem very abstract indeed, failing to engage the practical interest of citizens and thereby draining the fertile principle from the conduct of British institutions. To use the expression in its pejorative form, the meaning of British would have become merely academic, a ghostly dance of bloodless categories.

The other side of that coin is that as interest in the institutions of fifth nation wanes, then the self-interest of devolved institutions waxes. Nevil Johnson (2001: 340–1) provided the clearest statement of this concern, observing generally how devolution of power from Westminster – if it were to respect the integrity of fifth nation – should require in the deliberations of the territorial institutions an explicit effort to uphold the idea of the UK 'as the overarching political structure within which devolution is embedded'. In the specific case of Scotland, Johnson thought, this was entirely lacking. There was 'no overt requirement that the new Parliament should in the use of its powers respect the needs and interests of the other parts of the United Kingdom'. Insofar as Westminster retained formal sovereignty but experienced restricted scope for action, the likelihood of fifth nation losing out by default was built into the new dispensation. Equally, and something which Isserlis also feared, Westminster 'no longer has much reason for devoting time to debating Scottish, Welsh or Northern Irish issues'. If the institutional life of the UK becomes understood by the public as distinct national interests jostling for precedence then the particular could become more important than the whole. Bogdanor (2009a: 111), for example, believed that it was undeniable that 'devolution threatens the power of the government of the United Kingdom to secure equal social rights for all its citizens. It is difficult to see how the state can secure these equal rights if it has been fragmented and cut into pieces by devolution'. This is not a problem peculiar to the UK as traditional notions of citizenship are challenged by a culture that stresses personal choice and individual rights (see Stoker 2006).This fragmentation of the older assumptions of political association may be compounded in further ways.

The third challenge is the challenge of programmatic diversity. Rose's fifth nation supposed that policy unites what territory divides and this has become much less obvious after devolution. Now it tends to be policy divergence across the UK – on such things as university tuition fees, health care, water charges, prescription charges – and differentials in public spending which attract media attention, insofar as they are acknowledged at all (Greer 2007: 136–59). Of course, the very point of devolution is that there *should* be diversity in public provision albeit within the limits of broad financial equity throughout the UK. The original justifications for devolution were negative as well as positive: negative, in that Scotland, Wales and Northern Ireland could prevent the imposition of central policies lacking local public support (and the *cause celebre* here was the imposition of the poll tax in Scotland); positive, in that the devolved institutions could experiment in the development of policy agendas either particularly suited to local need or which could then be generalised throughout the UK (Mitchell and Bradbury 2004). Of course, doing things differently does not necessarily mean doing things better (for example, see Miers 2010) but the thesis of devolution is that institutions making their own decisions, successful or otherwise, is valuable in itself. This is the 'inherent' value of devolution: that it is has a non-instrumental worth which cannot be entirely resolved into its instrumental consequences. This is perhaps most obvious in the case of Northern Ireland where for the moment the existence of devolved institutions – that they 'are' – is of as much or even greater significance than policy output – that they 'do', though this is likely to change. But that factor is important in Scotland and Wales too, where the evidence suggests that there is often more difference in the 'how' than in the 'what' of policy (Keating, Stevenson, Cairney and Taylor 2003: 131). Devolution has secured legitimacy in Wales, something that would not have been obvious at the time of the referendum in 1997 which was only carried on a vote of 50.3 per cent to 49.7 per cent. Compare that with the referendum on according legislative powers to the Welsh Assembly in 2011 which was carried on a vote of 63.49 per cent to 36.51 per cent. This has happened largely because in the devolved territories 'self government has come to be viewed as the appropriate political expression of how they wish to be governed' (Wyn Jones and Scully 2009: 14). In short, devolution allows for the recognition that different parts of the UK have different centres of political gravity (even though England's centre of gravity remains *centralised*). As Greer (2005: 503) reminds us, policy divergence pre-dates devolution because distinct policy communities already existed and 'while Northern Irish, Scottish, and Welsh debates came to matter more and gained participants with devolution, they were already like their societies present and distinct before devolution'. What has changed may be detected in Bogdanor's (1984: 76) former questioning of the reality – about which James Kellas (1973) had written – of a Scottish political *system*. Then Bogdanor had argued with some justification that there was no political system but that there were policy networks. It is now the case (Greer 2005: 514) that policy divergence is a simple reflection of the existence of different political systems and, because of its permissive multinationalism, the UK 'is a particularly likely case for divergence'.

Certainly, reading policy divergence through media headlines often conveys a sense of nations drifting apart and these headlines are often taken to reflect a mood of grievance when it comes to differences in public expenditure across the United Kingdom. As 'Bagehot' (2007) observed in the *Economist*, what is most damaging to a sense of common Britishness (or fifth nation) 'is the fact that the devolved Scots now enjoy important perks, such as some paid-for medicines and (soon) free university education, that the English don't – preferential treatment that violates a deep if illogical English expectation that government should treat everyone everywhere the same'. That it does have an effect can be shown in some alarmist headlines such as: 'A deeply divided kingdom: Scots each get £1,600 more state cash a year spent on them than the English' (*Daily Mail*, 30 August 2011) and 'Government spending gap between England and Scotland widens' (*Daily Telegraph*, 30 August 2011). Here is a disposition that implies the end of multinational solidarity, sacrificed on the altar of national self-interest. This intimates a 'velvet divorce' or what McLean and McMillan (2006) called the 'Slovak scenario', one encouraged by the perception that the English are being exploited in the new dispensation (see Chapter 8). Again, one should always be wary of reading one's politics through the headlines. It has been a common complaint of British politicians (Wallace 2011: 18) that 'grown-up politics' are rarely reported in a 'grown-up' way, with every difference and divergence becoming a life-threatening UK 'split'.

If the post-war model of social citizenship (which Rose took for granted in 1982) has now been cut into pieces by the impact of devolution (as Bogdanor thinks) a countervailing consensus about what solidarity means in modern fifth nation politics has been slow to emerge. According to Walker (2010: 241), the old 'conversation' fails to engage so effectively and the new one has been fragmented and often ill-focused. It has often appeared that the debate has hastened in the opposite direction as devolved policy is discussed as if it exists in a sphere unrelated to UK-wide conditions. Jeffery (2009a: 289) came to much the same conclusion, arguing that one of the most significant features of the devolutionary process is that 'there has been no sustained attempt to review and renew the purposes of union since devolution'. Here is a distinct echo of Rose's concern that the fate of the UK could be threatened by well-meaning politicians at Westminster thinking about the Union when they had never done so before and either making the wrong choices or making no choices at all (Rose 1982a: 222). A sense of perspective is required because there is a history to this as well. Walker showed how the debate in Northern Ireland in the late 1940s about 'dominion status' provides an example which cautions against a certain type of devolutionary self-absorption (Walker 2010: 241). This is another example of 'Kant's dove' politics which sometimes informs thinking about devolution and its effect.

By that is meant the illusion that the distinctive policy paths of devolved institutions would somehow be better without the institutional context of fifth nation. That is the reference which Walker makes to dominion status, the illusion of some Ulster Unionists that self-government could flourish and prosperity grow by diminishing the constraints of UK membership. Today devolved governments have been able to give different emphases to social policy but this has been done mostly at the level of organisation rather than of entitlements. Greer (2010: 191) states 'Kant's dove' succinctly. 'If they had to sustain themselves on taxes, or negotiate their subsidies from the UK state on a programme-by-programme basis, the effects might be very different – with their organisation more to Westminster's taste, possibly, and their levels of services tailored to different taxing capacities (reliance on own revenue without subsidies would be a disaster for Northern Ireland and Wales; Scotland's future fiscal stability is more contestable because it depends on assumptions about oil reserves, offshore drilling rights and oil prices).' For true nationalist believers such instrumental considerations would not apply – independence is an intrinsic, non-instrumental good. It is expected that prosperity will be its consequence, of course, but ultimately such consideration must be of secondary importance. Nevertheless, this perspective is often fostered and fed by not only the possibilities which devolution delivers for things to be done differently but also by the negative claim that the main value of devolved institutions is the ability to 'stand up' to Westminster. This may be no more than political rhetoric but it can also foster a popular belief that the policy of Westminster is somehow alien and in each and every case inimical to local interests, a point made strongly by the Secretary of State for Scotland (McNab 2011). And devolution may over time encourage that belief in an unforeseen way and effectively drain the solidarity from fifth nation politics.

The fourth challenge is the challenge of party politics. Rose believed that the dynamics of party competition were a countervailing force to the politics of national identity. Since devolution inevitably means that matters of national identity are paid greater attention, the opposite effect may be detected, an effect which raises and does not subdue issues of territoriality. Devolution can advantage nationalist parties because when it comes 'to arguing about who can best stand up for Scotland or Wales, a party that is only concerned with Scotland and Wales has a huge advantage over ones which are trying to balance those concern's with UK ones' (Trench 2008a: 6). Fifth nation politics here could become a potential liability since the increased strength of the SNP, for example, can be traced directly to the establishment of the Scottish Parliament. Further proof for this may be taken from the disappointing performance of the Ulster Unionist and Conservative Party alliance in the General Election of 2010 (see Chapter 9). This inversion of effect could also happen by accident, irrespective of the historic commitments of political parties. For example, the proposal to end the equal voting rights of all Westminster MPs which has appeared in their manifestos consistently in recent years would mean that the 'Conservatives could no longer claim to be Unionist, but would have become an English party'. To be an English party does not 'sound like a party of government' but this would only be true in the context of the old British, fifth nation state (Hazell, 2006: 226). In the devolved state it could become – and dangerously so for the integrity of the UK – an electoral advantage. Indeed, devolution poses a doubly existential problem here. Westminster remains the sovereign Parliament of the UK; but in the absence of devolution for the largest nation it is also the Parliament of England. The tension is between Parliament seeking to legislate for England, though that legislation is potentially determined by non-English votes (the celebrated West Lothian Question); seeking to legislate for England alone but also affecting every part of the UK; and seeking to legislate directly for fifth nation or British interests. 'The British government, similarly, has a dual role. It remains a government for the whole of the UK, part of whose responsibility is to arbitrate between the different parts of the United Kingdom, and also a government for England' (Bogdanor 2009a: 115). That tension is complemented by the other side of the post-devolution coin. According to Johnson (2001: 341), Westminster 'can hardly avoid becoming more and more a purely English Parliament, notwithstanding the responsibilities it still has for matters of great importance affecting the United Kingdom as a whole'. Westminster could become a proxy for an English Parliament such that it could no longer claim to represent *the* fifth nation, not even *a* fifth nation, but to represent only one nation, England. As Bogdanor (2009a: 113–14) noted, it is 'difficult to resist the conclusion that Westminster in practice is no longer sovereign over the domestic affairs of Scotland and Wales; or that, at the very least, the sovereignty of Parliament means something very different in Scotland, and to some extent in Wales, from what it means in England'. Only with regard to England do the parties at Westminster continue to enjoy the policy remit they hitherto enjoyed for the whole of the UK. These matters are considered further in the next chapter where the character of a fifth nation in UK politics is explored institutionally. These challenges are serious ones but they are not determining ones and the enduring substance of fifth nation (until now) may be outlined directly.

Devolution paradox

The argument is that even though the delivery of major public services has been devolved a fifth nation perspective continues to be essential for common funding, irrespective of how that common funding is or should be allocated. For example, the conclusion of the Calman Commission on Scottish Devolution (2009) was that the 'UK is an economic Union with a very integrated economy, with goods and services traded within it all the time. We are absolutely clear that this economic Union is to Scotland's advantage and in considering how devolution should develop we have been very careful not to make recommendations that will undermine it'. In the consultation document (2008: 2–3) which preceded that report, the two truths of devolution set out at the beginning of this chapter were clearly identified. On the one hand, devolution admitted the principle of difference, allowing 'in principle' for different welfare provisions especially in relation to health and education. On the other hand, welfare is based on a principle of 'sharing risks and pooling resources' and driven by ideas of equity and parity. 'It does not matter whether an individual is ill in Caithness or Cornwall: he or she has access to free health care when and where it is needed, supported by taxes paid across the UK.' Excepting the possibility of the break-up of Britain, Calman obviously expected a concept of fifth nation to remain crucial to meeting those universal *and* particular needs. As a consequence there would continue to be across the UK 'expectations among citizens and political elites alike that common standards, particularly with respect to public services, will be maintained', irrespective of proposals for amending the common funding of public services (Tierney 2007: 747). These two truths together constitute what has become known as the 'devolution paradox'.

A study of devolution in practice by the Institute of Public Policy Research considered that the options for policy were either limited to variations in policy outcomes by territory, with a re-emphasis on the ideas of equity and parity such as Calman had identified; or unlimited policy variations within the UK in line with the differences in preference that Scottish, Welsh or Northern Irish communities might decide upon and express through devolved democratic processes. The evidence convinced the authors that the 'current devolution settlement treads something of a middle line, with core welfare entitlements reserved to the UK level, and therefore held in common, while other areas – most notably public services – are devolved with few legal constraints'. The paradox is this. 'Citizens appear to want devolved institutions to have more powers yet they appear also to be uncomfortable with territorial policy variation' (Jeffery, Lodge and Schmuecker 2010: 8). If this sounds familiar it is because it calls to mind again Kidd's remark (2008: 300) about 'the vast yet variegated terrain which constitutes the middle ground between the extremes of anglicising unionism and Anglophobic nationalism' which forms the dominant tradition of British politics in Scotland particularly, Wales and Northern Ireland.

An important Welsh study made the same point. It found that 'strong support in Wales for devolved decision government (indeed, for the strengthening of devolution) coexists with equally strong support for unified policy outcomes across the territory of the state, and for the transfer of resources from richer to less privileged areas within the state's boundaries' (Wyn Jones and Scully 2009: 15). Though Welsh people endorse the principle of self-government, they also favour uniform policy outcomes for everyone in the UK, supporting measures of territorial solidarity to ensure that differences across the whole country are, as far as possible, minimised. And this finding applied in a comparative basis across Europe. 'While there is general support for political participation at the regional level, only in a few cases – all of them, including Wales, "national regions" – does this extend to support for investing significant policy competences at that level' and in almost all cases, there was also majority support for uniform policy outcomes (21). What such studies seem to show is that a fifth nation dimension remains at work even in the policy divergence which is true now of Scotland, Wales, Northern Ireland and (it should not be forgotten) England. This would have been obvious to Isserlis (1975: 185–6) for whom there was no evidence or even prospect 'that individual citizens in any sizeable number in any part of Britain would for long, in practice, accept very material differences between themselves and their fellow citizens in other regions as regards either the methods and scale on which they are taxed or the broad priorities on which the proceeds of such taxes are spent'. Accordingly (Mooney and Williams 2006: 625–6), 'the dual national universes of the devolved nations and Britain here are reflected in successive attitude surveys that show continuing and widespread public support for the key institutions of the British welfare state'. The sting in the tail of this claim is that nation and welfare are now being 'mixed' in different ways which could threaten the middle ground of public support, especially in Scotland. And it remains to be seen if, when seriously tested, Isserlis will prove to be correct. Nevertheless, there still appears to be a 'primordial' dimension to being British which the experience of devolution has not erased.

Therefore, the question which Madgwick and Rose asked a generation ago – how do the distinctive parts fit together to form a United Kingdom? – remains the question today. It is a question of even greater salience because devolution has fostered the institutionalisation of distinctive politics in Scotland (now with the prospect of independence), Wales (growing in political self-identity and self-confidence) and in Northern Ireland (once again). The practice of self-government has encouraged differing expectations and modified policies and though devolution assumes a relationship within a larger political association recognised as possessing authority, it is that very authority which nationalism ultimately disputes on the basis of distinctive politics, differing expectations, unique policies and separate institutions. The British question has always been: how can the authority and utility of the UK be sustained under a new territorial dispensation? This can no longer mean the assertion of the rights of *the* fifth nation as described in *Understanding the United Kingdom* for, as previous chapters have argued, the evidence of both opinion polls and recent history speak against it (Curtice 2006a). Its authority cannot be found in some new 'project' either but only by securing the allegiance of citizens across the UK. How that allegiance can be articulated in the devolved UK without contradicting but instead complementing the distinctive politics of the nations is the real stuff of territorial politics. Westminster must give voice to a popular sense of being part of *a* fifth nation which the evidence of the devolution paradox shows is still widely held (how *deeply* held is likely to be tested in the next decade) and it requires on the one hand political sensitivity and administrative intelligence at the centre of British government and on the other hand acknowledgement of the UK's authority throughout the state. In short, it requires maintaining a fine relationship between the non-instrumental and the instrumental. In the first case, that being part of a fifth nation does remain important was expressed by a surprising source, the comedian David Mitchell (2011). He wrote that 'Scotland's fate mustn't be decided by people who consider themselves to be primarily English, Welsh or Northern Irish. But I'm sad that, as a result, most of those whose emotional investment is in the union, we children of this potential divorce, won't have a say.' He concluded that, if the Scots did choose independence, the British 'will have lost their country'. That is the sort of sentiment which contradicts the 'four nations and a British funeral' mood which one more frequently encounters in English discourse (see Chapter 8). If the UK is to survive it is the sentiment which needs to be generally evoked. In the second case of political and administrative sensitivity, Robert Hazell (2008) has argued that whatever about its enduring 'values' it is the common interests of the UK which help to underpin it. The practical difficulties of holding together this union of sentiment and interest are considered in the next part of the book.

Part III
Agendas

7

Institutions and directions of travel

The previous part of the book concluded with the suggestion that the meaning of being British today is somewhere between definite and indefinite articles, between *the* fifth and *a* fifth nation. To use the terminology of the first section, the fifth nation is how people in the UK – Northern Irish, Scottish, Welsh and English – read their own differences into the commonality of British. By contrast, a fifth nation means that what is common in being British is read into the differences of being Northern Irish, Scottish, Welsh and English. This may appear to be a mere semantic distinction but there are important institutional and conceptual consequences in the distinction. Institutionally, Westminster was the exclusive democratic representative of the fifth nation (Northern Ireland excepted between 1921 and 1972). Pre-devolution it was a 'three-in-one Parliament' operating as the legislature for the individual needs of Scotland, Northern Ireland and England *and* Wales, as well as being the one legislature for the whole of the UK (Hazell 2001: 269). Post-devolution, Westminster is no longer the exclusive legislative body and Rose's old maxim that policy unites what territory divides no longer operates. The shift from the UK as the fifth nation towards the UK as a fifth nation intimates a new way of conceiving relations between the parts and the whole. For example, Mitchell imaginatively identified a further modification to the familiar distinction between unitary state and union state. As we have noted, in the 1970s and 1980s students of British politics, under the influence of scholars like Rose, came to accept that the term 'unitary' was inappropriate to describe the UK and shifted to the use of 'union' state. Devolution in its present asymmetrical form has rendered even that term questionable and for Mitchell (2007: 35), devolution now means that the UK has the character of a state of diverse unions. The term 'union state' is no longer adequate 'to capture the variety of forms that devolved government takes and the different institutional forms and practices that have been adopted at the centre in response'. Mitchell thought it best to describe the UK as a 'state of unions'. To conceive of the state in this fashion implies that diversity is now much more pronounced – he believed the UK will become 'an ever looser union' – but this is not the same thing as claiming that the state will inevitably break up (Mitchell 2009: 225–6). Indeed, this understanding of the UK as a state of 'different unions' was adopted and used positively in the very unionist Final Report of the Commission on Scottish Devolution (Calman), a Commission (2009: 57) dedicated to confirming the proposition that 'Home Rule within a Wider Union can work'.

In attempting to capture the changes taking place, Schopenhauer's (1892: 142) fable of the porcupines suggests itself as a useful metaphor. A number of porcupines, Schopenhauer wrote, huddled together for warmth on a cold day but as they pricked one another they were forced to disperse. The cold drove them together again and the process was repeated. After many turns of huddling and dispersing they discovered that a comfortable relationship involved maintaining a little distance from one another. It is only when we discover a moderate distance, Schopenhauer believed, that life becomes tolerable: we can be distinct, our mutual needs can be reasonably satisfied and, as far as possible, we can avoid pricking one another. He used an English expression to capture the wisdom of this association: 'Keep your distance.' Of course, this fable concerns the worth of individuality and the limits of sociability not of nationality and it cannot be pressed too far. However, it does have a certain explanatory appeal. Translated into terminology appropriate to the constitutional structures of the UK, the fable of porcupines implies that association within and between the countries is always changing but in renovating their association – in modifying the distance if you like – between themselves, the nations are capable of recovering or instituting degrees of autonomy without sacrificing their solidarity. One might think this to be a very British compromise, the political equivalent of the historical metaphor of the dry wall, and it appears to describe the sort of middle ground between union and separation which devolution was intended to occupy. On the one hand and unlike endism, this fable does not assume some necessary direction of movement though Schopenhauer did think that a porcupine of some heat would prefer to remain outside the huddle neither pricking nor being pricked and this was clearly his own preference for *personal* association. *Politically*, it may be that the Scots will come to think that life outside the UK is not the cold house some have predicted, especially if the SNP can convince enough voters that the European Union provides 'alternative accommodation for the dysfunctional family' of British nations (Weight 2002: 731–5). That is a possibility but not yet a probability and as the first part of the book tried to show, a change in how the nations stand in relation to one another does not imply the end of the UK. On the other hand and unlike the old providential story, this fable does not expect a UK without tensions and difficulties but accepts those tensions and difficulties as part of political life. There will be pricking between institutions and prickly relations between administrations on important issues and this will now be based on different democratic mandates. For most of the twentieth century the distinctive national characters of the porcupines appeared irrelevant to issues of collective or individual need. This was expressed most famously by Aneurin Bevan's reference to the *British* irrelevance of the distinction between Welsh and English sheep. That old, transcendent and absolute belief has certainly diminished as Chapter 5 indicated.

If one tried to characterise the poles of debate about the future, a political rule of thumb would be that nationalists stress the painful antagonisms of the UK and the constraints of huddling together. For example, Alex Salmond (Fraser 2007) once used a very porcupine-like reference to Scottish independence, claiming that it would mean England losing a surly and prickly lodger but gaining a good neighbour instead. Reversing the claims of traditional unionist argument, he argued that mutual warmth comes from benign separation which for all concerned, English as well as Scots, is preferable to the cold house of the UK. Of course unionists continue to stress the warmth and security of the UK and the real freedom which multinational association brings. If pricklish national grievances make being British uncomfortable at times, the solidarity experienced by most people makes it worthwhile, sustaining common citizenship within the shared space of the UK. Maintaining that association in a state of unions means reconciling institutionalised national differences with multinational allegiance, permitting territorial diversity but without widening territorial disparity (Morgan 2001). That is a tall order. In short, how can British government best guarantee the interest of fifth nation, satisfying mutual needs and, as far as possible, avoid pricking the nations into disaffection? And how might of this be secured institutionally and operated politically?

Mitchell again provides useful guidance here. He noted that there have been two competing tendencies evident in central government policy after 1997. The first is what he called the 'diffusionist tendency' which has looked favourably upon the devolution of power away from Westminster and Whitehall. The second is the 'sovereigntist tendency' which has tried to resist that leaching of power from the centre. 'Devolution involves a case of the diffusion of power alongside the assertion of parliamentary sovereignty' (Mitchell 2009: 134). Certainly, the diffusion is often exaggerated for as Hazell's analysis (2007: 260) showed, on a crudely quantitative measure Westminster 'continues to be the most important source of primary legislation for each part of the country and the UK government continues to be the most important source of secondary legislation'. These two tendencies co-exist as one might expect in a political culture which prefers to justify change with the language of constitutional continuity and, of equal significance, confirms continuity in the language of constitutional change. Mitchell's tendencies can be re-described as the tension between thinking still of Westminster, or the centre, as *the* fifth nation – sovereigntist – and thinking of Westminster, or the whole, as *a* fifth nation – diffusionist. The *British* task is not only to prevent diffusion becoming dissolution but also to be mindful of the dangers of thinking only in terms of sovereignty. What is clear is that devolution has put the politics of territory and therefore the national question on the agenda in a way which (Northern Ireland excepted once more) would have seemed very unlikely a generation ago. The national question (rather, national questions), Hazell observed (2008: 290), is one 'which will never be fully resolved (short of independence), and managing it wisely will be a permanent task and permanent challenge for the UK government'. That is a sound assessment. The suggestion of this chapter is that two truths are in play in this case as well. If devolution does give voice to nationalism – the expectation of its supporters, of course, was that it would be only lower case nationalism – at the same time it seeks to transcend nationalism of the upper case, separatist, variety. This may sound contradictory but these are the two truths which it is the object of territorial politics to hold together (Bogdanor 2009a: 119). However, if the UK can be described as a state of unions, with the implication of loose association (not *loosening*, which is a very different notion), it is important to acknowledge that there is another reality. A diversity of unions does not mean that there is any necessary common interest between the devolved institutions which can fashion a countervailing power to Westminster or the centre. Thus the communiqués which follow trilateral meetings between the leaders of the devolved administrations often stress a common agenda and a collective interest (see for example Scottish Government 2011) but this is more presentational than actual. The reality is more often divergence of interest, particularly over finance. Gerry Holtham (2010) revealed the implication for financial equity in the way the devolved administrations generally relate to the centre. 'Wales', he argued, 'is by far the politically least influential part of the UK, with no credible threats to the centre, no senior politician in the coalition government, few Parliamentary seats, fewer marginals.' But this was not only a case of Wales being taken less seriously by the centre but also a case of differential influence exercised by devolved institutions. Westminster, which is 'extremely sensitive to the reaction of Scottish and Northern Irish politicians and give them the benefit of the doubt', simply has much less reason to do so when it comes to Wales. In short, if the UK has become a state of unions this may not always work to the individual or even to the collective advantage of the devolved territories and Wales does have a very good case to feel aggrieved.

Others have adapted the distinction between self-rule and shared-rule, often applied to federal systems, to make a similar point about the new devolved condition. Trench (2007a: 281) thought that after 1997, while the UK had adopted a system which combines shared-rule with self-rule, the relationship between devolution and institutional power in that system remains uncertain. It is often thought that uncertainty about this relationship continues to be a flaw in the arrangements which cannot benefit the cohesion of the UK. For example, Swenden (2010: 13) argued that the UK has gone a long way towards accepting the fact of self-rule but that insufficient attention has been given to the provisions for shared rule. Rather, self-rule has come at the expense of shared-rule and this makes the UK rather unique internationally. The 'mechanisms to tie or integrate the minority nations in the UK as a whole will continue to weaken', Swenden thought, and if something was not done to redress this tendency it could become the 'Achilles' Heel' of devolution. In other words self-rule, if it is not balanced by a continuing sense of fifth nation allegiance, will increasingly promote an exclusively national self-regard, encouraging the 'narcissism of small differences' between the parts *of* the UK and between the parts *and* the UK (Mitchell 2010). That is the route to fragmentation of interest and possibly separation. And though it is often said that breaking-up is hard to do, this may not be true at all of devolution. Indeed, one constitutional theorist (Wicks 2006: 170) controversially claimed that devolution is not an easy option at all for the UK to manage because secession 'is far less problematic in constitutional terms than an arrangement which seeks to reconcile devolved powers with a unitary constitution'. Scottish independence 'would involve little more in legal terms than the repeal of the Acts of Union of 1707, whereas the solution achieved in 1998 of Scottish devolution requires far more complex legal and constitutional restructuring'. This overstates the difficulties of devolution and the simplicities of secession but it identifies the challenges facing central government in the new dispensation. There is always the temptation in conditions of political complexity for people to long for simple 'clean starts' and 'clean breaks' and nationalism is nothing if not a great simplifier.

However, the notion of 'shared-rule' may not be an appropriate description of how the UK functions for there seems to be too much of the federal or even the confederal about that term (and perhaps even the frequently used term 'quasi-federal' may go a bit too far). At any rate, it seems inappropriate insofar as it implies equality in the sharing of rule between Westminster and the territorial institututions. The SNP, for example, has been concerned to assert a framework such as this and has been both consistent and logical in arguing for the enhancement of those institutions which at least intimate the progression of self-rule into shared-rule between (ultimately independent) equals. This explains the interest shown in the British–Irish Council established after the Belfast Agreement of 1998, the permanent secretariat of which is located in Scotland and to which, as Salmond confirmed (Scottish Government 2010), the Scottish government remains highly committed. It is represented in the guise of an intergovernmental institution which can deliver regular and constructive cooperation between the member administrations. Indeed, some (Nairn 2000: 278) have seen in the British–Irish Council a possible template for intergovernmental relations 'after Britain'. This is an imaginative aspiration – and it has a certain 'porcupine' logic – but it is no more than that at present. In his oral evidence to the Scottish Commission on Devolution, Bogdanor (2009c) explained why and dealt directly with the question of there being a possible institutional mechanism to resolve 'head-to-head' disputes between the UK and the devolved administrations. 'No. The UK Parliament sees itself as sovereign, and would not accept an arbitrator, which would seem to be a new sovereign.' Westminster, he thought, would see that as 'too important a power to surrender'. As the discussion of fifth nation tried to show, devolution is not just a Welsh, Scottish or Northern Irish matter. The UK perspective (Winetrobe 2011: 99) is fundamental and not just additional 'and the priorities and imperatives of a centre which ultimately controls the devolution scheme will continue to have a huge, even decisive, say in the future'. And so long as the centre's overriding imperative is the maintenance of the UK that will be the 'policy yardstick by which any territorial governance proposals will be measured'. Self-rule is still within the framework of *shared-out* rule from a powerful centre, placing a large responsibility on that centre to manage affairs sensitively and intelligently, confirming Mitchell's view (1996) that the break-up of Britain, if it were ever to happen, would not be so much a consequence of devolution but a failure of the UK.

It was observed in Chapter 6 that one important aspect of devolution has been to call into question that very principle of Parliamentary sovereignty, intimating a modification of the way in which UK politics works.

Walker (2000: 397) argued that in recent years, and as a consequence of constitutional change, the British state has come closer than ever before to accepting parliamentary sovereignty as a matter of form rather than substance; 'in other words, while ritual deference continues to be paid to the legal theory of the unitary state, the developing culture of negotiation and balanced settlement reflects a rather different political understanding'. There seems to be some wishful thinking informing this view, however. Devolution is asymmetric but power is also asymmetric. If things have changed – Bogdanor's notion of power being cut into pieces – things have also remained the same – the centre retains unique resources of power, political and financial, unavailable to the devolved institutions (Marinetto 2003: 606). In this relationship the sovereignty principle (Hadfield 2005: 294–5) continues to play a key role in how devolution is conceived and for 'all the talk of decentralisation and constitutional reform which devolution has engendered, the central principle of executive dominance remains untouched'. This was certainly true of the first years of devolution though the question is whether it always will be so, especially with the success of the SNP in Scotland. The task of achieving sufficient harmony between the asymmetry of devolution and the asymmetry of power has become a key task of British politics. For this reason the fundamental issue in the politics of the UK is to make constitutional and political forms congruent with changing public philosophy (Bogdanor 2009b: 77). This is a two-sided coin. For nationalists this means persuading Scots, Welsh, Northern Irish and English that state should correspond with nation. For those wishing to maintain the UK it requires persuading citizens of the enduring value of the multinational Union.

Practical experience

If this is one of the fundamental issues in British politics, then quite a few critics believe it is not being properly addressed. On the one hand, Flinders (2009: 385) invented the striking term 'constitutional anomie' to describe what he took to be the 'debilitating condition' of modern British governance. The symptoms of this condition include 'the introduction of reforms in a manner bereft of any underlying logic or explicit principles, combined with the inability to adopt a strategic approach that is sensitive to the inter-related nature of any constitutional configuration'. Though this criticism is addressed to the incoherence of general contemporary constitutional thinking in government, it applies in particular to reflection on devolution. Like Norton (see Chapter 3), Flinders repeated a commonly held view about the absence of a master plan for this revolution of practice, agreeing with Marquand (1998) that it lacks theory, is muddled and un-intellectual, a programme 'of sleepwalkers who don't quite know where they are going or why'. Flinders concluded (405) with the observation that Labour had 'deconstructed' the UK's venerable constitution without providing an alternative set of values or principles. 'The old rules do not appear to suit the new game, and yet the government continues to insist that the old rules apply'. This is a forceful argument and the case is argued with imagination and style but much of its authority lies in the frequency of its academic repetition. Though one can agree with the argument that times have changed, that old models of governance are no longer appropriate and that there was a cavalier quality to Labour's approach, there is a degree of rationalism inherent in this criticism, a rationalism one might call anticipatory coherence, one which seems at odds with the practice of politics. What may be academically magnificent may not be possible politically and the rationalism is doubtful if only because political practice is often un-theoretical, pragmatic and uncertain, a condition not confined to British politics alone. The argument that contemporary problems lie in the absence of a master plan assumes a certainty which is rarely evident and may expect too much.

On the other hand, and while sharing the concern about strategic thinking, Trench (2009a: 69) believed that a lot of academic energy was wasted on trying to find a clear rationale for devolution, especially a definitive master plan which would resolve all its inconsistencies, anomalies and asymmetries. 'As the present arrangements represent a largely pragmatic and ad hoc response to a broad political demand, it is not surprising that it is hard to find a golden thread of rationality or consistency in them, and that even when assessed against a set of models of ideal types designed largely for the UK case it is impossible to relate the present situation to any of the models proposed'. In other words, devolution owed a great deal to the past both in the relationship of the parts to the centre and in the way the centre managed its constituent parts (see also Mitchell 2007: 47). Certainly, this is what the 'state of unions' understanding suggests. As Trench (2009a: 70) defined it, the purpose of devolution for Westminster was utilitarian rather than idealist since the intention was to deliver constitutional mechanisms to deliver what people appeared to want. For the people of Scotland and Wales this meant 'a greater sense of devolved autonomy, but without creating either a federal system or leading to larger-scale change'. That purpose was not absent in Northern Ireland either but in addition there the objective was to underpin a fragile peace. This is not to excuse political leaders, to exonerate lack of imagination or to assume that things were either inevitable or that what was legislated for ensured that all is for the best in the best of all possible worlds as was sometimes implied (Falconer 2006). It is merely to put things into a 'dry wall' perspective and to warn against expecting too much of politics. Nevertheless, it is important to consider the cause for concern about Westminster's lack of systematic engagement with the devolved institutions and the substantial criticism that the arrangements now appear increasingly incoherent.

In an updating of the Westminster tradition, Rhodes, Wanna and Weller (2009: 118) argued in 'dry wall' style that 'British traditions of responsible government emerged through accretion. Separate and different conventions were amassed slowly into a recognisable but ever-changing form'. This was no abstract idea or master plan but a concrete manner of politics. Devolution adds to and modifies that accretion thereby modifying how things stand in relation to the UK as a whole. Critics would argue that the Westminster 'system' is just another way of talking about whatever politicians decide to do and in this regard devolution is taken to be nothing other than a collection of ad hoc responses to events (King 2001: 100). This was something which Brendan O'Leary (1987: 24) suggested was often the case in Northern Ireland and best illustrated by the Anglo-Irish Agreement of 1985. While at the time and subsequently the Agreement was defended as an act of strategic, intergovernmental, political imagination, it is better understood as the result of a pragmatic logic on the part of the government. The logic was not inherent in some great master plan but in the practical necessity 'to do something about Northern Ireland'. The Agreement was that something and there was incentive enough to do it. Far from being a dramatic departure it was better described as 'the outcome of the policies and actions of state institutions'. This was the substance of Bradbury's (2006: 576) perceptive view that when it came to devolution, Labour ministers became adept at making a constitutional virtue out of a reluctant necessity. Indeed, Tony Blair's only major speech on the constitution was, appropriately enough, his John Smith Memorial Lecture in 1996 which committed the party to fulfil the devolutionary commitment of his predecessor (but for the seriousness of Blair's interest, see Norton 2007). This is not all there is to be said of the British political tradition but it identifies an important aspect of it.

Certainly it has been well said of British administrative practice that what some academics see as revolutionary, most practitioners see as Whiggishly evolutionary (Rhodes, Wanna and Weller 2009: 472). Indeed, reviewing the state of reflection on the constitution by scholars and practitioners, Alison Young (2005: 170) thought that there was still little theorising from first principles or any appetite for cutting and thrusting about ideology. It is perhaps unsurprising that this tradition amongst civil servants and politicians should make the constitution so dependent on practical circumstances. With regard to the character of the UK as a territorial state, she thought that 'for the future, pragmatism is all'. Yet in that pragmatism – if one looks hard enough – a principle can also be found. When interviewed on the impact of devolution Sir Richard Wilson (2002), former Secretary of the Cabinet and Head of the Home Civil Service, answered that there is no 'five-year plan' if only because change (and the implication was *political* change) cannot be planned for. 'In a very British way we have taken where we were and adjusted it to reflect the new world we are in, but we have kept what was good and what was working and we have changed what had to be changed. That is what we will go on doing.' Of course, it is wise to treat this evidence with a degree of Mandy Rice-Davies scepticism – 'they would say that, wouldn't they' – and one should also be aware of bureaucratic professionalism which prides itself on adapting to new challenges without openly questioning the rationality of those challenges. Nevertheless, the pragmatic principle was confirmed by one of Wilson's successors, Sir Gus O'Donnell (2008) when he reflected on the changes that had taken place in the course of the last decade and the changes that were likely to be made in the course of the next. Development of relationships between administrations in a more formal manner was likely but how far and in what configurations needed to be established 'in the light of experience'. The key issue O'Donnell identified was the need for sustained effort to ensure that devolution matters get the priority they deserve in the policy-making process. That sounded very much like business as usual.

There is certainly evidence of such pragmatic adjustment and bureaucratic professionalism in the evidence given by officials to Parliamentary select committees at the beginning and at the end of devolution's first decade. As the Report of the House of Lords Select Committee on the Constitution (2002: 10) so felicitously put it, devolution was simply accepted as a settled part of the UK's constitutional arrangements and what the Committee sought to examine was 'how it works at present, and its implications on a more day-to-day, practical level'. The evidence from those responsible for the administration of the devolved settlements was at least reasonably consistent. In its submission to that Lords Committee, the Northern Ireland Executive stated that relations were set out in documents such as the Memorandum of Understanding between the UK government and the devolved administrations, the bilateral concordats between devolved departments and their UK counterparts and the consultative guidance notes issued by the Cabinet Office in London. These documents, the Lords committee was reminded, did not have the force of law but stated 'the principles of consultation, communication and confidentiality which are central to the good working relationships which have been established and maintained between the four administrations'. The conclusion was that the new system was already working well and that the informality of understandings ensured the smooth operation of devolution, a point which was emphasised as well by the evidence of the Welsh Assembly Government (WAG). Its submission pointed out that difference is not the same thing as criticism and that it would be wrong for the machinery of intergovernmental relations to be obsessed with eliminating all differences of view. The principle enunciated by the WAG was 'policy divergence is the welcome consequence and not the weakness of devolution' and the personal conclusion of the then First Minister, Rhodri Morgan (2008), added a political coda to that benign policy view: 'The question is whether devolving power has added to that allegiance variegation to the extent that a weakening of the union becomes more likely. I do not believe there is any evidence for this.' This too sounded very much like business as usual.

In his evidence to the House of Commons Justice Committee in 2008, reflecting on a decade of devolution, the then Permanent Secretary to the Scottish government, Sir John Elvidge, conceded there was always a risk that the different circumstances of Scotland, Wales and Northern Ireland would be overlooked at UK level and he saw his role to be 'the boy at the back of the class putting up my hand and saying, "Please, sir, there is another dimension to this"'. There were, of course, well-publicised disagreements on policy between the Labour government and Scotland, for example on community care for the elderly (Marnoch 2003) and some in Welsh Labour wished to put 'clear red water' between the party in Cardiff and the party in Westminster (Davies and Williams 2009). Even in these instances, the impression was not one of constant friction, a point emphasised by the then Secretary of State for Scotland, Des Browne (2008): 'Actually, despite what may surface occasionally and make people think that there is constant tension, there is nothing of the sort; people are getting on with it at bilateral levels.' On the whole these informal arrangements did seem to facilitate the operation of devolution and to contain potential disagreement. Indeed, the evidence from central government was even more categorically positive.

For example in its rather declaratory memorandum to the Justice Committee, the Ministry of Justice (2007) praised the UK's unique flexibility which had enabled the country to evolve and accommodate change such that a decade after devolution the 'UK Parliament remains sovereign, but the Union now functions in a more inclusive and consultative way'. Moreover, the 'state of unions' was singled out as a great strength because its asymmetry reflected the different historical circumstances and political ties between the nations of the UK. Certainly there was no indication whatsoever here of constitutional anomie. Indeed, the then Lord Chancellor and Secretary of State for Justice, Jack Straw (2008), showed his annoyance at academic criticism of the pragmatic and piecemeal accommodation by central government to the challenges of devolution. He could not understand the point of questions about the role of central government. 'What is the centre for? The centre is to deal with reserve matters and to ensure good governance across the United Kingdom as a whole.' And it was taken as axiomatic that the tasks of the 'centre' as they were carried out ensured the best outcome for everyone, irrespective of where they lived. Criticism that responsibility for devolved policy was fragmented ignored the proper, three-fold division of responsibilities at the centre: individual settlements were looked after by the Scotland, Wales and Northern Ireland Offices; wider constitutional matters were dealt with by the Ministry of Justice; and the Cabinet Office coordinated the inter-departmental work of government. Straw's response, then, was an accurate reflection of the insider view that things were as they ought to be. This was government as usual.

However, it was Hazell's opinion (1998) that in its early years at least, Labour government practice had been rather cavalier, assuming devolution to be a case of 'been there and done that' such that central government could now move on with little disturbance to traditional behaviour. This certainly appeared to be Tony Blair's attitude. 'One can imagine', Bradbury and Mitchell wrote (2005: 302), 'that issues of territorial politics, other than the vexed question of Northern Ireland, rarely crossed the Prime Minister's mind with any sense of urgency.' It is quite remarkable that so little about relations with devolved institutions appears in the published political memoirs and diaries from the Labour years 1997–2010 and there is hardly anything at all about what might be called a territorial strategy. Furthermore, when former junior ministers reflected on their periods in office little mention was made of their experience of or thoughts about territorial politics. 'Given that many consider Labour's constitutional agenda to have been one of its most successful areas of policy, it's telling that middle-ranking ministers simply never even noticed this particular part of Labour's record' (Trench 2010a). In other words, for these politicians too it seemed just like business as usual. The main criticism of this approach to devolution (as with other areas of policy) has been its informality and lack of structure. There is a big difference between the absence of a rational plan for devolution and not paying attention to or showing great interest in devolution. The first may be excused as traditional British pragmatism but the second sounds very much like carelessness. An IPPR report thought that relationships between London, Cardiff, Belfast and Edinburgh had been for too long 'based on gentlemen's agreements and Blair's sofa-style approach to politics' such that with the emergence of 'new territorial politics, characterised more by conflict and confrontation than in the past', central government appeared ill-equipped to deal with the challenges (Lodge and Schmuecker 2007: 93). Originally there may have been very good administrative reasons for this lack of institutional structure. For example O'Donnell's (2008) justification was that busy politicians and officials just found that formal institutional structures – like meetings of the Joint Ministerial Committee (JMC) apart from the JMC (Europe) – 'added insufficient value to justify the heavy burden of work that (especially because of the need to travel) they created'. In the press of modern government and the call on ministerial and official time that certainly is a very good, pragmatic reason.

What connected institutional practice and constitutional justification in this distinctive approach was another well-referenced aspect of devolution, the electoral factor. Labour (and Liberal Democrat) commitment to devolution in Scotland had been – in part – to provide electoral insurance against any future Conservative majority at Westminster, a legacy of Margaret Thatcher's terms of office. That consideration was also a strong factor in Wales and it was not entirely absent in Northern Ireland, albeit for very different reasons. Devolution, then, was intended to counterbalance Conservative electoral strength in England, particularly in the south. This represented a 'nationalisation' of electoral mandates, raising implicit questions about the scope of the UK or 'fifth nation' mandate, especially if the Conservatives got back into office. Of course for most of recent history, Labour was in office in Westminster, Wales (either alone or in coalition with first the Liberal Democrats and later with Plaid Cymru), and until 2007 in Scotland (in coalition with the Liberal Democrats). Before the return of stable devolution to Northern Ireland in 2006, Labour Secretaries of State had governed by direct rule. This meant reliance on the informality of party relations to secure goodwill with Edinburgh and Cardiff and on executive authority in Belfast to deal with matters there. It was also the case, as Paul Murphy (2008) admitted, that neither central government departments nor MPs at Westminster were really prepared for devolution and the prospect of policy divergence. Arrangements were designed for the convenience of the Labour Party and these seemed perfectly adequate given its expectation of electoral dominance in Scotland and Wales. What has happened since 2007, especially in Scotland, has disordered those expectations.

Certainly, one recommendation of the Lords Select Committee was quite prophetic in that, while it acknowledged that informal arrangements for intergovernmental relations were probably sufficient they were likely at some point in the future to seem merely *sufficient unto the day*. In 2002 the extensive use of formal mechanisms for intergovernmental relations might have appeared a bit excessive. The committee proposed that it was wise to assume a time when governments of different political persuasions had to deal with one another and when the structures of devolution might change, such as the Welsh Assembly acquiring primary legislative powers (2002: 6). The committee, while acknowledging that devolution had bedded in remarkably smoothly and praising especially the professionalism of the civil service in ensuring that this was the case, believed it would be prudent to put in place a more structured process. However, interviews with officials showed how 'excessive' that sort of recommendation seemed for it was generally accepted that politicians would gravitate towards informal procedures but the important thing was that the formal machinery was there to be used if necessary (see Horgan 2004: 120). This sounded very British and very pragmatic. Interestingly, there was some praise from a comparative point of view for the foresight of the civil service arrangements which were designed as much for collaboration as they were for dispute resolution (Greer 2010). This captures well the problem: the assumption that collaboration would always be the case and that disputes would easily be accommodated by informal understandings. The later House of Commons Justice Committee report on the experience of ten years of devolution was more critical. Firstly, it did welcome the reconvening of the JMC in domestic as well European formats following the formation of an SNP government in Edinburgh. On the other hand, it expressed concern at the 'patchy performance' of central departments in adjusting to devolution and thought that a strategic approach was now vital to strengthen the UK interest as a whole. In its response to that report (2009: Cm 7687), the government's line was again business as usual. It noted how procedures had been put in place to ensure that the devolution settlement would be observed within and across departments. Whether this is sufficiently 'robust' to secure a fifth nation interest remains to be seen. What would that interest look like anyhow?

Directions of travel?

Until quite recently we seemed to know what it looked like, for it had an ideological label, an appropriate form of governance and again Bogdanor (2010: 171) identified succinctly the change that has taken place. Devolution, he thought, has not undermined the UK but it has undermined an ideology, the ideology which had dominated much of post-war politics and which not even Thatcher could entirely destroy. What devolution has undermined is the ideology of British social democracy which, in principle at least, put mutual satisfaction of needs ahead of national distinctiveness. This is a passing which has not gone without mourning, though that mourning has been muted by the '1066 and all that' line of reasoning that devolution is self-evidently 'a good thing'. As one such critic wrote (David Walker 2010: 84), ostracism from polite society awaits the person who dissents from that polite consensus. Though this was a criticism of local government just as much as national devolution the argument remains the same. In an earlier sustained criticism along similar lines, Walker (2002: 5) claimed that major differences in resources between areas and nations in the UK still required the attention of government in order to provide not only efficiency but also equity. This meant 'a strong, self-confident centre' and in a powerful re-statement of the non-instrumental values of fifth nation politics, Walker (22) insisted that the debate which takes place about the allocation of public spending across and between the territories of the UK 'implies the UK is and remains a political entity within which the assent to redistributive taxation is wholehearted. That means the UK continues as a moral community with social democratic potential, able to assess geographically dispersed need and apply financial remedy appropriately'. The concern expressed here is that the attenuation of the very real, instrumental benefits of common rights and entitlements would tend towards fragmentation under devolution. As the previous chapter's discussion of the devolution paradox showed, the notion of the UK as a non-instrumental community which entails civic equality in public services still has purchase for most people, irrespective of place of residence and irrespective of existing diversity in public services (Jeffery, Lodge and Schmueker 2010: 15). It is in Scotland in particular where the ideology of social democracy is supposed to be alive and well and it is a national self-understanding upon which nationalism seeks to build a case for independence against the supposed market individualism of England (Beland and Lecours 2008: 127–8). Nevertheless, attitude surveys confirm that the supposed distinctiveness of Scottish public opinion in favour of welfare disappears when compared with Wales, Northern Ireland

and the English regions. Indeed, the (Calman) Commission on Scottish Devolution (2009: 65) even went so far as to suggest that if there were a compelling need, one could envisage shifting responsibility from the devolved institutions to Westminster for matters that ought to be uniform across the UK.

Yet there is about the argument for returning powers to the centre an echo of James Fitzjames Stephen's (1967: 156) view of mass democracy: 'The waters are out and no human force can turn them back' but there was no good reason 'why as we go with the stream we need sing Hallelujah to the river god.' Or, to adapt one of Wittgenstein's expressions, trying to refashion the social democratic tradition of centralism out of the changes which have taken place since the 1980s would be like trying to mend a torn spider's web with one's fingers. Not only would this be politically very clumsy and intrusive but also it would be likely to end in disaster. Therefore, the possibility of some reversion to central control is not only conceptually difficult, if not impossible, to imagine but also politically fraught. However unlikely, it at least draws attention to and insists on respect for that public expectation of UK-wide equity – fifth nation perspective – because it remains a truth of modern British life. Indeed, it was this case which the Labour administration (HM Government 2008) made in its submission to the Commission on Scottish Devolution, one which defined parity of social citizenship – 'this pooling of resources and risks' – as a key part of British citizenship. Devolution, it stressed, has not diminished the UK's role in that regard and sharing revenues of the different parts of the country according to need was still 'a very tangible sign of the solidarity that binds the different nations of the UK together'. The meaning of the Labour government's version of 'social union' defines nations bound up in a political association of enduring close warmth where the resources of the whole (fifth nation) promote the well-being of the national parts. And though that re-distributive language may not come so easily to the lips of Conservative politicians it continues to inform the party's unionism. Unfortunately, whatever the rights and wrongs of any proposal for the administration of policy, Isserlis (1975: 174) had predicted that after devolution questions of responsibility for policy could no longer be discussed relatively calmly within a single, sovereign legislature (or as it proved in the first years of devolution, within a single political party) but would be done 'amid a clash of actual or would-be sovereignties'. The pressure, he thought, would be for the pieces to be separated even more and not for them to be re-connected. That was an old-school fifth nation perspective.

Of course nationalists, in principle if not always in practice, favour the complete separation of the pieces. The SNP, for example, has promoted its own idea of a social union – a social and cultural sphere but one made up of politically independent nations. It asserts, as Margo Macdonald (Lee 2007) put it, that the political institutions of the UK have become disjointed, frustrating and lacking in public esteem. The UK is not worth saving but the 'social union' is worth preserving, one which would encompass all the distinctive national and regional communities formerly governed by Westminster. This is a formula intended to counter the arguments of those who claim that independence will separate families and relatives throughout the UK and what it entails is the (former) Union becoming, like the Monarchy, a dignified but no longer efficient association. Welfare would be a national, not a UK matter, and there would be no more shared rule (though there might be some shared functional services), only self-rule. This logical, if exclusive, view was set out in the Scottish government's memorandum to the Justice Committee where the political existence of a fifth nation was only acknowledged *de facto* and *pro tem*. The declaration – as an indefeasible right and as a constitutional fact – was that as a sovereign people 'it is for the Scottish people to decide how they are governed'. The SNP was at pains to stress that Westminster's 'claim' to sovereignty was qualified by the so-called Sewel Convention – that Westminster does not legislate on devolved matters in Scotland without the consent of the Scottish Parliament – and that it would be against the spirit of the new dispensation (*contra* Calman) for any competence so devolved to revert to the UK level. There was a keen interest in intergovernmental relations being formalised in the JMC system as well as in the abolition of the territorial offices (Crawford 2010). The significance of formal intergovernmental relations here is ideological – promoting the devolved administrations as equals to Westminster – rather than practical – there is little evidence that collectively devolved administrations either wish to or have sufficient common ground to act as a political counterweight to Westminster (Hazell 2007: 587). For nationalists, in Scotland primarily but also in Wales, if the *question* of independence has been brought back onto the agenda without shedding a single drop of blood then the *achievement* of independence by institutional means can be accomplished with the 'mutual good will' which has defined devolution so far (see MacCormick 1999: 204). The implication, of course, is that any lack of goodwill would be the result of intransigence at Westminster.

If re-centralisation is highly unlikely and independence remains speculative what would constitute that middle ground where the two truths of autonomy and commonality can co-exist? This question was asked by Jeffery, Lodge and Schmuecker (2010: 20) and they identified two possible answers. It is possible to reflect the 'ongoing attachment to a sense of community at a UK-wide scale and an ongoing sense of

UK-wide solidarity'. Or it is possible for central government to do nothing, to privilege the demands of self-rule and 'let the flowers of diversity bloom'. These are not absolutely exclusive answers but they do imply different expectations of what the UK as a polity would look like. Jeffery (2008) spelt these out clearly in his memorandum to the Justice Committee. The first of these options would 'embed expressions of union more explicitly in the operation of the devolved state' and to clarify, in the language of this book, the terms and requirements of fifth nation solidarity. Jeffery had expressed concern about the understated conception of the UK since devolution and that so far insufficient attention had been paid to the whole. As this chapter has discussed already, the reasons were historical (the state was addressing different 'unions' in each case), institutional (the role of the Labour Party until 2007 as a party of government across the parts of the UK) and cultural (the self-confidence of administrative elites that, when required, the necessary machinery was already in place to deal with any future intergovernmental problem). However, this configuration could otherwise be judged negligent and reactive rather than pragmatic and assured. Jeffery certainly thought that all the prospective challenges could be arranged under one problem: the failure to re-state what the UK is for and how the parts combine to form a single state (the sort of criticism which provoked the wrath of Jack Straw). This was the point, as we noted in Chapter 4, which had been made consistently by Trench (2007b) who, in his written evidence to the Commons Justice Committee, argued that there is a 'hollow centre' when it comes to devolution. If true, this would constitute a most disturbing 'lack', politically and administratively, because it would mean that 'no-one is able to take a view of the territorial make-up of the UK as a whole and of the constitutional and policy issues that affect it'. Departmentally and politically there needed to be a filling up of the centre to ensure that the system operated systematically rather than inconsistently, the conclusion to which the House of Lords Committee had already come and a policy which the Constitution Unit had long advocated. Trench's fear was that fragmentation of responsibility reflected lack of sustained interest in territorial matters. Indeed, he had predicted correctly in his evidence to the Commission on Scottish Devolution (Trench 2009a) what that lack of coordination and disjointedness on university tuition fees might do to policy coherence across the UK.

This criticism has not convinced everyone. Michael Keating, while partially accepting the point about fragmentation, thought that the implied direction of such arguments would indeed be towards re-centralisation and encourage the imposition by Westminster of arbitrary limits to policy divergence. Moreover, such interference by a strategic centre would no longer be the articulation of a British, or fifth nation, interest but would 'in fact be formed by English departments and policy co-ordination would be on their terms'. In short, any attempt to develop mechanisms for UK-wide policy coordination would 'undermine the dynamic of devolution' and contradict its very purpose to encourage the autonomous formation of policy. The term Keating coined (2010: 385) for this disposition was 'neo-unionism', a disposition to see the UK still as a 'nation-state'. Unlike traditional unionism, it favours devolution but is averse to large-scale policy divergence and to the territories working out their own forms of social settlement or welfare nationalism. There is a contradiction in Keating's assessment of 'neo-unionism' however. On the one hand, he presents it as a proposition which needs to be exposed and countered. On the other hand, he accepts the venerable thesis of Jim Bulpitt and believes that neo-unionism is incompatible with the traditional concern of the Westminster and Whitehall elites to secure 'central autonomy'. If Keating's thesis were true, these elites should have little interest in neo-unionism and even less in building an integrated polity and he could point in evidence to the absence of reflection on devolution in those diaries and memoirs of Labour ministers. He is not alone in that view and the lack of a well-thought-through constitutional settlement struck others as having a very Bulpittian feel (Bradbury 2006). Nevertheless, there seems to be a problem with an argument which holds that traditional unionism is dead and yet relies on traditional unionist practice to sustain the weight of its assumptions.

The second direction of travel which Jeffery outlines is the one to which Keating himself would subscribe. In this case autonomy of the devolved nations would be enhanced as the corresponding responsibilities of the UK diminish, a process leading either to a confederation for all, or to independence for some, of the nations. Keating has explored this possibility with subtlety and at length in his book *The Independence of Scotland* (2009). Though he nowhere defines himself as a 'neo-nationalist', his vision is of a UK radically disaggregated into its national parts. Keating's interpretation is too intelligent to accept the simple logic of endism but what he shares is a framework of analysis which looks to the transformative influence of global networks and European integration along with the acceptance that large states are unlikely to prevail in the contemporary world. These are, of course, equally large assumptions though not necessarily false ones. However the framing of the argument suggests, rather like Parnell's view of Ireland: that no boundary should be fixed to the march of a stateless nation. This really does render the UK level 'residual' and would hollow out of the term

British any political meaning. What is absent is a sense of mutuality which, as we noted in the previous chapter, Johnson (2001: 340–1) believed was necessary to uphold the idea of the UK as the overarching political association within which devolution is embedded. Of course, Keating is consistent in believing that this does cut along the grain of Bulpitt's thesis of 'centre autonomy' but that thesis presupposed compliant elites whose interest coincided in sustaining and not in dismantling the UK. It may very well be that – as some still believe that Home Rule would have kept Ireland in the Union – there *are* limits to autonomy and that a mutually self-interested arrangement of constitutional laissez-faire between centre and periphery is what is required, either by choice or by necessity. According to Jeffery (2009b: 120), without some institutional framework for shared interests across the UK and between jurisdictions the likelihood is a centrifugal drift. 'And continued centrifugalism suggests, more or less by default, that a much looser kind of UK is set to evolve, perhaps as a set of relationships between autonomous nations contained within a single state, perhaps as a set of unusually close and interdependent relationships between two or more different states.' In these circumstances, as Keating himself concluded (2009: 178–9), the problem for the Union may not lie in Scotland, Wales or Northern Ireland but rather in England. And it is the question of England which is addressed in the next chapter.

8

The matter of England

One of the closest students of the English question (Hazell 2001: 5) once remarked that 'England remains the gaping hole in the devolution settlement. It is the space where everything is still to play for.' Michael Forsyth (cited in Bogdanor 1999b: 228) used more colourful language and described it as the 'Bermuda Triangle' of devolution. For Forsyth, of course, the English Question was employed to reject the *principle* of devolution while for Hazell it was an anomaly in the *practice* of devolution. It was Hazell's expectation that in the course of time the gaping hole would be filled by the development of stronger forms of English regional governance (then promised by the Labour government) along with the evolution of distinctive procedures for dealing with English business at Westminster. Neither of these expectations has been fulfilled. Firstly, the problem with Labour's original project of English regionalism was that it did not map onto regional affections. Tony Blair admitted (Parker 2003): 'People have got to want it. You have to be sure that this is what I call a people's desire and not a desire of the political class.' And the people did not want it. In an all-postal referendum for an elected assembly for the North-East in November 2004, 78 per cent voted against and only 22 per cent voted in favour. As a consequence, plans for regional referendums elsewhere in England were abandoned. It was once said that the English regions had never barked (Harvie 1991) but now that they had barked, devolution was not what they wanted. However, as the work by Sarah Ayres and Graham Pearce (2004; 2005) showed, English *regional* devolution was never envisaged to have the same constitutional significance as *national* devolution in Scotland, Wales and Northern Ireland. Compared with the political character of devolution elsewhere in the UK, the networked form of governance tentatively envisaged for the English regions was intended to deliver central policy more efficiently rather than to disrupt or to supplant the Westminster-Whitehall model. It was intended to be exclusively instrumental and there was little expectation that it would foster non-instrumental attachments. But as Mark Sandford concluded (2009: 190), the proposals for elected regional assemblies was a 'part-time policy', one not properly thought through and perhaps this judgement could be applied to devolution policy as a whole. The exception to this English rule was the directly elected Mayor of London and the 25-member Greater London Authority, approved in a referendum in 1998. London not only has a distinctive identity within England (and the UK) it is also a 'world city' (Travers and Kleinman 2003) yet it still conforms to the policy concerns of Westminster-Whitehall. Secondly, aside from the Labour government's brief experiment after 2007 with regional ministers and regional select committees of the House of Commons, English structures at Westminster remain to evolve. The Coalition government did not continue with the regional experiment and its programme for government (Cabinet Office 2010a) agreed only to establish a Commission to examine the West Lothian Question (the ability of non-English MPs to vote on mainly or exclusively English legislation), one which would need to take account of reform of the House of Lords, changes to House of Commons business and amendments to devolution. What defined this approach was its obvious lack of urgency. So a decade after Hazell's assessment it can still be said that England remains the gaping hole and that everything is still to play for. How can it be that England remains devolution's unfinished business and what explains the hesitancy to do anything about it (Mitchell 2006)? These questions can be examined by way of an initial paradox.

On the one hand, according to the former editor of the *Daily Telegraph* Charles Moore (1995: 5), the word 'England' is 'an immensely powerful and poetic one, but one that resists clear definition'. He distinguished England from 'Britain' which, by contrast, 'has different overtones, more official and less likely to be used in conversation' because it is 'fundamentally a political word'. The word Britain 'does not evoke so much a series of pleasing sensory images, like well-mown lawns or warm beer or whatever your particular fancy may be, but rather a way of running things, or to be more exact a whole collection of ways of running things, an intricate network of institutions'. Moore's reflection on English identity is one which has traditionally exhibited a distinctive character, defined in terms of cultural 'listing', rich in particular associations or 'sensory images'. This does appear to be a characteristic of English reflection and it is one which has been confirmed by academic research (Ribeiro, 2002). Indeed, David Willetts (2009: 54) observed how in England national ties have not been diminished in an era of globalisation. They mean as much as ever though the English (of course) 'have celebrated these ties with nothing as vulgar as a clear theory'. Instead the English tend to offer 'lists of associations' and Willetts thought that they conveyed a potent sense of shared understandings. This was not political but cultural (58), and he subscribed to Moore's view that there are British political institutions but no English ones. For Willetts at any rate, if one was looking to define the English Question that was it – there are British political institutions but no English ones. If that seems an overly conservative understanding it also informs Marquand's judgement (2008a: 225) that there has always been a lot of poetry about England, good and bad, but not much politics. England, then, 'was intimate, cosy, *home*: the place to be when Browning's April was here'. By contrast, Britain 'was the place for politics, government and the state'. Or, as Rose (1965) described it in a celebrated reference, England is a state of mind but not a state and though one could write of politics *in* England, the politics *of* England were British.

On the other hand, there is A. V. Dicey's observation (2008: 329) that the secret of English liberty lay in the absence of any popular or romantic national idea: 'The singular absence in England of all popular traditions causes some natural regret to poets and even to patriots. Yet it has assuredly favoured the growth and preservation of English freedom.' What distinguished England was its institutions especially the distinctive balance which had been struck between law and public opinion. And in his accustomed manner, David Starkey (1999) differentiated between the 'Celtic-fringe' nations of Scotland, Wales and Ireland which had taken on board the whole panoply of cultural nationalism and England which had taken a different route. In re-stating the case for exceptionalism, he argued that what the English celebrate is not cultural symbolism but political institutions, such as Parliament and the common law. 'In so far as they had national symbols, they were the crown and the Church of England, with its Shinto-like worship of the royal family.' And though Marquand used Powell's famous Royal Society of St George speech of 1961 to illustrate the sort of poetic patriotism which Dicey would have deprecated, it is interesting to note that – certain rhetorical flourishes apart – it was the political institutions of England to which Powell generally referred. What endured, he thought (1969: 339), now that the experience of empire had gone, are 'the qualities that are peculiarly England's: the unity of England, effortless and unconstrained, which accepts the unlimited supremacy of Crown in Parliament so naturally as not to be aware of it'. There is some historical substance to that ideological claim since the constitution and its providential development were central to the Whig interpretation of history (Kidd 1999). Again, if this seems an intrinsically conservative vision, consider

Robert Colls's view (2002: 28) that it was the bonding of people with their common law which was the basis of English national identity. And when this older sense of the law became bound up in the celebration of the constitution, this too was 'a people's story' for what radicals demanded was a constitution that accepted them as equally English. If in the nineteenth century this was a political matter of citizenship in the twentieth century it became a matter of equal social citizenship. In short, England was always a place for politics, government and the state and that great institutional strength underpinned the stability of the UK.

Marquand (2008a: 225) demonstrated how that seeming paradox has been traditionally resolved. In the course of the last three centuries the 'English Parliament had become the British Parliament; the English monarchy, the British monarchy' such that things British came to take on appropriate associations and pleasing images for English people. In this regard, the general principle which Moore applies to the poetic quality of Englishness and the political character of the UK is another example of *distinctio sed non separatio* – it is possible to distinguish between the political character of 'British' and the emotional quality of 'English' but it has been (hitherto) impossible to separate them (see Guiberneau 2006: 67). Because of the sheer size and predominance of England in the UK, the imaginative life of politics could be led as if only England existed and the important thing for continuity in the state was not that the Scots, Welsh or Northern Irish felt British but that the English continued to do so (Canovan 1996: 79). The other side of that British coin is that the Scots, Welsh and Northern Irish can feel themselves dominated by England (and its institutions) even if that feeling cannot be so readily acknowledged by the English. From that angle of view (what used to be patronisingly described as the view from the 'Celtic fringe'), what is British may seem very English indeed. Again, devolution has an effect here because if it addresses the desire of the non-English territories for some security against England it also highlights the political difference not only between what is English and what is Scottish, Welsh or Northern Irish but also, perhaps for the first time, between what is English and what is British. Some had anticipated this positively, with Bernard Crick (1991: 104) writing that the English must stop infusing 'everything that is English into the common property of Britishness'. There are a number of questions here. Has a new political self-consciousness developed in England after devolution? If so, what are its characteristics? Is it possible, as Crick hoped, to distinguish English from British without threatening the break-up of the UK?

British England

The House of Commons Justice Committee investigation into the experience of ten years of devolution devoted a significant amount of time to consideration of the 'English Question'. Its final report summarised fairly the complexity of the matter but also the profound difficulty of addressing it, especially those procedures at Westminster which Hazell believed would have evolved already. Though the governance of England was acknowledged to be 'unfinished business', there was no agreement on what should be done to finish that business. The Justice Committee (2009) identified the main issue to be the West Lothian Question which it defined as follows: government in England remains centralised under the UK Parliament and UK government and is 'therefore subject to Ministers and MPs who do not represent England and whose own constituents come under devolved governments'. Nevertheless one can abstract from the expert evidence submitted to that committee certain arguments which may be said to constitute established wisdom about England's new standing-in-relation to the other parts of the UK.

In the introduction to a comprehensive study of the English Question, Hazell (2006: 20) had argued that 'the English seem broadly content with the status quo' but he thought that the situation was fluid. If there was such a thing as English nationalism it had, in G. K. Chesterton's oft-quoted phrase, 'not spoken yet'. Indeed, there was a general view that it would be best, if it did speak, that it spoke with circumspection. This was really a footnote to Canovan's point that the important thing for the future of the UK is that the English continue to feel British and it was put succinctly by Bogdanor (2008b): 'the price that has to be paid for keeping the Union, which I think is very important for all of us, is English self-restraint'. As Bogdanor pointed out to the Justice Committee, the most significant constituency pressing the English to take a more advanced position were Scottish nationalists and for obvious reasons. This was an agitation at least as old as Nairn's *The Break-up of Britain* (1977: 294–5) where it was argued, with no reference to Dicey's view, that there was 'no coherent, sufficiently democratic myth of Englishness – no sufficiently accessible and popular myth-identity where mass discontents can find a vehicle'. Romantic nationalism (Dicey's bugbear) 'is not only a matter of having common traditions, revered institutions, or a rich community of customs and reflexes'. Nairn thought that England – as Moore and Marquand would agree – already had these in abundance but that English nationalism was 'precluded, above all, by those features of which English ideology is most convinced and proud, her constitutional and parliamentary evolution'. Nairn's purpose, as Pocock (2000a: 46) described it, was to encourage the English to stop thinking of themselves as British. 'All Nairn wants to say by these means is that it is absurd for the English to think they can bring about a multinational politics. In fact, he is more afraid that they will do so than that they won't. The aim of his satire is to lessen their political will, not to transform it.' Nairn's satire may eventually prove successful, but for the moment Bogdanor's view – the established consensus view – is that it is important that the English do *not* stop being British and that it is crucial to sustain their will to do so if devolution is to uphold multinational politics.

For example, Labour's Lord Chancellor and Justice Secretary Jack Straw (2007) once argued that pursuing 'Little England' policies that 'create resentment between the peoples of Britain is a sure means of destroying the union'. Straw's message was really an old liberal one: the failure of Irish Home Rule because of partisan political manoeuvring should remain an object political lesson for England. Therefore, those who criticise devolution should 'learn from that experience and understand that it is by embracing devolution that the union has been able to survive and to thrive'. Interestingly, in his later evidence to the Justice Committee, Straw (2008) used Bogdanor's expression to describe England's place within the Union. He thought that the English could completely dominate the UK if they wished but that this was not in the character of British politics. The Union would endure provided each part of it accepts – the English part above all – 'a degree of self-restraint' and the devolutionary settlement was something about which the English *should* show self-restraint. When it turned its mind to the matter of England, that theme ran like a thread through Labour and Labour-associated thinking (see for example Blunkett: 2005 and Kenny, English and Hayton 2008). Though it may have been expressed differently, the official Conservative view actually dissented little in substance. Kenneth Clarke (2008) thought that 'to rely on English tolerance would not be good enough' but he also thought the reason to answer the English Question was to nip in the bud potential political irritation 'by some sensible constitutional minor change'. This unfinished business was of only limited significance in the larger schemes of things. 'I think resentment could certainly well be sorted out so long as you could tackle what I regard as this niggle that sometimes English matters are settled against the majority votes of the English MPs.' Clarke was aware of the calls for devolution for England but, he queried, 'what is the point of going down that road?' He certainly did not see any point. This view informed the deliberations of the Conservative Party's Democracy Task Force's report (Conservative Party 2008) which Clarke chaired. His report was a form of 'anticipatory conservatism', designed to avert any prospective constitutional deluge. It advocated reform in order to prevent the storm clouds forming and it was a plan deeply conservative insofar as it proposed a modification of existing circumstances rather than radical change. Though the Task Force believed that the present devolutionary arrangements were a threat to the Union because the likely build-up of English grievances 'could undermine the current constitutional arrangements', it concluded that it was important to avoid the 'sort of alienation' experienced in Scotland in the 1980s and 1990s being replicated in England. If English nationalism has remained a mood and not a movement then this is mainly because the Conservative Party has refused to mobilise it as such. The Task Force's objective confirmed the Unionism of the Conservative Party, which is something David Cameron has taken every opportunity to repeat since becoming leader. If the position which became associated with Labour was: dealing with English matters at Westminster is a question which should *not* be asked (Hadfield 2005: 293) – then the Conservative position appeared to be: dealing with English matters at Westminster is a question which *should* be asked but a definitive answer should *not* be forthcoming. Consider Philip Norton's view (2011) that there 'was a need to answer the English question but without doing anything about it'. On reflection, he wondered if there was a stronger case for doing something, or rather some things, to mitigate the problem but without actually answering the question. The Liberal-Democrat policy of dealing with the English Question as part of a new federal settlement for the UK shared the same concern to avoid agitation on the subject if only because the policy was comprehensively unlikely. What has been the view of English public opinion?

There are obvious signs that people in England have become more willing to call themselves English rather than British and there is some support for doing something about the English anomaly but in neither case does it seem to be deeply rooted (Curtice 2006b: 138). In short, the distinguishing characteristic of English public opinion has been its readiness to accommodate the other nations of the UK and this can be attributed to the curious mismatch between constitutional irritation and lived experience. On the one hand, as a leader in *The Observer* of 2 July 2006 remarked, if 'the English are told often enough they should feel aggrieved at the results of devolution, they'll start to believe it'. Certainly, when they are made aware of it, people in England express dissatisfaction with the effects of asymmetrical devolution. On the other hand, because of the sheer size and predominance of England-in-the-UK, life can still be led as if only England existed. Ironically, size and dominance actually limit the calls for English devolution since most people can ignore the anomalies of devolution because, for most of the time, they have not readily impinged on their daily lives. For the English, the challenge appears to come less from the process of devolution and more from the process of European integration. As Curtice (2009) told the Justice Committee, 'one of the intriguing things about England is that, although national identities may be changing, so far at least it is not clear that even those who feel English necessarily particularly feel that that Englishness needs to be reflected in distinctive political institutions'. If one were to summarise the main academic findings about public opinion, the prevailing consensus would seem to be this: the majority accept that other parts of the UK should have some form of self-government; English self-identification has increased since the new millennium but this has not meant an increase in English nationalism; there is still little sign that English support for the UK has been eroded following devolution; and most English people prefer England to be governed by Westminster, not by a separate English Parliament, though they would – when it is called to their attention – like something to be done about the West Lothian Question. As Richard English (2011) concluded, if this is nationalism it is very un-nationalistic.

Again, Hazell made the classic statement about the challenge of devolution to popular political attitudes. The English Question, he argued (2006: 241), 'is not an exam question which the English are required to answer'. It can remain unresolved 'for as long as the English want'. This is the position he has taken consistently: that English people deserve nothing less than being allowed the time it takes to get the answer right. Beyond the academic sensibility expressed here, the crucial point is that the question of what to do about England has not appeared sufficiently pressing for politicians if only because the touted English backlash never seems to happen. H. G. Wells once said that: 'In England we have come to rely upon a comfortable time-lag of a century intervening between the perception that something ought to be done and a serious attempt to do it' and this could be true of devolution as well. As Condor has shown (2010: 539–40), once devolution was implemented there has been frequent talk of an 'English backlash', a backlash which Scottish nationalists welcome, and indeed invite, as the necessary precondition of England ceasing to be British (as Nairn expected). 'Since the alarm was first raised concerning the impending English reaction to the Scotland Act, false sightings of an English backlash on the political horizon have become a regular feature of media reports on matters relating to devolved governance.' Condor found a disconnection between these predictions and the general experience of most of those expected to lash back. 'However, whilst issues relating to the devolution settlement clearly continue to excite media commentators, politicians and academics', she thought, 'ordinary English people by and large remain stubbornly galvanized into inaction.'

However, the historian (and now cross-bench peer) Peter Hennessy (2011), when asked how stable was English support for the Union, replied that the measure of English attitudes was not what was said publicly or measured statistically but what was felt personally. The word he used was 'irritation' and he thought that if the English became seriously irritated by the operation of devolution, then the UK would really be under threat. In that response, he was confirming the interpretation of English nationalism as a sort of irritable growl syndrome – a complaint of varying intensity about present conditions which are felt to disadvantage England but a syndrome with no obvious remedy. This can always change and change rapidly. It does not mean the emergence of a political party of significance – the English equivalent of the SNP for example – but a movement of opinion away from that self-restraint which is the bulwark of the UK (exemplary fifth nation thinking) to self-interest (exemplary separatist thinking). This is a rather different conception of backlash from the dramatic suggestion one finds in newspaper commentary but some think that this should actually impart a greater sense of political urgency. In Christopher Bryant's words (2008: 681): 'The many politicians who acknowledge the anomalies and inequities attached to England's current place in the union but who prefer not to address them until the non-existent easy solution presents itself risk an eventual English backlash.' For many students of the subject, this suggests a rather un-English style of politics. Kumar has written (2010: 481) that for England 'the option of a strong political nationalism is neither a realistic nor a sensible one. It goes against the grain of its whole history – its whole temperament, we may say'. Kumar highlights a useful rule of political thumb: persuading English people to think *nationalistically* involves persuading them to think very differently about themselves and about their country *in the UK*. Nevertheless, there have been counter-indications and others perceive subterranean changes in attitude which herald something which may not be quite 'a strong political nationalism' but which could have a significant effect on England's relationship with the devolved parts of the UK. This has been alluded to by Michael Kenny (2010: 648) who argued that one of the trends since the new millennium is the rise of 'a more salient sense' of English identity. 'Though shunted to the margins of political debate by such pressing concerns as the recession and MPs expenses scandal, this phenomenon may well come to be seen as of equal importance, given its ramifications for the constitution and governance of Britain, by historians of the future when they come to form their judgements of the dog-days of the Brown premiership and the rise of the Lib-Dem/Conservative coalition.' Perhaps an indication of this 'salient sense' can be found in an article in *The Spectator* by Matthew Parris (2010). It was only a brief 'think piece' but its significance lies in the way in which it disorders those consensual assumptions about Englishness, politics and the future of the UK.

With a shrug of the shoulders?

In summary, here is what can only be called Parris's English moment of epiphany. He was listening to the presenter on BBC Radio 4's *Today* programme doing a quick round-up of the weather in December. It is very cold all over Britain, the presenter said. Later there would be 'snow in the north of the country'. Parris asked himself: 'Which country?' And the realisation dawned: 'As an Englishman, and as 2010 drew to a close, I was experiencing for the first time the thought that, when directed towards a predominantly English audience, the ordinary and natural meaning of "the country" might now be England.' Though it is often said that English nationhood is 'resurgent', Parris thought something else was happening: 'Englishness isn't growing at all; it's just unmasking itself.' Devolution of power to Scotland, Wales and Northern Ireland had slowly impinged on English consciousness and people were now reacting in a politically understated but very English way. According to Parris, the English only used the term 'Britain' because they thought it pleased the Scots. 'Now we discover they've gone off the idea. Fine. So let's call it England again.' Here he was unconsciously repeating Stanley Baldwin's old wish (1927: 1) that he could use the word 'English' in his speeches without someone at the back of the hall always interjecting 'British'. But Baldwin made it plain that he was speaking about English culture and was certainly not making any political point about the enduring value of the UK. Parris accepted that his view was a bit of a caricature but then all nationalist thinking involves caricaturing itself and others. What he detected was a 'collective shrug of English shoulders' and he believed there was now a palpable mood for people to say: very well then, 'England'. If the break-up of Britain is in prospect, it isn't Scotland, Wales or even Northern Ireland which are drifting away. 'It is England.' Nationalists who have difficulty persuading Scots, Welsh and Northern Irish to support separatism are finally succeeding by example – as Pocock thought they would *not* – in persuading the English to cease being British. At least that *would be* the case if Parris's view had already become representative of public opinion. This may appear unlikely since what he has to say sounds a bit like Willie Whitelaw's old reference to Harold Wilson in the 1970 General Election: that he was going around the country 'stirring up apathy'. How, one may ask, can an apathetic 'shrug of the shoulders' become a stirring political act? The political implication of this sort of shoulder-shrugging is evident because it challenges academic wisdom on three different but related matters.

The first is a matter of identity. It has been said (Rhodes, Wanna and Weller 2009: 229) that: 'The Scots, the Welsh, and the Northern Irish can and do debate national identity at length and with arms. The English can mount the occasional sortie but, like sex and religion, it is not deemed a suitable dinner table topic.' This may always have been an illusion and the English are probably never *more* English than when either they self-consciously ignore nationality or when they think they *aren't* talking about themselves. That, at least, is how Scots, Welsh and Irish critics have traditionally interpreted the confusion of English with British, the very observation that was made by Seton-Watson about policy-makers in London (see Chapter 6). Roy Hattersley captured this temperament in his collection *In Search of England* (2009: 5) where he devoted a lot of space to listing the qualities of English life but yet saw no point in making a fuss about it. Indeed *not* making a fuss about being English seemed to him an essential ingredient of Englishness. This could be defined as traditional shoulder-shrugging: *of course* our identity is English. That sort of cultural insouciance implies that persuading English people to think nationalistically would mean persuading them to think very differently about themselves and about their country. In other words, the distinction which Moore and others have made between cultural Englishness and political Britishness remains deeply characteristic. Yet it is Parris's suggestion that a change has taken place already and that shoulder-shrugging means something rather different now. It is a gesture signaling that the English *do* think differently about themselves and their country: to use the Moreno scaling, they have become significantly *more* English than British because the trend is for them to think of themselves as English and *not* British. To put this simply, who needs 'arms' (either national militancy or organised political agitation) when you have 'shoulders' (English nationalism represents a loss of interest in the UK for it is Britishness which is being shrugged off). The English nationalist blogger Gareth Young (2011) translated this (once again in the words of Baldwin) to mean that the distinction between culture and politics is collapsing such that 'England is the country, and the country is England'.

There is empirical evidence to support Parris's epiphany. Though 'Britishness has long been no more than a secondary identity both in Scotland and Wales' the most dramatic trend was for it to become a secondary identity in England as well. 'Already relatively weak in Scotland and Wales, Britishness now appears to have lost some ground in England to a sense of feeling English instead.' Britishness as the primary identity of residents in England is thought to be only 48 per cent (Heath, Martin and Elgenius 2007: 11–13). However, as Chapter 4 tried to show, an exclusive focus on the issue of identity may miss what remains of political importance for the maintenance of the UK: allegiance to common sovereign institutions. So long as English people continue to think of Westminster as their Parliament then the prospect of imminent disintegration appears to be limited. If, however, the political consequence of Parris's reflection was the establishment of a separate English Parliament then this would eviscerate the old Westminster. It would, thought Anthony King (2007: 206), leave little for a 'leftover' UK institution to do and in such an eventuality, it would be best to 'make a clean break all round'.

The second is a matter of disposition. The work of Susan Condor (see, for example 2000) has been influential in defining what might be called the English disposition. Condor's extensive interviews discovered something interesting about English responses. Rather than presupposing an 'other' against which to define itself, Englishness tends to function as its own 'other', constructed not in relation to Scotland, Wales and Northern Ireland but self-referentially. This has operated mainly through contrasts with the English past, different places (for example North versus South or urban versus rural), different social classes and different political persuasions. By and large, then, this work has tended to show that the English do not lack a sense of national identity nor do they fail to recognize how devolution has changed the UK. These findings challenge in part Kumar's claim (2003: 34) that there is 'the absence of a tradition of reflection on such questions' as national self-definition and that there is a 'blankness of the English tradition on just this matter of English national identity'. The important point seems to be that neither this sense of identity nor this recognition of the effect of devolution has (as yet) altered significantly the disposition towards the devolved territories. This is another example of benign shoulder-shrugging. The Scots, the Welsh and people in Northern Ireland now have some self-government? Well, we wish them good luck. Parris's argument, however, puts both this self-referential disposition and this acquiescent mood into a very different perspective. He describes an English disposition which is becoming self-regarding though not in an aggressive manner. It implies that the other parts of the UK are fading from consciousness and perhaps even from conscience.

It has happened before, of course. Between the wars, the historian G. M. Young (1947: 104) wrote that it was difficult for his generation, which rarely thought of Ireland at all, to imagine the fervour of the previous generation which appeared to think of nothing else. The (mainly) English amnesia which applied to Ireland after 1922 could now apply to Scotland, Wales and Northern Ireland. Andrew Marr (cited in English, Hayton and Kenny 2009: 361) speculated intelligently on this. He thought that the challenges to English identity did not come from within the UK at all but from trends in globalisation. 'Just as the creation of the Irish Free State had virtually no impact on British identity, so Scottish independence, should it happen, will have little impact on English identity.' There would be no open hostility and the disposition would have little to do with what Bulpitt (1992: 271) once called 'the English "Sod Off" school of Anglo-Scottish relations'. As Parris implied, it is complaisant rather than implacable. If English people now assume that the Scots want to be independent then good luck to them in that as well. This (potential) mood corresponds with the argument found in some recent books which claim, like Parris, that the national disposition has changed already and that England is – in spirit if not yet in fact – already *'after Britain'*. As Perryman (2008: 31–2) proposed, this new state of affairs does not exist 'solely in our imagination' if only because politics is not founded solely on reality. The 'fantasy land we like to call England is taking shape' as people now 'piece together this imagined nation out of the wreckage of broken-up Britain'. A very different England – no longer cultural alone but also political – 'will take shape out of a modern separation as well as ancient origins'. And this is the conclusion at which Bryant (2003: 409) had already arrived, expecting that further constitutional evolution in Britain would prompt more searches for distinctive political expressions of Englishness. Nationalism, as Nairn might say, had finally caught up with the English.

The third aspect is the matter of political imagination. We noted how Rose thought that England existed as a state of mind but not a state. There is also a long tradition here with a celebrated literary connection. In *News from Nowhere*, for example, William Morris wrote (1977: 63; 72): 'I must now shock you by telling you that we have no longer anything which you, a native of another planet, would call a government.' His message was ironic but could also be taken as self-satisfied. The English 'are very well off as to politics – because we have none'. Again, Parris challenges the self-satisfaction of that view, suggesting that the backlash which Condor could *not* detect will come in a very different form. It will be *another* shoulder shrugging affair, not an assertive demonstration of will. In other words it will be a very English form of British dissolution – the UK will go with a whimper, not a bang and possibly many in England will not even notice the passing of the Union. Almost without thinking about it, just as it helped to construct and then deconstruct an empire, England will have become the politics, and the politics, England. Indeed for some, Morris's irony no longer describes an English utopia but an English dystopia. The message here is that it is necessary to politicise England because, in Billy Bragg's terms (1995), as the other nations are coming out from under the safety blanket of Britishness, the English are threatened to be smothered by it. This is not thought to be so much a political as a psychological problem. The confusion of English and British is no longer just a failure to acknowledge the proprieties of the multinational UK. It is a failure to acknowledge the world the English are now in. There is a longing to define a clear identity in order that England will avoid becoming some sort of 'British rump'. This conveys a palpable sense of living amid the decay of an old state and a fear of becoming historically superfluous, of being left behind, of failing the test of modernity. It has encouraged some on the left and on the right to propose that the choice for England is either to continue within a decadent UK and/or to recover or re-imagine that popular Englishness long suppressed by the British connection. Just as the Scots can proclaim their identity to be an exclusively civic one (Ichijo 2005) then the English can do the same (Goodhart 2008).

That notion of the British suppression (or *thwarting*) of England has become quite widespread, again with echoes of Chesterton's famous reference about the people of England who have never spoken yet. The language used shares much in common with traditional nationalist voices of the 'Celtic fringe'. Thus it has been claimed that there 'is a political void where England should be' and while the rest of the UK enjoys self-government, Westminster, the traditional assembly of the English people, speaks for the Union and not for them. 'England, as a political nation, has no body and cannot speak', a perspective which often involves a strong degree of self-pity. The English are 'now a nation with a history but no destiny. We exist; we have needs, but no sense of self. We are baggage-laden travelers with no clue about where we are going, or why, or how' (Glasman 2010). In Scotland, the demand for organising affairs in a distinctively Scottish manner is to be called a nationalist. If the English call for their interests to be respected in a similar manner they are called bigots (Morrison 2008). It is an attitude which crosses the divide between culture and politics, even intersecting with the sacred cow of the national football team. Other states take football failure seriously and devote the resources to dealing with it. 'England has yet to make its footballing debacles an affair of state. But then that's not difficult because England does not have a state' (Younge 2010). Even those not normally associated with this style of thinking have also been influenced by its frequent repetition. Marquand (2008b), for example, thought that unless there was the promotion of a positive 'English national myth' the English will 'not be fit for self-government'. Until such time as they do they are condemned to conduct their affairs within 'an increasingly threadbare Britain', a state which is also increasingly dysfunctional. In short, England once first among nations is now the laggard of history (thus reversing the notion of an English centre and a Celtic periphery). Nevertheless, what Marquand proposed was completely in tune with a possible English nationalist project: that intellectuals should recapture and revive 'the true glory of English history', the radical tradition of Milton and Blake, so that it would have 'twenty-first century clothing', thus making the English fit for self-government. In summary, then, Parris implied an inversion of effect – that English insouciance, once sustaining of the UK, has now become subversive of it. It is important to stress, this is a *mood* and not a *movement* but as Parris intimates, perhaps there is a shift taking place such that the mood may be changing. Here may (at least) be that Chestertonian moment when the people of England finally speak, of political freedom this time and not of cultural ale (for a contemporary expression see Wheatcroft 2009). If all of this sounds quite negative, what are the positive arguments which might impart movement to this mood?

The first argument is institutional. Simon Lee (2007: 158), for example, has argued that devolution has created 'deficits in citizenship rights, democratic accountability and the denial of the expression of England's national identity as a distinct political community'. The political case for England, then, must involve 'the self-determination to vote on policies and issues that affect it alone that devolution has extended to the other constituent nations' of the UK (244). The language here carefully avoids nationalist rhetoric but others have identified a policy to keep the 'English question' out of political debate. As a proposition this is not original. Lord Crowther-Hunt (1976) claimed that the devolution proposals of Harold Wilson's government had given English people a false prospectus about the extent of devolution for Scotland and Wales. What particularly irritated him was 'the false impression that England has nothing to worry about' when obviously its interests would be seriously affected. This 'nothing to worry about' prospectus was sustained by the Labour government after 1997. This view has an interesting intellectual lineage. For example, Bulpitt's thesis in *Territory and Power in the United Kingdom* (1983: 237) was that the multinational Union presented a problem for the 'Centre' in that it had to manage a difficult 'estate'. Though in the history books it was usually recounted as a problem of managing the non-English, a 'less obvious problem', he observed, 'though in many ways a more intractable one, has been that posed by England and the English'. England and the English certainly dominated and continue to dominate the UK in terms of wealth, resources and population but 'the English have never taken the Union seriously. They have either ignored it, or regarded it as a mere extension of England and Englishness'. This was only one side of the question. The other side was that 'England has always been an incredibly localized society, exhibiting a strong distaste for positive peripheral government from any quarter' and, as a result, most of the English have been unwilling to take territorial politics seriously. So here is the conundrum, exaggerated and compounded by devolution today: 'how to run a territorial Union not taken seriously by this peculiar dominant section', a problem which dogged consideration of the Irish Question (Jackson 2004). This English unthinking-ness about the UK and this indifference to devolution for themselves used to be the ballast of the British state but it could also, when alarmed into reflection, become a crisis for any programme of constitutional change, creating uncertainty for territorial politics. Therefore, it can be argued that the UK has involved a deliberate misrecognition of the English Question by successive British governments (see also Guthrie and McLean 1978). According to Bulpitt (1983: 238), the centre 'attempted to relate to (or distance itself from) all parts of the periphery in similar fashion. For the Centre then, if not for the English, England was part of the periphery'. If devolution has significantly disturbed that 'efficient secret' of multinational stability it may have done so not, as the newspaper headlines would suggest, in Scotland, Wales or Northern Ireland, but in England.

The second argument is economic: the case is commonly made in the popular press that the English now need to assert themselves not only for the purpose of patriotic dignity but also for sound material reasons. There are insistent voices claiming that when it comes to public spending, devolution shows how England's lack of political identity is a handicap. Shoulder-shrugging is no longer an option. English nationalists think that governments are buying political quiescence on the 'Celtic fringe' and paying for it with English money (Young 2007). What is commonly identified, in litany form, are the advantages experienced by other citizens in the UK at the expense of the English: certain cancer drugs available in Scotland but not in England; free prescriptions in Scotland, Wales and Northern Ireland but not in England; tuition fees for English university students but not for the Scots and Welsh; subsidised residential care for the elderly in Scotland but not in England. These concerns about England's pecuniary sacrifice and the disharmony between England and the rest of the UK, (especially) Scotland, are often badly misinformed (Bell 2011) – which does not mean that the stories are not repeated. The distinguishing theme of a recent style of English journalistic commentary has been an exaggeration of language at odds with the economic or institutional effect of devolution but not at odds with a certain existential mood. One even wrote that the project of devolution had so 'discriminated against' England that it had created a situation resembling that of the American colonists in 1776 (Rees-Mogg 2005). Here is a trope very familiar in English cultural history, conjuring up that image of Orwell's gentle people, a people with a profound sense of justice and fairness but a people difficult to rouse and slow to criticise. But when the time comes it is a people stubbornly determined to do what is right and to re-claim their rights. There is a serious element to it, however, because a sense of fairness is important not only to English sensibility but also to equity in the UK.

As 'Bagehot' (2007) observed in *The Economist* for example, what is most damaging to the Union is the perception that those with devolved powers now enjoy important perks that the English do not, 'preferential treatment that violates a deep if illogical English expectation that government should treat everyone everywhere the same'. In sum, devolution comes to look like *subsidised* self-determination. The Scots, the Welsh and the Irish get the self-determination and the English do the subsidising and the issue of University tuition fees has put this firmly in the public mind. Even here, of course, the truth is that it is not a case of discrimination against the English but nationalists in England, like those in the Campaign for an English Parliament or in the small party of English Democrats, expect that subterranean changes in mood – those about which Parris writes – will have a decisive impact at some stage on politics. For example, the Labour MP Frank Field (2011) recounted the views of one of his constituents which he took to be representative of wider opinion: 'Why is it, Frank, that if I lived in Scotland, I would have free medicines, free long-term care and my children would go to university without paying the fees they pay in England?' Despite all the talk about grants and their distribution, Field thought that there was 'no reply yet to our English constituents on those points'. As Field went on: 'I have affection for the way our different nations have been grouped into the United Kingdom, but I am anxious, because unless we start to face these questions and answer them soon a general sourness will enter into English politics, and we will not be able to judge where that sourness will lead us.'

There is no doubt, as Field made clear, that the politics of public expenditure has become an issue for English people and it can lead to absurd conclusions of the 'joking, but not joking' kind. As the *Liverpool Daily Post* (Merrick 2011) put it in a commentary on Fields's speech: 'It is now crystal clear what Merseyside needs to do to become an economic powerhouse – threaten to quit the United Kingdom. This is, of course, the action followed by the Scots, who are being love-bombed by the Treasury to bribe them into staying inside the Union.' This is particularly the case when levels of spending per head in Scotland are compared with those in England. Though this sense of grievance was muted in the early years of devolution, at least one in three English respondents now believe that Scotland 'receives more than its fair share', suggesting that the language of disadvantage has begun to make its mark on public opinion (Curtice and Heath 2009: 55). According to an IPPR study of the Barnett formula – used by the UK government to calculate a substantial element of the expenditure in the devolved territories – 'political parties, commentators and the media are increasingly drawing attention to the issue, which may further increase public awareness' such that current practice has the potential 'to become a major source of tension between the constituent nations of the UK' (McLean, Lodge and Schmueker 2008: 6). If you like, that is a measure of the Hennessy factor – a desire to prevent English irritation becoming English political disaffection. As that excellent IPPR study showed, there are regional variations in expenditure per head which qualify a simple nationalistic reading of the figures. Though Scotland and Northern Ireland have levels of public expenditure per head 21 per cent above the UK average and England 3 per cent below the UK average, it is in London where the deviation is highest (28 per cent above average). The North East and North West regions in England are 6 and 5 per cent respectively above the UK average. Yorkshire, the Midlands, East, South West and South East England are all below the UK average. Wales does badly out of the application of the Barnett formula too and is a more deserving case than any other (Independent Commission on Funding and Finance for Wales 2010). Of course, there is a certain irony to English criticism of the Barnett formula if only because it is a formula based on spending decisions in England. This has put the devolved administrations at the mercy of funding decisions made for England and limits their autonomy of action. However, as the IPPR analysis concluded (35), the system for the allocation of public finance needs to be addressed to promote public legitimacy and to enhance solidarity and cohesion throughout the UK. That remains to be done (Mellett 2009).

It is difficult to come to any clear conclusion about the politics of Englishness because things could change rapidly in the next few years. That is perhaps not unusual because things everywhere in the UK could change rapidly in the next few years. Some have dramatically predicted a 'velvet divorce' or what McLean and McMillan (2006) called the 'Slovak scenario', a scenario that 'would be driven from England', the result of that anticipated 'English backlash' to the perception that England was being financially exploited by the devolved territories. Others are genuinely – and with the best of intentions – keen to encourage the English along the road of political self-expression (Hassan 2009; 2011). Yet others show the same sort of impatience with English political reticence which was expressed by Nairn in the 1970s (Perryman 2009). As Pocock knew, the wish of these commentaries is that the English should be other than they are. For as a close analysis of survey opinion revealed (Curtice and Heath 2009: 52), firstly, that English people do *not* feel antipathy to British symbolism; and, secondly, do *not* think that the UK government is antipathetic to England's material interests. That survey concluded (61) with a suggestion how the two truths of English and British could be better related in present times. Englishness 'could be represented alongside Scottish and Welsh as one of a family of "British" identities. Only then are we likely to be able to say that England really is both English and British'. That conclusion corresponded with Richard English's thoughtful essay on Englishness.

According to English (2011: 7–8), what has resurfaced in recent times has been 'an English cultural sensibility, a feeling of distinct identity based on peculiarly English traditions, practices and attitudes' rather than a form of English nationalism. The emphasis here was a repetition of that familiar theme which can be found in Moore, Willetts and Rose – that Englishness is cultural rather than political. In sum, England has experienced a resurgence of cultural identity but not 'nationalism as such'. If this is so, then it has implications for any strategy to deal with the English Question. English thought that the particular matter of Englishness now became the general matter of Britishness. He acknowledged, again like Moore and others, that Britishness carried far less emotional force than attachments to particular nations but if the UK is to endure, its institutions need to accentuate 'the positive and emancipatory elements of British politics and identity, and to diminish those aspects of British nationalism which constrict and weaken, and which generate conflict'. His conclusion was ultimately the one Crick had suggested much earlier – there is little to fear in terms of English nationalism but much to be gained by greater recognition of English identity. 'The blurred lines between Englishness and Britishness, and the absence of a forceful English nationalism, mean that UK political parties can probably worry less about Englishness, and recognise it more openly, than has sometimes been the case.' Further survey work by the IPPR (Wyn Jones, Lodge, Henderson and Wincott 2012: 41) shows that such a definite 'stirring' of a political Englishness is now evident not as 'an unintended consequence of devolution, but also a political project (if that is not too portentous a phrase) enjoying significant levels of popular support in a country that appears to be increasingly conscious of a distinct national identity that is not simply reducible to Britain and Britishness'. The consequences of that 'stirring' remain unpredictable.

Current expressions of Englishness, of course, have a particular context: the new complexity of United Kingdom governance and the uncertainty of how England fits into it. Things have changed but things have also stayed the same. In sum, 'England' remains an immensely powerful and poetic reference while 'Britain' remains a collection of ways of running things and a network of institutions. It is still possible to distinguish between the political character of 'British' and the emotional quality of 'English', now with a greater political edge, but it is still not possible to separate them entirely, despite the claims and the promptings of nationalists. The same is true in Wales and Scotland. That may change and the tensions are clear but for the moment the English have not ceased to think of themselves as the ballast of the UK.

9

Respect and independence

The discussion of certain English attitudes in the previous chapter is reminiscent of Joseph Roth's lament for the demise of Austria-Hungary (cited in Aughey 2001: 182): if the break-up of Britain has become a possibility the reason cannot be attributed to those who wish to destroy it but to the ironic disbelief of those who should believe in and support it. In his magisterial study of the constitutional effect of devolution, Bogdanor (2009a: 108) thought that this analogy was somewhat overwrought. In his view such arguments – especially of those English commentators 'whose conception of England can be a somewhat dogmatic one' – mainly ignore the substantive issues of politics and the very practical benefits of continued Union. 'Too much self-consciousness, after all, is as bad for a nation as it is for an individual.' That is a very sensible position to take, an echo of Barker's view that the English (in particular) are not usually given to 'indulgence in *Weltschmerz*'. This reluctance to take nationalism seriously shows an aversion to (with apologies to Allen Ginsberg) the best minds of a political generation being destroyed by the madness of constitutional controversy, an aversion which applies as much to Europe as it does to the Union. It represents a concern not to let matters of process endlessly distract from matters of policy substance, a disposition which marries Westminster pragmatism with the utilitarian tradition of British policy-making. Bogdanor was really addressing what he termed the 'English Gaullist' mentality of commentators like Simon Heffer (2007) who were signed up members in Bulpitt's 'Sod Off Scotland' brigade and it is also a temptation for even the best of contemporary historians (Sandbrook 2011). As the previous chapter showed, however, there is another distinctive aspect to this fashion in England, that manner described by Alan Bennett (cited in Paxman 1998: 18) as joking but not joking, serious but not serious. Germaine Greer (2005) too has alluded to a 'chronic lack of seriousness' in English culture which frequently baffles outsiders and disorders neat definition. And it is often the case that outsiders, especially the

Scots, Welsh and Irish, encounter this lack of seriousness as itself a nationalistic move. George Walden (2004) admitted that if you probe English sensitivities on national identity too seriously either 'they get you for earnestness' or 'put you down with their toleration' since one characteristic of this disposition is to make other nationalisms appear vulgar. For example, it was something which John Lloyd (2005) amusingly encountered in conversation with a merchant banker and former royal courtier. When Lloyd objected to his use of the term 'English' instead of 'British' when speaking of the UK, the response was 'none of your Scottish nationalism here!' The insight which stayed with Lloyd was that, despite national caricatures to the contrary, it is the Scot who is more likely to be unionist by reason and the English by casual emotional attachment. And it is casual emotion, and not reason, which is susceptible to ironic disbelief. As the previous chapter explored with the example of Parris's 'shrug of the shoulders', disappointment of casual emotion and the consequent rise of ironic disbelief can account for much of contemporary English discontent with devolution. The evidence for this is not hard to find, where jokiness can intimate a serious conclusion and this is important since it is often to England – which constitutes 85 per cent of the UK's population – that much of nationalist argument is actually addressed. As a *Comres* poll for the BBC discovered (Devlin 2011) about one-third of English respondents now appear to favour both an independent Scotland and an independent England – though how serious were these opinions it is difficult to tell.

Two illustrations of this 'joking, but not joking' form of ironic disbelief in the UK are taken not, as one might expect, from columnists in those newspapers consciously addressing middle England, like the *Daily Mail* and *Daily Telegraph*, but from those who write for the newspaper of the British left, the *Guardian*. The occasion in both cases was anticipation of a referendum on Scottish independence following the SNP victory in the Scottish parliamentary elections of May 2011. Firstly, Simon Hoggart (2011) joked that the advantage of Scottish independence would mean the BBC being relieved of the duty of saving the Union by pretending that anyone in England is interested either in Scottish football or in documentaries about standing stones near Stornoway. 'I'm afraid', he concluded, 'I don't see any real disadvantages for either side except the end of a 304-year experiment which worked some but not all of the time. So why do politicians talk as if it desperately matters?' Ironic disbelief could not be better put. Secondly, and despite being a 'gut unionist', Michael White (2011) wrote (in the style of Norman Davies's *The Isles*) about the historical malleability of state boundaries and especially the changing allegiances within them. He was not concerned to think through a rational defence of his gut unionism but to accept the comforting proposition that things will carry on regardless – 'life will go on', even if the SNP calls an independence referendum and wins it. This is ironic disbelief differently, though equally authentically, expressed. Either looking to the future or looking to the past, the consoling message seems to be that the imminent breaking up of the UK is a matter of little consequence, especially for England. Though things may fall apart and the centre may not hold, the second coming of an independent Scotland is nothing to worry about. If that message does become the fashion then the political common sense which Bogdanor defends could well be discounted with a shrug of the shoulders. What that suggests in turn is a possible disconnect (as Hoggart intimates) between the intent of political leaders at Westminster and the mood of the electorate. Thus, it is possible to envisage the encounter of two very different political discourses.

At one level, as was the case in Northern Ireland for most of the Troubles, unionism and nationalism in Great Britain tend to talk past each other, no more so than in Scotland after 2007. There the National Conversation sponsored by the SNP government and the Calman Commission on Scottish Devolution supported by the Labour, Conservative and Liberal-Democratic parties came to their obvious conclusions: the former, independence and the latter, incremental modification of devolved powers. Beneath the surface of the respective conversations there exists on the one side a brutal discourse amongst the so-called 'cybernats' and an excited discourse of wild catastrophe on the other, even on the floor of the House of Commons (see for example BBC News 2011a). This is the familiar world of partisanship, point-scoring, winning and losing. It has its own logic since it takes its character from the sense that the UK is in a period of transition. As Ernest Gellner (1964: 66–7) explained, the crucial power in periods of transition 'is the power to decide which turning to take, being at the wheel at the big and rare road-forks'. Since 'some crucial road-forks generally only appear once' there will be no opportunity for those who are not in control at that moment 'to reverse the mistake made "last time"'. In a stable situation 'one can play for marginal advantages, and accept defeat, tolerate opposition, and refrain from pushing every advantage to its utmost in the knowledge that tomorrow is another day'. A transitional situation is far from stable and in this case 'tomorrow is not *another* day: it is an *other* day, altogether'. In this case, 'the game is played for the highest stakes' because each side knows that there can be no replay. That is why it is essential to struggle for control at these moments because the party which has control during the transition will determine the character of the transformation.

The crucial power in a period of transition, then, 'is the power to decide which turning to take'. Gellner's specification of this distinctive character of the politics of transition captures some of the frenetic spirit of constitutional debate in which the culture of winning and losing is so pervasive.

At another level, however, this all appears to be a clashing din of symbolism with little relevance to that solidly pragmatic, middle ground of British politics occupied by sensible politicians and their equally practical electorate. Transitions of the first sort are thought to be the stuff of fantasy because politics is all about the art of the possible. The expectation is that things will work themselves out for the best, in this case best for the UK. Unfortunately, this sort of non-symbolic politics can have unintended consequences. For example, Hazell (1998) outlined the lineaments of a devolutionary dispensation which he thought appropriate for a new vision of the UK. In order to come to terms with the new political culture, he thought, 'the centre will have to relax and be willing to let go'. The centre needed 'to understand and respect the political forces which have been unleashed, and to channel and direct them by working with the flow'. This required a strategic conception of relationships between the devolved institutions and Westminster, obliging the centre 'to give a lead, in its actions and its words, to bind the Union together in order to counter-balance the centrifugal political forces of devolution'. But the message of 'going with the flow' implied that greater autonomy for the devolved territories (and especially Scotland) was perfectly compatible with the continued integrity of the UK. On the other hand, Hazell was prepared to admit (1999: 88) the very different possibility of the genteel separation of Scotland in terms very similar to the SNP's own vision of 'social union'. If the Scots did choose independence 'many of the fundamentals in terms of people's everyday lives would remain surprisingly unchanged – the Scots would continue to live and vote here, we would be able to live, work and vote in Scotland. The two countries would remain close neighbours, closely intertwined, with a lot of movement and other links between the two, much as there has been between the United Kingdom and Ireland for most of this century'. The first alternative suggests that there is no need for separatism because the UK can modify itself sufficiently to accommodate nationalism. Hence former Secretary of State for Constitutional Affairs, Lord Falconer (2006), could argue with some conviction that constitutional change was designed to guarantee the rights of the nations and thereby help to maintain the UK, concluding that 'it has done exactly that. Separatists have been stymied by devolution'. The second alternative suggests that there is no longer any need to be concerned about the integrity of the UK because separatism will not mean radical dislocation of old associations. Therefore Lord Falconer could say with equal conviction two years later (cited in Lloyd 2008) that the 'Union is in play in a way it has not been before'. Of course, if Scotland did leave the UK, the allegiance of Wales, the position of England and the status of Northern Ireland would also be called into question. It would be a very different world indeed.

These two understandings of the constitutional moment run in parallel and it is difficult to know which is more threatening to the future of the UK: the first, which dramatises and polarises but at least in its provocation confronts the electorate with a radical choice (in the style of Nairn); or the second, which calms and mollifies but which may imply (in the style of Hoggart and White) that nothing much will change in the everyday life of most people. Indeed, the intersection of the two perspectives can be found in Trench's observation (2008b: 40) that while 'the effects of Scottish independence for the UK as a whole would be profound, it may be that the difference in the extent of autonomy of being in a separate state and remaining part of a further decentralised UK (which would be the price for remaining in the UK at all) would be modest'. This is an ambivalence which may be conducive to nationalist objectives but it can have – and has had – the opposite effect. Why is that so? It is so because popular opinion is disposed against radical change insofar as conservative modification appears to meet the concerns of 'everyday life'. For example, David Torrance (2011a) repeated the famous line from Lampedusa's *The Leopard*: 'if we want things to stay as they are, things will have to change'. He thought that such wisdom should act as a guiding philosophy for unionists throughout the UK who, in wishing to conserve the state, should be willing to act with imagination in changing things. Indeed, one could argue that the wisdom of *The Leopard* is a re-statement of Hazell's first proposition. However, with equal relevance, that line could be reversed to become a guiding philosophy for nationalists who, intent on dissolving the state, should also be willing to conservatively accommodate some aspects of it: 'if we want things to change, some things will have to stay as they are'. And one could argue that wisdom is a re-statement of Hazell's second proposition. In the first instance, the question is: how far can you change without either destroying the substance of what it is you wish to maintain or ceding the case of one's opponents? For example, Lord Forsythe claimed that proposals to extend the financial powers of the Scottish Parliament would make it hard to dispute nationalist calls for full fiscal autonomy 'when you have conceded the principle' (cited in Barnes 2010). In the second instance, the question is: how far can one accommodate the institutions of the UK without abandoning altogether the ultimate objective of independence? This has been the perennial question for Plaid Cymru, now also for Sinn Fein and in a more immediate sense for the SNP. As Harvie asked (cited in Brown and Barnes 2011): 'Independence was never off the agenda, but was it kept around to pacify the SNP faithful? By early 2011 was Salmond still pursuing this goal?' For all the sound and fury of the politics of transition, it is the ambiguity and fuzziness of the politics of pragmatism where debate about the future of the UK is located – Kidd's middling ground *par excellence*.

Respect agenda

To take Hazell's first alternative, a coherent British narrative would need to go some way towards treating devolved governments more like equal partners; respecting the political forces to which devolution has given institutional expression; and binding together the UK, counterbalancing the centrifugal tendencies of territorial mandates. The thrust of the criticism in Chapter 7 was that this had not been done sufficiently or consistently enough and if such a narrative had been lacking under Labour – when the going was good both economically and politically – then it was going to be all the more difficult in times of financial austerity. Devolution in a cold climate would test the imaginative resources of any British government especially when, after May 2010, that government was a Conservative-dominated Coalition with the Liberal-Democrats committed to a policy agenda at odds with the political centres of gravity in Scotland, Wales and Northern Ireland. Concern about the potential for conflicting mandates had informed David Cameron's leadership of the Conservative Party after 2005. Cameron was intent on recommitting the party to its traditional unionist vocation as well as confirming the long-standing cross-party consensus at Westminster: that the UK contributes to the security of all its component parts; gives its citizens a more powerful voice in the world; best secures economic prosperity; promotes fairness through commonly financed health and social services; and has a common cultural inheritance in which all can share equally (Cameron 2007a). Addressing what bound the United Kingdom together, Cameron deployed the familiar language of One Nation Toryism, exemplified in the call to his Party Conference (2006; see also Jones 2010: 268) that 'we are all in this together'. That 'we' was everyone in the UK, irrespective of territorial location, whose interests a future Conservative government was pledged to protect. It is easy to be cynical about political motives, of course, and yet Cameron's dedication to the Union must never be discounted. 'If it should ever come to a choice between constitutional perfection and the preservation of our nation', he told an Edinburgh audience (2007b), 'I choose our United Kingdom. Better an imperfect union than a broken one.' The implication was that the Conservative Party would accept all the 'anomalies' of devolution if that were the price of keeping the UK together (even though it might confuse the objective of answering the English Question). In May 2010 one could argue that it was also better to have an imperfect coalition if that meant averting threats to the UK's stability, either financial or constitutional. And Cameron was certainly sincere when, walking into Downing Street as Prime Minister, he claimed to be deeply conscious of his responsibility for the future of the UK: 'When I say I am prime minister of the United Kingdom, I really mean it. England, Scotland, Wales, Northern Ireland – we're weaker apart, stronger together, so together is the way we must always stay' (Cameron 2010). As Anthony Barnett (2010) wrote at the time (and which private sources have subsequently confirmed), 'the desire to preserve the Union and prevent a boost for the SNP in Scotland was an important motive for Cameron's offer of a coalition'. There has long been speculation about the party's potential temptation into an English nationalist position – Lord Blake's best-selling history (1985: 361–2), for example, had pointed to the conundrum of a party overwhelmingly English in its support being so vigorous in its defence of the UK – but Cameron's commitment seemed to reflect accurately the sentiment of the membership. A *ConservativeHome* online survey (Montgomerie 2011) showed that while there was a general and fatalistic expectation amongst party supporters that Scottish independence would happen at some point and that independence would even help to underwrite Conservative dominance at Westminster, it was still the case that 72 per cent agreed that England, Scotland, Wales and Northern Ireland 'are better together' with only 17 per cent dissenting. If Cameron (cited in Mackie 2010) thought the UK remained 'a family' then the party agreed with him that keeping it together for better and for worse was preferable to divorce. How the family was to be kept together, and how close, was open to debate (Major 2011).

Cameron also wished to signal that the Conservatives did accept and understand the new political dispensation in Scotland and Wales and wished to work with, rather than against, differing institutional mandates. His proposed contract of governance intimated a willingness to treat the devolved administrations as respected, if not equal, partners. The message of this 'respect agenda' was that a Conservative government would deal seriously with those administrations which had a different political complexion and that to achieve the common objectives of the

UK, differences of approach should be acknowledged. Whether a respectful relaxation at the centre and a letting go – up to a point, with that point being the integrity of the Union – would be conducive to intergovernmental harmony was moot. But it was important for Conservatives to acknowledge that, if they were returned to office, the political order they would inherit was very different from the one over which they had presided in 1997. 'If we win the next election at Westminster', Cameron wrote (2009a), 'we would govern with a maturity and a respect for the Scottish people. I would be a Prime Minister who would work constructively with any administration at Holyrood for the good of Scotland, and I would be in regular contact with the First Minister no matter what party he or she came from.' Speaking later to the Scottish Conservative conference, he marked (2009b) the tenth anniversary of devolution by announcing: 'I stand here, the leader of the Conservative Party, and say loudly and proudly, we support devolution, we back it heart and soul, and we will make it work for everyone.' Cameron was not addressing here his own party or the members of the SNP. He was speaking to the traditional Labour-supporting Scot that a Conservative majority at Westminster would not be a threat to Scottish interests. If it was the lament of some in the party that Conservatives had blundered badly by getting themselves on the wrong side of the devolution debate in the 1980s and 1990s, it was also the case that there was a festering resentment at what was taken to be the political opportunism of Labour in that debate. According to Malcolm Rifkind (cited in Lloyd 2008), the great strategic mistake of Labour (which had forced the subsequent quest on Gordon Brown's part to define 'British values') had been to fall in behind the SNP's assertion that the Conservatives had no mandate north of the border. 'It was to be expected that the Nationalists would so argue. But the Labour party wished to form a British government. To use the "no mandate" argument was wholly unprincipled. It has left a legacy from which it, and we all, suffer – that a British government can lack legitimacy here.' This political legacy was perhaps not as deep in Wales given the weaker position of Plaid Cymru, but it was just as widespread. If this can be written off as a partisan gripe by a disgruntled Scottish Tory, consider Trench's view (2011a) that the Labour Party in Wales and Scotland have come perilously close to saying that devolution can only work if Labour is in office in Cardiff, Edinburgh and London 'which is pretty much an admission of defeat for the whole constitutional enterprise'. Speaking in Cardiff, Cameron (2009c) also confirmed that his would be 'the party that supports devolution and makes it work', establishing a relationship between the Assembly and Westminster that would be 'one of co-operation, not confrontation'.

Though this 'respect agenda' has been almost exclusively associated with Conservative – and subsequently, with Coalition – strategy, the term can also be found in Labour's White Paper *Scotland's Future in the United Kingdom* (Scotland Office 2009: 3–5). The objective was to ensure that the relationships between Scottish and UK institutions were 'based on mutual respect', sharing resources and pooling risks for the benefit of all citizens. By giving expression to the diversity of the UK, decisions could be made 'which reflect the different priorities in those diverse parts' thereby strengthening the Union in the process. All of this has become common ground amongst the major parties about what it means to be British such that there was little difference of substance on devolution in the manifestos of the three major parties in the General Election of 2010. On Scotland, they all promised to legislate on Calman's proposals. On Wales, they all agreed to support a referendum on primary legislative powers for the National Assembly under the terms of the Government of Wales Act 2006. On Northern Ireland, they all supported the power-sharing institutions established by the Belfast Agreement of 1998.

Moreover, when it came to negotiating a common programme of government, Conservatives and Liberal Democrats coalesced easily on devolution matters. The history of the two parties would have suggested that this was unlikely since the Conservative Party had traditionally opposed devolution (Ted Heath's 1968 Declaration of Perth notwithstanding) while the Liberal Democrats had long been advocates of federalism. Vince Cable (2007), for example, had voiced those old suspicions and raised doubts about Cameron's ability to change Conservative belief in a strong, centralised, Anglo-centric state. 'Although there is, now, more willingness to use the language of localism, nothing concrete has emerged. Devolution to Scotland and Wales is still regarded with great suspicion and regionalism in England is treated with ridicule.' By 2010, such a clear distinction could be made no longer since both parties had made localism a campaign issue. And in their foreword to the Coalition's programme for government (Cabinet Office 2010a), Cameron and Nick Clegg committed their parties to 'a radical redistribution of power away from Westminster and Whitehall to councils, communities and homes across the nation'. There seemed to be a coherent narrative in the grand belief 'that the time has come to disperse power more widely in Britain today; to recognise that we will only make progress if we help people to come together to make life better. In short, it is our ambition to distribute power and opportunity to people rather than hoarding authority within government'. Rhetorically at least, the respect agenda fitted in neatly with this commitment. Cameron fulfilled his promise to visit both the Scottish Parliament and the Welsh Assembly as the first official acts of his premiership. In Edinburgh (BBC News 2010a), he tied together the personal, the political and the constitutional (and repeating the language of the previous Labour government's *Scotland's Future in the United Kingdom*), announcing that the agenda 'is about parliaments working together, of governing with respect, both because I believe Scotland deserves that respect and because I want to try and win Scotland's respect as the prime minister of the United Kingdom'.

In the preface to *Strengthening Scotland's Future* (Scotland Office 2010) Cameron and Clegg repeated: 'Right from the outset, this Coalition Government has shown its commitment to making the Devolved Administrations work well, and pursuing an agenda of respect between our Parliaments.' And speaking to the National Assembly in Cardiff, the new Conservative Secretary of State for Wales, Cheryl Gillan (2010), tried to put institutional flesh on the words of the 'agenda of co-operation and optimism'. She argued that the 'solid proof of the government's commitment to work in collaboration with the devolved institutions, and to integrate devolution into our policy making' would be the more frequent meeting of the Joint Ministerial Committee 'to consider matters of common mutual interest'. This change, according to Gillan, indicated the way in which the Coalition intended to approach devolution and it has been repeated as a mantra on every subsequent occasion. Confirmation that the respect agenda was more than mere window-dressing came from an unexpected source. When the First Ministers of Scotland, Wales and Northern Ireland issued a joint declaration expressing reservations about the Coalition's spending plans they also 'welcomed the general spirit in which the new coalition government has approached intergovernmental relations' (BBC News 2010b). This was something which the SNP government had been advocating for some time. Moreover, the new draft Cabinet manual made this explicit, incorporating the respect agenda in paragraph 289: 'The foundation of the relationship between the Government and the Devolved Administrations is mutual respect and recognition of the responsibilities set out in the devolution settlements' (Cabinet Office 2010b: 103). There was acceptance that intergovernmental relations should be conducted more regularly through the JMC and its two sub-committees, JMC (Domestic) chaired by the Deputy Prime Minister and JMC (Europe) chaired by the Foreign Secretary. However, the three territorial departments, the Scotland, Wales and Northern Ireland Offices were maintained. The Coalition did not accept that there should be one central department for the nations and regions, dissenting from a long-held academic view that such a department could deliver a more coherent approach and help to harmonise UK-wide with devolved policy matters (Hazell 1998). This represented modification within continuity, an approach which seemed to chime well both with the respect agenda and with the pragmatic traditions of British governance. In short, necessity and aspiration appeared to coincide such that 'the very fact that electoral and parliamentary arithmetics will force the coalition to adopt a negotiated approach to governing the UK – working with the nations on a case by case basis – might help ensure that it succeeds in working with the devolved nations in an effective way' (Jeffery, Lodge and Schmuecker 2010: 26).

If one can detect an *ideal* formula linking together the elements of Coalition strategy then it was probably best captured by Cameron's remark about what was required of the Conservative Party in Scotland: that it needed to be both 'more Scottish and more pro-Union' (cited in Settle 2010). If this could be generalised into an operative principle of devolved relations then one would expect as well a complementary policy of 'more Welsh and more pro-Union' and 'more Northern Irish and more pro-Union'. It was still difficult to see what 'more English and more pro-Union' would look like, though one could imagine England having a distinct institutional identity at Westminster. And the reason for the prevarication on the English Question – and also its justification – was that the Coalition's overwhelming majority of seats in England was about as good as it got from the point of view of calming English worries about the extent of devolution elsewhere in the UK (Bogdanor 2011: 41). Representing 59 per cent of the United Kingdom vote, 64 per cent of the English vote, 46 per cent of the Welsh vote and slightly less than 36 per cent of the Scottish vote, only in Northern Ireland was there no explicit Coalition mandate. If this did not dispel the tensions of territorial policy it did put to rest for a while the 'Rifkind factor' – questioning of the legitimacy of Westminster.

Under the Coalition's Scotland Bill, taxation and expenditure were to be joined up in the name of greater accountability with the Scottish Parliament granted extra tax and borrowing facilities of about £12 billion. From 2015, the Treasury will deduct 10p from rates of income tax there and reduce the UK block grant commensurately. This will mean that the Scottish Parliament will become responsible for raising about 35 per cent of its revenue from designated 'Scottish taxpayers'. Scottish ministers will also be empowered to borrow in order to fund both current and capital expenditure. Stamp duty, land and landfill taxes will also be devolved and the Scottish Parliament may, subject to the approval of Westminster, propose new taxes. In June 2011, the Coalition amended the Bill with a package of measures to give Scottish

Ministers greater flexibility and more financial responsibility. Additionally, there was a new emphasis on strengthening intergovernmental dialogue on matters of welfare policy. One further aspect of the respect agenda included in the Bill is the statutory recognition that the term 'Scottish Government' should replace 'Scottish Executive'. Jim Gallagher (2010), who had been Secretary to the Calman Commission and formerly Director-General, Devolution Strategy, in Whitehall, almost echoed Cameron's words about 'more Scottish and more Union' when he described the Coalition's Scotland Bill as 'obviously in Scotland's interest, but it will be good for the entire UK too'. The Coalition's commitment to introduce a referendum on further Welsh devolution represented both continuity with previous policy and also consensus amongst the parties in the Welsh Assembly and at Westminster. If in the referendum a majority voted 'yes', then the Assembly would be able to make laws in those areas for which it has responsibility without Westminster's agreement. On 3 March 2011, 63.5 per cent voted in favour – on a low turn-out of just over 35 per cent – and the general view was that this represented a boost for the authority and standing of the Assembly. The wording of the Programme for Government on the future financing of Welsh devolution was a curious composite. The Coalition recognised the concerns about the system of devolution funding but stated that 'at this time, the priority must be to reduce the deficit' though, depending on a positive vote in the referendum, the Coalition promised to 'establish a process similar to the Calman Commission for the Welsh Assembly'. The logic here also seemed to be that there was no contradiction in an Assembly being both more Welsh and more pro-Union linking, as in Scotland, the power to spend money with some responsibility to raise it. In Northern Ireland, the Coalition supported the devolved institutions but inserted the language of the Conservative manifesto to work 'to bring Northern Ireland back into the mainstream of UK politics'. The key policy proposal was to produce 'a government paper examining potential mechanisms for changing the corporation tax rate in Northern Ireland'. Speaking to the Northern Ireland Grand Committee at Westminster, Secretary of State for Northern Ireland Owen Paterson argued for dovetailing strategies between London and the Northern Ireland Executive. 'I do believe that devolving powers over corporation tax could play a major role in attracting significant new investment into Northern Ireland and, over time, reducing its dependence on the public sector' (Northern Ireland Office 2010). The question of varying the corporation tax was not new. It had been considered by Sir David Varney under the previous Labour government. Varney was critical of the proposal on two counts. For Northern Ireland, there was no clear case for a reduction to 12.5 per cent and the estimated loss of revenue was over £300 million with little expectation of recovering such a sum in the medium term. For the United Kingdom, the case against was even more marked because the likelihood was a displacement of capital and profits from Great Britain to Northern Ireland resulting in an estimated loss to the Exchequer over ten years of about £2.2 billion (Varney 2007). Devolving corporation tax would certainly mean, in Cameron's term, more Northern Ireland, but it was difficult to understand how it was more Union. Indeed, it suggested a lack of strategy and it certainly encouraged the SNP to demand that Scotland should also have control of corporation tax. As a concerned editorial in the *Financial Times* (2011) noted, the constitutional implications of intra-state competition on corporation tax are huge and 'a heavy price to pay for a reform that will produce at best marginal economic benefits'. It advised the government to go back to the drawing board.

Sceptics, then, would take some convincing that much had really changed. Admiration for the quick formation of the Coalition at Westminster was contrasted with what one commentator (Mitchell 2010) described as the 'stumbling approach' to its implications for the UK as a whole. If the criticism of the previous government has been that it acted in an ad hoc way on devolved matters, then there seemed to be little acknowledgement of the unintended consequences of central decisions which continued that tradition of ad hoc-ery. For example, the lack of consultation on the proposal for fixed-term Parliaments and on the date of the Alternative Vote referendum (held on the same day as elections to the Scottish Parliament and the Welsh and Northern Ireland Assemblies) suggested that the mantra of 'taking devolution seriously' had not been entirely absorbed by decision-makers at Westminster. It was still moot, then, whether central government was capable of following Trench's wise injunction (2010c) 'to think territorially, and act carefully'. Furthermore, some thought that what had occurred in 2010 was the re-assertion by the Treasury of its traditional position as the driver and arbiter of policy across the UK (Grant 2010). The territorial concern was that, despite the fine sounding words about respect, the drive to reduce public expenditure outlined in the 2010 Spending Review would override all other considerations and severely qualify the ability of devolved governments to take different decisions. To these qualifications of the workings of the respect agenda can be added the key question: is it, as currently understood, really fit for purpose? This was a question which became even more pressing when the SNP won its dramatic victory in the Scottish Parliament elections in May 2011 with 45 per cent of the vote, giving it an overall majority of 6 seats. The SNP, having dropped from its own legislative programme in the previous Parliament the promised referendum on independence, now moved confidently onto different political territory. The prospect of independence (for Scotland) was now up for serious consideration. Nationalists were now clearly setting the agenda there and the reform agenda, designed to make separatism irrelevant, had stumbled badly.

Independence agenda

When the SNP formed a minority government in Scotland in 2007, the alternative was either the generation of momentum towards independence or the pressure for greater transfer of devolved powers. It was thought that either possibility was contingent on its performance in office and the response of other parties (Lynch 2009: 635). In the period 2007–11, the SNP never made any detailed or explicit case for independence reflecting its judgement that – to use an old Irish term – advanced nationalism was far too advanced for Scottish people (Mullen 2009: 37). However its success in 2011 suggests the possibility once more of McLean and McMillan's (2006: 265) 'Slovak scenario' or, as Anthony King (2007: 214) waspishly put it, Edinburgh at some point in the near future becoming 'the Bratislava of the north'. It did seem to substantiate a nationalist belief that the future belonged to them, where it can be seriously argued that the SNP 'wins even when it loses' (MacWhirter 2010). But this is pure hubris and it only promotes a number of myths. The first is that the UK is constitutionally inflexible whereas the evidence is actually otherwise. The second is that the vote for the SNP represents a statement of Scotland's faith in itself thereby associating authentic expressions of Scottish identity exclusively with separatist politics. The third is that a change of 'cultural gear' has taken place in which Scots move forward confidently on a social agenda more progressive than elsewhere in the UK, especially England. Together these myths perpetuate an exaggerated sense of destiny often expressed in an inflated language. Thus Libby Brooks (2011) could write of 'seismic' change in Scottish identity while the normally sensible online forum *Our Kingdom* (2011) could run a series of articles under the silly heading of 'The Scottish Spring'. Times had changed and it appeared that the SNP would now be leading Scotland off the low road of devolution and onto the high road of independence (Lynch 2005). If it is appropriate to be sceptical of how thoroughgoing have been changes at the centre it is equally appropriate to be sceptical about the onward march of nationalism.

The difficulties for the SNP have nothing to do with the economics of independence. In any case, for the convinced nationalist economic arguments are – or should be – marginal considerations. This is not to disparage the work of economists or of those concerned to model the impact of independence on Scottish finances, merely to argue that serious nationalists would not make their political objective dependent on material calculations. A Kant's dove nationalist – or a 'believer in better' – has implicit faith that only the removal of British constraints will allow Scotland to flourish as it should, like those cited in the SNP's manifesto (2011) 'who set out the ways Scotland can be better as an independent country'. What they expected ranged from ending child and pensioner poverty to Scotland becoming an international centre for science and innovation. Others can make perfectly rational arguments based on the prospect of green energy, North Sea oil revenues, low corporation tax and the reinvigoration of domestic industry. In both cases they may well be right but these expectations generally do not convince people to become nationalist; rather they are the consequence of already being convinced of the virtue of independence – which is why the SNP could in recent years adopt Ireland and Iceland as models of independence and then just as easily drop them when they became inconvenient references. The simple response to the question: is it possible for Scotland to become independent can only be: yes, of course, why not? Nationalists are correct on that point. Anatole Kaletsky (2007) put this very well. The honest answer to all questions about whether Scotland (or Wales) would gain or lose financially from independence is that one cannot answer with any certainty. Revenues vary from year to year and there are so many unpredictable factors, the crucial one being the price of oil. Moreover, he thought such calculations are irrelevant 'to affect the balance between the immense historical arguments on both sides of the independence debate'. The statistical details encourage a lot of sound and fury but the economic bombardments of either side rarely inflict serious damage to the respective positions. Predictions of economic penury were as misdirected as predictions of a *Wirtschaftwunder* (see Salmond and Alexander 2006). In the end, Kaletsky thought, arguments about independence depend on attitudes to risk. The weakest arguments were the Kant's dove ones – if the Scots or (at some point) the Welsh and the English really were determined to make their respective economies amongst the most competitive in Europe they could do so whether the UK broke up or not. According to the director of the Fraser of Allander Institute for economic research, Brian Ashcroft (cited in Carrell 2011), all that one can say for certain is that there is 'fantastic uncertainty' about the balance of financial matters. If one is not a convinced nationalist it is the calculation of risk which calls into doubt the enterprise of dismantling the UK. That is the doubt which, despite its electoral success and the force of its arguments, the SNP has yet to dispel, and which explains why the rhetoric of endism is so prominent in nationalist discourse. If people can be convinced that independence is *bound to* happen – as Tam Dalyell now believes (Peterkin 2011) – they are already half way to being persuaded that it *should* happen. Four years of responsible minority government after 2007 were intended to persuade Scots that destiny and desire should now harmonise in the collective purpose of independence. That did not happen but some expect that it will now happen at some point in the next four years. The question raised here is what precisely did the SNP victory in 2011 represent for the future of the UK?

According to Wayne Norman (2006: xvi) 'we will miss much of what is interesting about nationalism if we think of it primarily as the ideology of national communities seeking self-determination'. That certainly applies in Scotland (and elsewhere in the UK) where 'nationalism' may be a rattle-bag term comprising 'nationality', 'nationhood' and 'national identity'. Equally, we may miss much of what is interesting about the vote for the SNP if it is assumed to be a vote for separatism. Curtice (2007) predicted the likelihood of a result such as that in 2011 in his oral evidence to the House of Commons Justice Committee. The view he had come to about people's motivation to vote in Scottish Parliament elections was that 'they seem to think it is quite important to have an administration in Edinburgh that they regard as standing up for Scotland's interests – and that does not just simply mean effectively and efficiently disposing of the devolved powers. It also means representing Scotland's interests within the Union'. He further suggested that there was an element of ambiguity here but that it was vital not to subsume complexities of political identity into a simple, nationalist one. Therefore, 'while it may be true that having a more voluble government in Edinburgh might persuade the Scottish electorate that perhaps the Union is not worthwhile, it is also at least as plausible that a more voluble government in Edinburgh may actually convince people that Scotland is now being more adequately represented within the Union and that therefore as a result people may become rather happier with the devolution set-up than so far appears to be the case'. That appeared to capture very well the popular mood and subsequent events have confirmed his view. For example, shortly after the SNP's victory in May's Scottish parliamentary elections, Labour was able to hold on to its Inverclyde Westminster seat in the byelection there in June 2011. Tom Devine (cited in Bolger 2009), for example, had thought the likelihood of an SNP majority administration at Holyrood was increased by the prospect of a Conservative-dominated Westminster. By voting nationalist Scots would be electing a defensive force in a period of austerity. 'By voting a Nationalist government into power, and by remaining within the Union, Scots get what they are very good at: having their cake and eating it'. That may be a desirable position but it may not be a permanently sustainable position. That old law of unintended consequences could come into play engineering a situation most Scots – and most people in the UK – would not choose.

Curtice (2011) also assessed the outcome of the May 2011 election in much the same way as Devine's prediction but there was a significant qualification to the 'cake-and-eating-it' syndrome. By voting SNP many electors had clearly backed a party with whose central agenda on independence they disagreed. Curtice speculated that these voters had assumed that so little headway had been made towards that goal in the previous four years that it was unlikely to happen this time either. 'But with a SNP majority now ensconced in Edinburgh that will no longer be the case.' The best laid plans as Scots should know better than anyone else – even having your cake and eating it – gang aft agley. David Trimble used to argue that constructive ambiguity was necessary to sustain Northern Ireland's position within the UK and constructive ambiguity has, for the most part, operated in a benign way in Scotland too. The pragmatic tendency in the SNP hopes to sustain that ambiguity until such time as the substance of political Union has disappeared like the smile of a Cheshire cat. Advanced nationalists in the SNP would like to end that ambiguity in a final vote for independence. Their question of the pragmatic tendency would also involve the smile of a Cheshire cat, but in this case the line from the English indie rock band Milburn's song of the same name: 'If you wanted to leave so much then why are you still here?' There is a real tension and weakness in nationalist argument such that Trench (2011b) believed the SNP's supposed 'win–win' or 'trying to have their cake and eat it' strategy was ultimately incoherent. The battle for that vital middle ground of Scottish opinion is far from lost to those who wish to sustain the UK. For although Alex Salmond (cited in Maddox 2011b) has pronounced in venerable endist style that Scottish independence is indeed 'inevitable' that inevitability is far from self-evident. The certainty of the end is now presented in a very uncertain way because that end remains unpopular. That is why the party's leadership is trying to promote the idea of what has become known as 'independence-lite' – 'trying' because as one leading SNP figure told the journalist Eddie Barnes (2011) 'the SNP doesn't have the words yet to say what they mean'. And it is having difficulty because what most Scots seem to be saying about the UK is: 'We don't want to leave so much and that's why we are still here.' That at least was the view of Alan Massie (2011a) who, taking a longer historical view than the breathless historicism of endism, thought the UK (as fifth nation) would survive the SNP just as Scotland and the idea of Scotland survived in the nineteenth and twentieth centuries.

This is nothing new either. When the minority SNP government published its White Paper *Choosing Scotland's Future* (Scottish Executive 2007) to promote the conversation on independence, critics observed how flimsy the prospectus was in the apparent attempt to make it palatable to middle Scotland. Norman Bonney (2008: 563–4) wrote that the whole thrust of the argument was that independence need not be disruptive because the new Scottish state would continue to share not only a 'social union' with the rest of the UK but also to share some common institutions and regulatory regimes. 'An obvious rejoinder to these suggestions that seek to allay worries about the implications of independence is why go to all the effort required to dismantle the United Kingdom and then re-assemble aspects of pre-existing cooperation in a new or similar pattern.' And Tom Gallagher (2009b: 543) also challenged the SNP to define the problem for which independence is actually the answer, arguing that the SNP is fooling itself if it believed that dealing with the hard questions of domestic governance could wait until after Scotland had left the UK. Others took the view (Miers 2010) that, despite the interest of the SNP in proving itself both efficient and effective as a party of government, nationalists had no vested interest in making devolution work in the long run but only in demonstrating the limitations of existing powers. The object is to encourage the Kant's dove syndrome and to promote it as accepted political wisdom. So 'independence-lite' on the one hand seems rational, reflecting the state of Scottish public opinion, but on the other it seemed to lack all conviction (in the long run even nationalists are all dead). As Hazell commented (cited in Barnes 2011), to suggest that important issues of collective defence, macroeconomic policy, foreign affairs amongst others would remain shared with the rest of the UK makes of Scottish statehood a very fuzzy concept, one which raises the question: 'Does the SNP want Scotland to be independent or not?' Torrance (2001b) retailed one explanation of it as follows: 'The point being made here is that independence (in relation to the rest of the UK) is not about separation, ripping Scotland out of the UK etc, but about building a better relationship on the basis of equality.' Torrance felt that this was politically contrived and that in practice it would prove to be unworkable. And this only underlines Bonney's point: if the SNP is tentative about independence and finds it hard to explain what sort of Scottish state it wishes to establish, how can voters be expected to support independence in a future referendum?

This is a point which has not gone without comment amongst the intelligent SNP blogging community (Bella Caledonia 2011). That question illustrates why the ground rules for the Scottish referendum have become such a vital issue of political debate.

Chapter 6 considered briefly the issue of the referendum on Scottish independence in terms of the idea of 'fifth nation'. There are two issues here. The first is whether or not there should be two referendums. That there should be two makes good constitutional and political sense. The Scottish Parliament has only the power to call an advisory referendum, Westminster the power to call a determinative one. The time in between, assuming Scots voted in favour of independence, would be devoted to political negotiation on the details of separation, for example on the division of the national debt. A second referendum would allow Scots to vote on the precise terms of independence. At this final stage there would be no certainty that these terms would be attractive enough for Scots to relinquish their place in the UK (Murkens, Jones and Keating 2002). This sequencing would mean that the idea of fifth nation is present in deliberations at each stage though it could very well test that idea to destruction, especially in England. Whether holding two referendums is politically wise is another matter because of the potential for promoting bad feeling and heightening tension. The Secretary of State for Scotland, Michael Moore, stated that two referendums should be required, though he later admitted that this was only a 'personal view' (BBC News Scotland 2011b). When Vernon Bogdanor supported the proposition, the response of an anonymous Scottish government spokesman indicated the potential for political polarisation: 'Scotland's future will be decided by the people of Scotland, not by Oxbridge professors' (cited in Johnson 2011). Nationalists have some justification in their concern that the principle of a second referendum gives Westminster an incentive to put up obstacles during negotiations. But the greater worry is the unionist one: that there would be an incentive in the first referendum for people to vote for independence on the understanding that they would have another chance to change their mind. The unintended consequence might be irreversible momentum in favour of independence irrespective of the ultimate details for it would be a strange nation indeed which was only *instrumentally* patriotic when given the chance. It would be a demeaning position for any self-respecting Scot. The advantage of a single referendum is that it compels a simple choice and encourages popular responsibility rather than any hedging of bets. This approach has its advocates at Westminster as well as its supporters at Holyrood but it has its obvious risks for both sides. Unionists worry that it encourages the SNP to define independence as a wish-list and to campaign on a Kant's dove agenda. In this case, however, the nationalist worry is more profound: that even a narrow defeat would set back their cause for generations.

The second issue is the wording of the referendum itself and the number of options on the ballot paper. Anticipating the election of a Conservative government in the General Election, the Constitution Unit (2010: 32) considered how it should respond to the prospect of an independence referendum. Its advice was that it should act in a measured way and certainly avoid any legal challenge to Holyrood. It warned against being 'led into supporting a multi-option referendum which includes further powers for the Scottish Parliament' for the very reason that it would likely confuse voters. A similar argument was made by Trench (2011c) who put the matter with admirable clarity. There should not be multiple options because the object in a referendum is to produce both a clear choice and a clear result which a multi-option 'preferendum' was very unlikely to do. 'The effect of a referendum is not just to establish what the public think, but to demonstrate it' and Trench's conclusion was that the SNP's argument for having a multiple choice referendum came close to implicit acceptance of the need for two referendums. It is possibly truer to say that it is tacit admission that independence is incapable of commanding majority support. What *would* satisfy both the Scottish desire for autonomy (to be more Scottish) and the desire to remain within the UK remains uncertain and that leaves much still to play for – the future of the UK no less. Never was Trench's motto 'to think territorially, and act carefully' more apposite.

10

Concluding remarks

The former Conservative MP Michael Portillo called his radio series on history and public memory: *Things We Forgot to Remember*. What Portillo's broadcasts explored intelligently was how our understanding of the past often conceals truths which cut across familiar narratives. If that is true of the past – to use Chandler's definitions, warming (or chilling the heart) is valued more than lighting the way – it is all the more true of the future. This final chapter is titled 'Concluding remarks' rather than 'Conclusion' if only because it is difficult to be certain about what may happen in British politics even in the course of the next five years (Nelson 2012). If we can forget to remember significant historical events, how much more likely is it that we will forget to anticipate significant ones? Or to put that in Chandleresque fashion, how likely is it that we will impose either heart-warming or wished-for patterns or will resort to prophesies of doom? As it is said of Tarot readings, the cards never lie but that is because we interpret them to confirm what we already want.

As Chapter 2 attempted to show, the ideological substance and the political intent of those who proclaim confidently that politics is already 'after Britain' is to promote (and with some success) apathy and resignation on the part of those who wish to maintain the UK. It is designed to encourage the belief that the future of the UK is behind it and the proclamation of defeat and humiliation encourages a vision of political development which is beyond one's power to influence. It is the future understood in terms of that old novelistic formula, 'with a leap and a bound', a predictive formula which leaps and bounds over details and practicalities in order to arrive at a happy ending. It complements that disposition in politics which we also identified in Chapter 2 as 'Kant's dove syndrome', the expectation of nationalists that free from the constraints of the old UK order the constituent nations will soar in prosperity and influence. It should be stressed that this is not an ignoble position to take. Even if the sceptic can point out that nothing, certainly not independence, is an unmixed blessing, a legitimate response is: so what? Nationalism is an act of faith and independence in this sense is not a means to an end (instrumental) but an end in itself (non-instrumental). It is probably not wise, from this nationalist perspective at least, to exhaust oneself with detailed schemes if that detracts from summoning the final energy to achieve the goal of separating from the UK. Certainly it is clear in the Scottish case that the SNP feels no pressing obligation to respond to opposition demands for 'spelling out' the consequences of independence. This is consistent with that broader Kant's dove narrative which assumes that everything will be different anyway when Scotland exits the UK. What is more, even if policy outcomes are mixed these are acceptable consequences according to the higher and general good of national self-determination.

For instance, the First Minister of Scotland (copying former Plaid Cymru MP Adam Price) announced a programme of government for the 'independence generation' even though what independence means in practice has not been defined. For Salmond (Gardham 2011), the people accept his political ambition to take the country further on its journey, understanding that 'the SNP believe in independence. They understand that and they do not fear it.' Normally it is the unknown that people *do* fear and one is tempted to categorise Salmond's statement as a very good example of Kant's dove syndrome. It is a sign of the times that the phrase 'independence generation' can be used and be taken seriously by the media without much critical examination. It also says much for the disarray of the SNP's opponents, and not only within Scotland, as it does for the imagination of nationalists. At least this is the language of political conviction and should be respected as such. It was observed in Chapters 8 and 9 how there has developed a reactive and complementary disposition amongst some influential voices in England, sometimes fatalistic sometimes angry, which speak the language of indifference about the UK rather than conviction about the nation. According to Jeremy Paxman (2011), following Parris, if and when Scotland and Wales opt for independence, 'the English will shrug their shoulders' and he thought that if 'our political masters have their way, England will have no say in the divorce and will remain sat upon by "Great Britain" forever. For the most part, the English seem committed to the union – in a dozy "what's the point of changing things?" sort of way' but that was no reason for going on with things as they are. 'The Westminster dullards' inability to imagine casting off a surplus piece of political clothing is no reason for the rest of the English to feel the same way indefinitely.' This is the intellectual territory on which political conviction and political indifference combine with subversive panache, where Salmond's expectation and Paxman's anticipation share common ground and both expectation and anticipation intimate the necessary end of the UK. Nevertheless, this is all rather simplistic and one-dimensional. However convinced nationalists may be about its end, and however indifferent some commentators may be about its undoing, that does not require those who wish to maintain the UK to respond with fatalism. There is just as much likelihood that expectation and anticipation will not be fulfilled.

Living with paradox and ambiguity may not be the easiest thing to do but it is the only thing we can do. And that truth applies to all political configurations on the British Question. As this book has tried to show, living with paradox has been, and remains, a very multinational thing. One is tempted to say that acknowledging paradox and ambiguity is one of the strengths of the UK. Chapter 4 noted James Tully's reflection on a decade of constitutional transformation in Europe, a reflection that multinational democracy today, like the UK's, appeared to run against the prevailing norms of national legitimacy. However, it was Tully's further observation that those 'norms' were not universal but only the particular norms of single nationhood. This was the insight which informed consideration of the so-called 'devolution paradox' in Chapters 6 and 7, for that paradox suggested that there are many possible directions of travel in the UK and not just one, as endism asserts; that a sense of multinational belonging can continue to co-exist with strong expressions of national identity; that political allegiance to multinational institutions is much more complex than a Moreno-scaling of national preferences would make one think; and that constitutional change is not incompatible with multinational stability. In short, the devolution paradox identified popular support for devolved institutions to have greater powers to meet local needs without displacing the equally popular belief that common standards of service should be maintained throughout the UK. It was argued in Chapter 9 that, in principle then, 'more' Scotland, 'more' Wales and 'more' Northern Ireland (and by implication, 'more' England) has not removed for most people the claims of multinational democracy, that common allegiance to, sympathy with and willing participation in the larger political life of the UK. In Chapter 6 this was called (after Madgwick and Rose) 'fifth nation'. To sustain that multinational, fifth nation, allegiance requires a sense of belonging which is not instrumental but authoritative in two senses: the first, symbolised by the Crown, acknowledges that the UK is sovereign; the second, accepts that it is the relationship from which the functional benefits of being British flow. Like all such associations, the multinational UK is an artifice and therefore contingent, as historians like Davies continue to point out. It may indeed dissolve soon but the devolution paradox at least implies that there is life yet in fifth nation allegiance, a life which surveys of identity do not properly record.

Ironically, Northern Ireland may show this most dramatically in the practice of devolution. Where once no-one talked of anything else but the 'constitution' and 'break-up', what is noticeable is the absence of any serious debate on the subject – apart that is from the unilateral 'national conversation on the future of this island' in the run-up to the centenary of the Irish rebellion of 1916 announced by Deputy First Minister, Martin McGuinness, at Sinn Fein's *Ard Fheis* in September 2011. It would certainly be a difficult task, even in the new climate of political detente in Ireland, to persuade unionists 'of the merits of a new republic and of their treasured place in it' (de Breadun 2011). The proposition here is a rather Whiggish one: that the UK is much more adaptable than its critics give it credit for. This point is not made within the framework of assumptions which complacently accepts, as Chapter 1 explored, the Whiggish 'evolutionary genius' of British constitutionalism. It is only a Whiggish-*inclined* point drawn from the 'dry wall' experience of Northern Ireland where for a generation the 'inevitability of Irish unity' was the anticipated or feared sub-text of all debate. This was the political condition of 'wild catastrophism' (Aughey 2009), one slowly, though not entirely, displaced since the new millennium by a politics of cautious adjustment. Things have changed but also stayed the same; things have stayed the same but also changed. The contest of Union, nothing but the Union and unity, nothing but unity, between which positions catastrophe seemed to lie, has become muted and given way in large part, though not entirely, to debates about political consent and inter-institutional relations. Fifth nation, in its instrumental and non-instrumental aspects, is alive and well and living at Stormont. The perspective on the UK from Northern Ireland unionists used to be like that of the biblical watchmen in Sion (Elliott 1985), alert to the dangers for Britain, always ready to speak and forever giving warning. They are not shouting with joy today but the message is more relaxed and secure, ironically so at a time when some voices in the rest of the UK are insistently prophesying doom. It is not faith in the great wisdom of Whiggish constitutionalism which suggests that further modification of the UK does not mean its disintegration. No one in Northern Ireland, observing the course of policy since the 1980s, could ever have faith in that proposition. It is simply the observation that the resources of Kidd's (2008: 300) 'vast yet variegated terrain which constitutes the middle ground between the extremes of anglicising unionism and Anglophobic nationalism' in Scotland, Wales and Northern

Ireland have yet to be exhausted. And in the case of England the flow of British sympathy, if modified in its unthinking expression, continues to be strong.

Nevertheless things are not so simple even from this relaxed perspective for there are, of course, counter-indications. If the devolution paradox reveals a political condition in which the growth of national identities also confirms popular acknowledgement of a UK reference, it is possible to identify another paradox today which suggests an opposite tendency. The paradox is what might be called the 'paradox of externality': though the international conditions for the break-up of the UK have never seemed less propitious, the advocacy of break-up has never been stronger or seemed so persuasive. This paradox is clearest in Scotland; in Wales the paradox is certainly more muted but it is still detectable; and as Chapter 8 shows, it is one consequent aspect of the debate about Englishness. On the one hand, and to use a serviceable term of Jim Bulpitt's, the external support system which according to nationalists affirms the *instrumental* case for independence has become very uncertain. For Bulpitt (1983: 64) such an external support system would 'attempt to minimise the impact of external forces on domestic politics, or ensure that these forces are favourable to the maintenance of domestic tranquillity'. The irony of this reference is that it is the collapse of the imperial 'external support system' which endists (see Chapters 2 and 5) believe has undermined the instrumental purpose, or 'project', of the UK. Thus, globalisation, which is supposed to have changed the international equation in favour of small nations such as Scotland, allowing them to reap the benefits of adjusting nimbly to changes in world markets, looks much less persuasive in the light of recent economic events. Similarly the prospect of European Union, which is supposed to have changed the opportunity framework for national independence, providing a secure and sustaining association for the exercise of self-determination, now looks much less sure as well. Whatever the fate of the Euro and the institutional response by Germany and France, the opportunities are not as encouraging as they once were for (in Nairn's words) new, small communities of will and purpose in the 'springtime of victorious dwarves'. Equally, if independence is a serious option – for Scotland initially – but requires keeping the pound then representation at Westminster is lost and along with it any direct influence over monetary policy. The general case which is always made for membership of the European Union – that it is important to be a member of an association the decisions of which will materially affect the welfare of the state – would be ignored. Fiscal policy made in London would not have to consider Scottish interests at all and the best that could be said of that proposition – for those who are not committed nationalists – is that it looks like a questionable political bargain (Trench 2011d). As Financial Secretary to the Treasury, Danny Alexander (2011), put it in a summary of the fiscal options for an independent Scotland, all of them are 'less optimal' than the current UK arrangements. In essence, Alexander was drawing attention to the weakness of the Kant's dove, leap and a bound, tendency in nationalist argument, which always responds by shouting 'scare tactics' rather than a serious consideration of the mutualisation of risk in the UK, not only fiscally but also diplomatically and militarily. This should be the political spectre haunting the claims of nationalists but despite the efforts of critics it has not really done so.

The other side of the paradox of externality is that the attraction of independence (or apathy about the UK) is making advances. Indeed, the crisis in the European 'support system' and the UK government's response to it has been cited as further evidence of the value of self-government and the real limits of the 'respect agenda'. It is here that the different centres of gravity between (in particular) Scotland and England could have significant disintegrative effect. When David Cameron refused to accept the proposed treaty changes to save the Euro, some commentators took this to indicate a distinctive breach between Eurosceptic (and Conservative) England and Eurofriendly (and nationalist) Scotland. According to John Lloyd (2011), for example, this has allowed Salmond to re-assert the potential of a distinctively Scottish, as opposed to UK, external support system and to remind voters 'that an independent Scotland would be Euro-friendly, with a place at the top tables of the Continent. It would have nothing to do with foreign wars, in which Scots soldiers have died. It would renounce nuclear weapons. And it would lay claim to the oil which, though dwindling, will still gush up from the bed of the North Sea, off Scotland, for some years yet'. However, this assumes that the Scots and the Welsh *are* more pro-EU than the English for which there is little evidence, and ideological repetition of the 'fact' does not constitute 'evidence'. For instance, a *ComRes* poll carried out for ITV found that Scots tend to be more Eurosceptic, not less, than the English; and *YouGov* found that those who self-identified as Welsh tended to be more in favour of leaving the EU than either English or British self-identifiers (see details in Toque 2012). This is hardly the solid basis for such a radical alternative external support system, confirming the similarity not the difference in popular attitudes across the UK. Yet again there is another related paradox: it could very well be the increasing similarity of views across the nations of the UK which, ironically, encourages an emphasis on 'difference', difference which is not only culturally but also institutionally driven under devolution (Massie 2011b). And this differentiation is having an effect as some polls reveal.

A Scottish social attitudes survey showed that the price the majority of Scots put on the maintenance of the UK was £500 per year (BBC News Scotland 2011c). Nearly two-thirds of respondents (65 per cent of the sample) said they would support independence if they were £500 better off. That result would confirm a UK understood in purely functional and instrumental terms and as Chapter 5 suggested, that would be hardly conducive to long-term allegiance and constitutional stability. Moreover, it also seemed to confirm the confidence of those in the SNP who believed that the Scots no longer feared independence and that time was on their side. However, the evidence is not so straightforward here either. Though the media generally reported that survey to mean that a majority of Scots valued UK citizenship at £500 per year, another way of looking at it was that a majority of Scots were entirely instrumental about independence. Only 21 per cent supported independence if they thought they would be £500 worse off. This is hardly the stuff of a new dawn or a 'Scottish Spring'. The message was that Scots still wanted 'more' Scotland – there was a consensus that Holyrood should have more devolved powers – but that Scotland should still stay part of the UK. The 'vast yet variegated terrain which constitutes the middle ground' of Scotland-in-the-UK is where most Scots still feel at home. That also is the message from Wales and one of the most insightful students of devolution believes that there is little appetite for Wales to do other than 'stick with union arrangements' (Holtham 2011). What those 'union arrangements' will be is the open institutional question. The outcome is not exclusively dependent upon the opinion of people in Scotland, Wales and Northern Ireland but, as Chapter 8 illustrated, it is dependent on public opinion in England as well.

George Dangerfield's study of Anglo-Irish relations was called *The Damnable Question* (1979) and there is a certain irony in the thought that today it is not Ireland (or even Scotland) but England which is the damnable question in British politics if only because political leaders have reckoned that they are damned if they do and damned if they don't. If the English Question is not properly addressed, then the integrity of the UK could be threatened; yet the integrity of the UK could come under threat when the English Question is properly addressed. This was put concisely by the House of Common's Justice Committee report (2009) on 'Devolution: A Decade On' which concluded that not only was there no consensus about solutions to the English Question but also that there was no consensus about the question. The English Question constitutes a sort of 'known unknown' but implementing a definitive answer risks opening up all sorts of 'unknown unknowns' for governing the UK. The instinct at Westminster, as Lord Norton so felicitously put it, is to ask the question but not come up with a definitive answer. However, as the 2012 IPPR report *The Dog That Finally barked: England as a Political Community* argued, the scope for such evasion is narrowing. That makes prediction even more uncertain but that is no good reason to assume that 'wild catastrophism' – the break-up of the UK – is any more likely than constitutional adaptation. In a sort of 'dry wall' manner Julian Baggini (2007: 32) put this well. The mistake people often make, he argued, is 'not that they are wrong to identify changes that have happened, but to see them as being fundamental when really they're not'. That rule of thumb can be applied to devolution as well. The 'process' of devolution does appear to mean, as James Mitchell has argued (2009), an 'ever looser' UK but that does not necessarily mean its end. Or to put that rather differently, there are always endings which are also beginnings but *the* end (despite the promptings of endists) does not seem to be nigh. It will be a different UK certainly but with intelligent political leadership and popular willingness its anomalies and paradoxes remain capable of standing reasonably solidly in relation. Time alone will tell.

Bibliography

Aaronovitch, David (2007) 'Don't spurn us – I don't want to be English', *The Times*, 1 May

Abizadeh, Arash (2004) 'Historical truth, national myths and liberal democracy: on the coherence of liberal nationalism', *Journal of Political Philosophy*, 12: 3, 291–313

Alexander, Danny (2011) 'Speech to the SCDI', *heraldscotland*, 9 December, www.heraldscotland.com/politics/background/danny-alexanders-speech-to-the-scdi.2011129596. Accessed 13 December 2011

Anderson, Benedict (1991) *Imagined Communities: Reflections on the Origins and Spread of Nationalism*, London: Verso

Andrews, Rhys and Mycock, Andrew (2008) 'Dilemmas of devolution: the "politics of Britishness" and citizenship education', *British Politics*, 3: 2, 139–55

Arditi, Benjamin (2004) 'Populism as a spectre of democracy: a response to Canovan', *Political Studies*, 52: 1, 135–43

Armstrong, Karen (2010) *The Case for God: What Religion Really Means*, London: Vintage Books

Aughey, Arthur (2001) *Nationalism, Devolution and the Challenge to the United Kingdom State*, London: Pluto Press

Aughey, Arthur (2005) *The Politics of Northern Ireland: Beyond the Belfast Agreement*, London: Routledge

Aughey, Arthur (2007) *The Politics of Englishness*, Manchester: Manchester University Press

Aughey, Arthur (2009) 'From wild catastrophism to mild moderation in Northern Ireland', in Mark Perryman (ed.), *Breaking-up Britain: Four Nations after a Union*, London: Lawrence and Wishart, 76–84

Aughey, Arthur, Bort, Eberhard and Osmond, John (2011) *Unique Paths to Devolution: Wales, Scotland and Northern Ireland*, Cardiff: Institute of Welsh Affairs

Ayres, Sarah and Pearce, Graham (2004) 'Central government responses to governance change in the English regions', *Regional and Federal Studies*, 14: 2, 255–80

Ayres, Sarah and Pearce, Graham (2005) 'Building regional governance in England: the view from Whitehall', *Policy and Politics*, 33: 4, 581–600

'Bagehot' (2007) 'Jock v Posh', *The Economist*, 28 June

Baggini, Julian (2007) *Welcome to Everytown: A Journey into the English Mind*, London: Granta

Baldwin, Stanley (1927) *On England*, London: Philip Allan

Barker, Ernest (1927) *National Character and the Factors in Its Formation*, London: Methuen
Barker, Ernest (1942) *Britain and the British People*, Oxford: Oxford University Press
Barker, Ernest (1947) 'An attempt at perspective', in Ernest Barker (ed.), *The Character of England*, Oxford: Clarendon Press, 556–8
Barker, Ernest (1961) *Principles of Social and Political Theory*, London: Oxford University Press
Barker, Rodney (1995) 'Whose legitimacy? Elites, nationalism and ethnicity in the United Kingdom', *new community*, 21: 2, 58–66
Barker, Rodney (1996) 'Political ideas since 1945, or how long was the twentieth century?', *Contemporary British History*, 10: 1, 2–19
Barnes, Eddie (2010) 'Lord Forsyth demands new Holyrood referendum', *The Scotsman*, 28 December
Barnes, Eddie (2011) 'What the new form of independence is all about', *The Scotsman*, 15 May
Barnett, Anthony (2010) 'Twelve reflections now we have Coalition government', www.opendemocracy.net/ourkingdom/anthony-barnett/twelve-reflections-now-we-have-coalition-government. Accessed on 19 April 2012
Baumeister, Andrea (2007) 'Diversity and unity: the problem with "constitutional patriotism"', *European Journal of Political Theory*, 6: 4, 483–503
Bayard, Pierre (2007) *How to Talk about Books You Haven't Read*, London: Granta
BBC News (2007) 'Most support English Parliament', 16 January, http://newsvote,bbc.co.uk/mpapps/pagetools/print/newsbbc.co.uk/1/hi/uk_politics/62548i. Accessed on 17 January
BBC News (2010a) 'Cameron calls for Scots "respect"', 14 May, http://news.bbc.co.uk/1/hi/scotland/8680816.stm. Accessed on 12 September 2011
BBC News (2010b) 'Devolved leaders' cuts pleas in full', 7 October, www.bbc.co.uk/news/uk-scotland-11493649. Accessed on 12 September 2011
BBC News Scotland (2011a) 'Storm over MP Ian Davidson's SNP 'neo-fascist' remark', 22 June www.bbc.co.uk/news/uk-scotland-13874842. Accessed on 12 September
BBC News Scotland (2011b) 'Michael Moore: independence needs two referendums', 6 June www.bbc.co.uk/news/uk-scotland-13671907. Accessed on 12 September
BBC News Scotland (2011c) 'Scots count price of independence', 5 December, www.bbc.co.uk/news/uk-scotland-scotland-politics-16024399. Accessed on 12 December
BBC News Wales (2009) 'Plaid MP tips future independence', 9 March, http://news.bbc.co.uk/1/hi/wales/wales_politics/7932649.stm. Accessed on 12 September 2011
Bechhofer, Frank and McCrone, David (2007) 'Being British: a crisis of identity?', *Political Quarterly*, 78: 2, 251–60
Bechhofer, Frank and McCrone, David (2009) 'Conclusion: the politics of identity', in Frank Bechhofer and David McCrone (eds), *National Identity, Nationalism and Constitutional Change*, London: Palgrave, 189–205
Beland, Daniel and Lecours André (2008) *Nationalism and Social Policy: The Politics of Territorial Solidarity*, Oxford: Oxford University Press
Bell, David (2011) 'Analysis: Scotland's spending binge is just a fantasy', *The Scotsman*, 31 August

Bibliography

Bell, Duncan (2003) 'History and globalization: reflections on temporality', *International Affairs*, 79: 4, 801–14

Bell, Duncan (2006) 'The idea of a patriot Queen? The monarchy, the constitution, and the iconographic order of greater Britain, 1860–1900', *Journal of Imperial and Commonwealth History*, 34: 1, 3–22

Bella Caledonia (2011) 'Independence-lite: the triumph of hope over reality' (posted by 'Doug the Dug'), http://bellacaledonia.org.uk/2011/07/06/independence-lite-the-triumph-of-hope-over-reality/. Accessed on 12 September

Benhabib, Seyla, Shapiro Ian and Petranovic, Danilo (2007) 'Editors' introduction' in Seyla Benhabib, Ian Shapiro and Danilo Petranovic (eds), *Identities, Affiliations, and Allegiances*, Cambridge: Cambridge University Press

Benner, Erica (1997) 'Nationality without nationalism', *Journal of Political Ideologies*, 2: 2, 189–206

Benner, Erica (2001) 'Is there a core national doctrine', *Nations and Nationalism*, 7: 2, 155–74

Berlin, Isaiah (1981) *Against the Current: Essays in the History of Ideas*, Oxford: Oxford University Press

Billig, Michael (1995) *Banal Nationalism*, London: Sage

Birch, A. H. (1976) 'The Celtic fringe in historical perspective', *Parliamentary Affairs*, 29: 2, 230–3

Blake, Robert (1985) *The Conservative Party from Peel to Thatcher*, London: Methuen

Blunkett, David (2005) *A New England: An English identity within Britain*, London: IPPR

Bogdanor, Vernon (1984) 'Richard Rose and territorial politics', *Local Government Studies*, 10: 4, 73–6

Bogdanor, Vernon (1995) *The Monarchy and the Constitution*, Oxford: Oxford University Press

Bogdanor, Vernon (1996) *Politics and the Constitution: Essays on British Government*, Sudbury: Dartmouth Publishing

Bogdanor, Vernon (1999a) 'Devolution: decentralisation or disintegration?', *Political Quarterly*, 70: 2, 185–94

Bogdanor, Vernon (1999b) *Devolution in the United Kingdom*, Oxford: Oxford University Press

Bogdanor, Vernon (2004) 'The constitution and the party system in the twentieth century', *Parliamentary Affairs*, 57: 4, 717–33

Bogdanor, Vernon (2006) 'Anocalyntic visions', in Tom Nairn (ed.), *Gordon Brown: Bard of Britishness*, Cardiff: Institute of Welsh Affairs, 56–60

Bogdanor, Vernon (2007a) 'The quiet revolution', *The House Magazine*, 2 March, http://epolitix.com/EN?Publications/House/1208_32/ce342dal-67e5-498c-b4d6-d3. Accessed on 27 May 2009

Bogdanor, Vernon (2007b) 'The constitution and the party system in the twentieth century', *Parliamentary Affairs*, 57: 4, 717–33

Bogdanor, Vernon (2008a) 'Review', *Parliamentary Affairs*, 61: 2, 409–10

Bogdanor, Vernon (2008b) 'Justice Committee – Minutes of Evidence – Devolution: A Decade On', 19 February, www.publications.parliament.uk/pa/cm200809/cmselect/cmjust/529/8021902.htm. Accessed on 20 January 2010

Bogdanor, Vernon (2009a) *The New British Constitution*, Oxford: Hart Publishing

Bogdanor, Vernon (2009b) 'Constitutional reform after the expenses crisis', *Public Policy Research*, 16: 2, 71–7
Bogdanor, Vernon (2009c) 'Oral evidence session', Commission on Scottish Devolution, 16 March, www.commissiononscottishdevolution.org.uk/uploads/2009-05-18-professor-bogdanor_note-of-meeting-(final)-1.pdf. Accessed on 10 June
Bogdanor, Vernon (2010) 'No turning back: the peacetime revolutions of postwar Britain', *New Statesman*, 17 June
Bogdanor, Vernon (2011) *The Coalition and the Constitution*, Oxford: Hart Publishing
Bolger, Andrew (2009) 'Nations confront question of identity', *Financial Times*, 13 May
Bonney, Norman (2008) 'Looming issues for Scotland and the Union', *Political Quarterly*, 79: 4, 560–8
Boucher, David (2005) 'The rule of law in the modern European state: Oakeshott and the enlargement of Europe', *European Journal of Political Theory*, 2005, 4: 1, 89–107
Boyce, David G. (1986) 'The marginal Britons', in R. Colls and P. Dodd (eds), *Englishness: Politics and Culture*, Beckenham: Croom Helm, 230–53
Boyce, David G. (1988) *The Irish Question and British Politics 1868–1986*, Houndmills: Macmillan
Bradbury, Jonathan (2005) *Union and Devolution: Territorial Politics in the United Kingdom under Thatcher and Blair*, Basingstoke: Palgrave Macmillan
Bradbury, Jonathan (2006) 'Territory and power revisited: theorising territorial politics in the United Kingdom after devolution', *Political Studies*, 54: 3, 559–82
Bradbury, Jonathan (2010) 'Jim Bulpitt's *Territory and Power in the United Kingdom* and interpreting political development: bringing the state and temporal analysis back in', *Government and Opposition*, 45: 3, 318–44
Bradbury, Jonathan and Andrews, R. (2010) 'State devolution and national identity: continuity and change in the politics of Welshness and Britishness in Wales', *Parliamentary Affairs*, 63: 2, 229–49
Bradbury, Jonathan and Mitchell, James (2005) 'Devolution: between governance and territorial politics', *Parliamentary Affairs*, 58: 2, 287–302
Bradley, Ian (2007) *Believing in Britain: The Spiritual Identity of Britishness*, London: I. B. Taurus
Bragg, Billy (1995) 'Looking for a new England', *New Statesman*, 17 March
Bragg, Billy (2006) *The Progressive Patriot: A Search for Belonging*, London: Bantam Press
Brockliss, Laurence and Eastwood, David (eds) (1997) *A Union of Multiple Identities: The British Isles c1750–c1850*, Manchester: Manchester University Press
Brooke, Basil (1950) 'Speech to Northern Ireland House of Commons', Northern Ireland Parliamentary Debates, 34: 21, 28 February, http://stormontpapers.ahds.ac.uk/stormont papers/index.html (I thank Carol-Ann Barnes for alerting me to this reference). Accessed on 12 August 2011
Brooks, Libby (2011) 'Salmond's Scotland has the faith but it needs a vision', *The Guardian*, 23 June
Brown, David (2007) 'Ethnic conflict and civic nationalism', in James L. Peacock, Patricia M. Thornton and Patrick B. Inman (eds), *Identity Matters: Ethnic and Sectarian Conflict*, New York: Berghahn Books, 13–33

Brown, Gordon (1992) 'Constitutional change and the future of Britain', Charter 88 Sovereignty Lecture, 9 March
Brown, Gordon (2004) *Britishness*, London: British Council
Brown, Gordon (2007) 'We need a United Kingdom', *Daily Telegraph*, 13 January
Brown, Gordon (2009) 'Introduction', in M. D'Ancona (ed.), *Being British: The Search for the Values That Bind the Nation*, Edinburgh: Mainstream Publishing, 25–34
Brown, Gordon and Alexander, Douglas (2006) *Stronger Together: The 21st Century Case for Scotland and Britain*, London: Fabian Society
Brown, Gordon (1992) 'Constitutional change and the future of Britain', Charter 88 Sovereignty Lecture, 9 March
Brown, Gordon and Straw, Jack (2007) 'Foreword' in *The Governance of Britain*, CM 7170, London: HMSO, 5
Brown, John (2005) 'The state of British political history', *Journal of Contemporary History*, 40: 1, 189–98
Brown, Keith M. (1994) 'The vanishing emperor: British kingship and its decline 1603–1707', in R. A. Mason (ed.), *Scots and Britons: Scottish Political Thought and the Union of 1603*, Cambridge: Cambridge University Press, 58–88
Brown, Rob and Barnes, Eddie (2011) 'Retiring SNP MSP in bitter attack on Alex Salmond', *The Scotsman*, 29 April
Browne, Des (2008) 'Justice Committee – Minutes of Evidence – Devolution: A Decade On', 29 January, www.publications.parliament.uk/pa/cm200809/cmselect/cmjust/529/8012902.htm. Accessed on 12 September 2011
Brubaker, Rogers (1998) 'Myths and misconceptions in the study of nationalism', in J. A. Hall (ed.), *The State of the Nation: Ernest Gellner and the Theory of Nationalism*, Cambridge: Cambridge University Press, 272–305.
Brubaker, Rogers and Cooper, Frederick (2000) 'Beyond "identity"', *Theory and Society*, 29: 1, 1–47
Bryant, Christopher G. A. (2003) 'These Englands, or where does devolution leave the English?', *Nations and Nationalism*, 9: 3, 393–412
Bryant, Christopher G. A. (2008) 'Devolution, equity and the English question', *Nations and Nationalism* 14: 4, 664–83
Buckle, Stephen and Castiglione, Dario (1991) 'Hume's critique of the contract theory', *History of Political Thought*, 12: 3, 457–80
Bulmer, Simon (2008) 'New Labour, new European policy? Blair, Brown and utilitarian supranationalism', *Parliamentary Affairs*, 61: 4, 597–620
Bulpitt, Jim (1983) *Territory and Power in the United Kingdom: An Interpretation*, Manchester: Manchester University Press
Bulpitt, Jim (1992) 'Conservative leaders and the "Euro-ratchett": five doses of scepticism', *Political Quarterly*, 63: 3, 258–75
Burke Edmund (1973) *Reflections on the Revolution in France*, ed. C. C. O'Brien, Harmondsworth: Penguin
Butterfield, Herbert (1924) *The Historical Novel*, Cambridge: Cambridge University Press
Butterfield, Herbert (1931) *The Whig Interpretation of History*, London: Bell and Sons
Butterfield, Herbert (1944) *The Englishman and His History*, Cambridge: Cambridge University Press

Cabinet Office (2010a) 'The Coalition: our programme for government', www.cabinetoffice.gov.uk/sites/default/files/resources/coalition_programme_for_government.pdf. Accessed on 12 September 2011

Cabinet Office (2010b) 'The Cabinet manual – draft', www.cabinetoffice.gov.uk/sites/default/files/resources/cabinet-draft-manual.pdf. Accessed on 12 September 2011

Cable, Vince (2007) 'Prospects for a post-Blair "progressive consensus"', *Public Policy Research*, 14: 2, 119–25

Cameron, David (2006) 'Speech to Conservative Party Conference, 4 October, www.guardian.co.uk/politics/2006/oct/04/conservatives2006.conservatives. Accessed on 12 September 2011

Cameron David (2007a) 'I support the Union for what it can achieve in the future', speech at Gretna Green, 19 April, www.conservatives.com/popups/print.cfm?obj_id=136389&type=print. Accessed on 12 September 2011

Cameron, David (2007b) 'Stronger together', 10 December www.conservatives.com/News/Speeches/2007/12/David_Cameron_Stronger_Together.aspx. Accessed on 12 September 2011

Cameron, David (2009a) 'I would govern Scots with respect', 8 February, www.conservatives.com/news/articles/2009/02/david_cameron_i_would_govern_scots_with_respect.aspx?cameron=true. Accessed on 12 September 2011

Cameron, David (2009b) 'Speech to Scottish Party Conference', 15 May, www.conservatives.com/News/Speeches/2009/05/David_Cameron_Speech_to_Scottish_Party_Conference.aspx. Accessed on 12 September 2011

Cameron, David (2009c) 'Speech to Welsh Conservative Party Conference', 29 March, www.conservatives.com/News/Speeches/2009/03/David_Cameron_Speech_to_Welsh_Conservative_Party_Conference.aspx. Accessed on 12 September 2011

Cameron, David (2010a) 'Speech to Conservative Party Conference', 6 October, www.telegraph.co.uk/news/newstopics/politics/david-cameron/8046342/David-Camerons-Conservative-conference-speech-in-full.html. Accessed on 12 September 2011

Cannadine, David (1987) 'British history: past, present – and future?', *Past and Present*, 116: 1, 169–92

Cannadine, David (2001) *Ornamentalism: How the British Saw Their Empire*, London: Allen Lane

Cannadine, David (2008) *Making History Now and Then: Discoveries, Controversies and Explorations*, London: Palgrave Macmillan

Canovan, Margaret (1996) *Nationhood and Political Theory*, Cheltenham: Edward Elgar

Canovan, Margaret (2000) 'Patriotism is not enough', in Catriona McKinnon and Iain Hampsher-Monk (eds), *The Demands of Citizenship*, London: Continuum, 276–98

Canovan, Margaret (2003) 'Wider still and wider may thy bounds be set? National loyalty and the European Union, in Michael Waller and Andrew Linklater (eds), *Political Loyalty and the Nation-State*, London: Routledge, 137–53

Carmichael, Paul, Knox, Colin. and Osborne, Robert (2007) *Devolution and Constitutional Change in Northern Ireland*, Manchester: Manchester University Press

Carrell, Severin (2011) 'SNP hopes a new wave can carry Scotland to independence', *The Observer*, 29 May

Catterall, Peter (2000) ' "Efficiency with freedom?" Debates about the British constitution in the twentieth century', in Peter Catterall, Wolfram Kaiser and Ulrike-Walton-Jordan (eds), *Reforming the Constitution* London: Frank Cass, 1–42

Cavallero, Eric (2003) 'Popular sovereignty and the law of peoples', *Legal Theory*, 9, 181–200

Chadwick, Andrew (1999) 'Aristocracy or the people? Radical constitutionalism and the progressive alliance in Edwardian Britain', *Journal of Political Ideologies*, 4: 3, 365–90

Chandler, Raymond (2007) *The Notebooks of Raymond Chandler*, New York: HarperPerennial

Charney, Evan (2003) 'Identity and liberal nationalism', *American Political Science Review*, 97: 2, 295–310

Chesterton, G. K. (1915), 'The secret people', in *Poems*, London: Burns & Oates, 243–6

Choudry, Sujit (2007) 'Does the world need more Canada? The politics of the Canadian model in constitutional politics and political theory', *International Journal of Constitutional Law*, 5: 4, 606–38

Clark, J. C. D. (1990) 'National identity, state formation and patriotism: the role of history in the public mind', *History Workshop*, 29: 1, 95–103

Clark, J. C. D. (2000) 'Protestantism, nationalism, and national identity, 1660–1832', *Historical Journal*, 43: 1, 249–76

Clark, J. C. D. (2003) *Our Shadowed Present: Modernism, Postmodernism and History*, London: Atlantic Books

Clark, J. C. D. (2010) 'Editor's introduction', in J. C. D. Clark (ed.), *A World by Itself: A History of the British Isles*, London: William Heinemann, xvii–xxvii

Clarke, Ken (2008) 'Justice Committee – Minutes of Evidence – Devolution: A Decade On', 19 February, www.publications.parliament.uk/pa/cm200809/cmselect/cmjust/529/8021902.htm. Accessed on 12 September 2011

Clegg, Nick (2010) 'Vision for political reform', 16 November, www.cabinetoffice.gov.uk/news/vision-political-reform. Accessed on 12 September 2011

Cohen, Robin (2000) 'The incredible vagueness of being British/English', *International Affairs*, 76: 3, 575–82

Cole, Laurence and Unowsky, Daniel (2007) 'Introduction', in Laurence Cole and Daniel Unowsky (eds), *The Limits of Loyalty: Imperial Symbolism, Popular Allegiances and State Patriotism in the Late Habsburg Monarchy*, New York: Berghahn Books, 1–10

Colley, Linda (1992) *Britons: Forging the Nation 1707–1837*, New Haven: Yale University Press

Colley, Linda (2000) 'Mongrels looking for a kennel, *Times Literary Supplement*, 10 March

Collingwood, R. G. (1978) *The Idea of History*, Oxford: Oxford University Press

Colls, Robert (2002) *Identity of England*, Oxford: Oxford University Press

Commission on Scottish Devolution (2008) 'The future of Scottish devolution within the Union: a consultation', http://news.bbc.co.uk/1/shared/bsp/hi/pdfs/02_12_08_calman.pdf. Accessed on 12 September 2011

Commission on Scottish Devolution (2009) 'Serving Scotland better: Scotland and the United Kingdom in the 21st century', www.commissiononscottishdevolution.org.uk/uploads/2009-06-12-csd-final-report-2009fbookmarked.pdf. Accessed 19 June

Condor, Susan (2000) 'Pride and prejudice: identity management in English people's talk about this country', *Discourse and Society*, 11: 2, 175–205

Condor, Susan (2010) Devolution and national identity: the rules of English (dis)engagement, *Nations and Nationalism*, 16: 3, 525–43

Connolly, Sean J. (1996) 'Eighteenth century Ireland', in D. G. Boyce and A. O'Day (eds), *The Making of Modern Irish History: Revisionism and the Revisionist Controversy*, London: Routledge, 15–33

Connolly, Sean J. (2000) Reconsidering the Irish Act of Union, *Transactions of the Royal Historical Society (Sixth Series)*, 10: 399–408

Conservative Party (2008) *Answering the Question: Devolution, the West Lothian Question and the Future of the Union*, London: Conservative Party

Constitution Unit (2010) *The Conservative Agenda for Constitutional Reform*, London: Constitution Unit

Cosgrove, R. A. (2008) 'A usable past: history and the politics of national identity in late Victorian England', *Parliamentary History*, 27: 1, 30–42

Costa, Josep (2003) 'On theories of secession: minorities, majorities and the multinational state', *Critical Review of International Social and Political Philosophy*, 6: 1, 63–90

Craig, David M. (2003) 'The crowned republic? Monarchy and anti-monarchy in Britain, 1760–1901, *Historical Journal*, 46: 1, 167–85

Crawford, Bruce (2010) 'Ten years of devolution', *Parliamentary Affairs*, 63: 1, 89–97

Crick, Bernard (1991) 'The English and the British', in B. Crick (ed.), *National Identities: The Constitution of the United Kingdom*, Oxford: Blackwell, 90–104

Crick, Bernard (1998) 'The decline of political thinking in British public life', *Critical Review of International Social and Political Philosophy*, 1: 1, 102–20

Crick, Bernard (2008) 'The four mations: interrelations', *Political Quarterly*, 79: 1, 71–9

Croce, Benedetto (2000) *History as the Story of Liberty*, Indianapolis: Liberty Fund

Croll, Andy (2003) 'Holding onto history: modern Welsh historians and the challenge of postmodernism', *Journal of Contemporary History*, 38: 2, 323–32

Crowther-Hunt, Lord (1976) 'Will England come off third best on devolution day?', *The Times*, 4 December

Cullen, L. M. (2000) Alliance and misalliances in the politics of the Union, *Transactions of the Royal Historical Society (Sixth Series)*, 10: 221–41

Curtice, John (2006a) 'A stronger or weaker Union? Public reactions to asymmetric devolution in the United Kingdom', *Publius*, 36: 1, 95–113

Curtice, John (2006b) 'What the people say – if anything', in Robert Hazell (ed.), *The English Question*, Manchester: Manchester University Press, 119–40

Curtice, John (2007) 'Justice Committee – Minutes of Evidence – Devolution: A Decade On', 13 November, www.publications.parliament.uk/pa/cm200809/cmselect/cmjust/529/7111303.htm. Accessed on 12 September 2011

Curtice, John (2008) *Where Stands the Union Now? Lessons from the 2007 Scottish Parliament Election*, London: IPPR

Curtice, John (2009) 'Is there an English backlash? Reactions to devolution', in Alison Park, John Curtice, Katarina Thomson, Miranda Phillips and Elizabeth Clery (eds), *British Social Attitudes: the 25th Report*, London: Sage, 1–23

Curtice, John (2010) *Is An English Backlash Emerging? Reactions to Devolution Ten Years On*, London: IPPR

Curtice, John (2011) 'Scottish election victory for the SNP is Labour's reward for devolution', *The Guardian*, 6 May

Curtice, John and Heath, Anthony (2009) 'England awakes? Trends in national identity in England', in Frank Bechhofer and David McCrone (eds), *National Identity, Nationalism and Constitutional Change*, London: Palgrave Macmillan, 41–63

Curtice, John and Seyd, Ben (2009) 'The citizens' response: devolution and the Union', in John Curtice and Ben Seyd (eds), *Has Devolution Worked? The Verdict from Policy Makers and the Public*, Manchester: Manchester University Press, 116–37

Daily Telegraph (2011) 'Foster parent ban: "this is a secular state", say High Court judges', 1 March

D'Ancona, Matthew (2009) 'Editor's Preface', in M. D'Ancona (ed.), *Being British: The Search for the Values That Bind the Nation*, Edinburgh: Mainstream Publishing, 19–24

Dangerfield, George (1979) *Damnable Question: Study in Anglo-Irish Relations*, London: Quartet Books

Davies, Nick and Williams, Darren (2009) *Clear Red Water: Welsh Devolution and Socialist Politics*, London: Francis Boutle

Davies, Norman (1999) *The Isles: A History*, London: Macmillan

Davies, Norman (2011) *Vanished Kingdoms: The History of Half-forgotten Europe*, London: Allen Lane

de Breadun, Deaglan (2011) 'SF calls for dialogus on a "New Republic"', *The Irish Times*, 10 September

Devine, Tom (2004) *Scotland's Empire 1600–1815*, Harmondsworth: Penguin

Devine, Tom (2006) 'The break-up of Britain? Scotland and the end of empire', *Transactions of the Royal Historical Society*, 16, 163–80

Devine, Tom (2011) *To the Ends of the Earth: Scotland's Global Diaspora, 1750–2010*, London: Allen Lane

Devlin, Kate (2011) 'English demand say on future of Scotland', *Herald Scotland*, 5 July

Dicey, A. V. (1886; reprinted 1973) *England's Case against Home Rule*, London: Richmond

Dicey, A. V. (2008) *Lectures on the Relation between Law and Public Opinion in England during the Nineteenth Century*, (ed.) R. VandeWetering, Indianapolis: Liberty Fund

Dyson, Kenneth (1980) *The State Tradition in Western Europe*, Oxford: Martin Robinson

Eliot, T. S. (1972) *Notes Towards the Definition of Culture*, London: Faber & Faber

Elkins, Zachary and Sides, John (2007) 'Can institutions build unity in multiethnic states?', *American Political Science Review*, 101: 4, 693–708

Elliott, Marianne (1985) *Watchmen in Sion: The Protestant Idea of Liberty*, Derry: Field Day

Elton, G. R. (1991) *Return to Essentials: Some Reflections on the Present State of Historical Study*, London: Verso

English, Richard (2011) *Is There an English Nationalism?*, London: IPPR

English, Richard and Kenny, Mike (1999) 'British decline or the politics of declinism?', *British Journal of Politics and International Relations*, 1: 2, 252–66

English, Richard and Kenny, Mike (2000) *Rethinking British Decline*, Basingstoke: Macmillan

English Richard and Kenny, Mike (2001) 'Public intellectuals and the question of British decline', *British Journal of Politics and International Relations*, 3: 3, 259–83

English, Richard, Hayton, Richard and Kenny, Mike (2009) 'Englishness and the Union in contemporary Conservative thought', *Government and Opposition*, 44: 4, 343–65

Evans, Jill (2011) 'Foreword', in Adam Price with Ben Levinson, *The Flotilla Effect: Europe's Small Economies through the Eye of the Storm*, www.english.plaidcymru.org/uploads/downloads/Flotilla_Effect_-_Adam_Price_and_Ben_Levinger.pdf. Accessed on 12 September

Evans, Stephen (1998) 'The Conservatives and the redefinition of Unionism, 1912–21', *Twentieth Century British History*, 9: 1, 1–27

Everson, Michelle (2003) ' "Subjects" or "citizens of Erewhon"? Law and non-law in the development of a British citizenship', *Citizenship Studies*, 7: 1, 57–83

Falconer, Lord (2006) 'Speech to ESRC Devolution and Constitutional Change Programme', Queen Elizabeth II Conference Centre, London, 10 March, www.dca.gov.uk/speeches/2006/sp060310.htm. Accessed 3 June

Fenton, Steve (2007) 'Indifference towards national identity: what young adults think about being English and British', *Nations and Nationalism*, 13: 2, 321–39

Field, Frank (2011) *HC Deb*, 21 June, c261-2, www.publications.parliament.uk/pa/cm201011/cmhansrd/cm110621/debtext/110621-0003.htm#11062211000661. Accessed on 12 September

Financial Times (2011) 'Devolution too far', 23 August

Fine, Robert (2007) *Cosmopolitanism*, London: Routledge

Finlay, Richard (2001) 'New Britain, new Scotland, new History? The impact of devolution on the development of Scottish historiography', *Journal of Contemporary History*, 36: 2, 383–93

Finn, Margot (1989) 'An elect nation? Nation, state and class in modern British history', *Journal of British Studies*, 28: 2, 181–91

Fitzjames Stephen, James (1967) *Liberty, Equality, Fraternity*, Cambridge: Cambridge University Press

Flinders, Matthew (2008) *Delegated Governance and the British State: Walking without Order*, Oxford: Oxford University Press

Flinders, Matthew (2009) 'Charter 88, New Labour and constitutional anomie', *Parliamentary Affairs*, 64: 2, 645–62

Fraser, Douglas (2007) 'England loses a surly lodger and gains a good neighbour', *Herald*, 21 March

Freeden, Michael (1996) *Ideologies and Political Theory: A Conceptual Approach*, Oxford: Oxford University Press
Fried, Charles (2004) 'Review of V. Bogdanor (ed.), *The British Constitution in the Twentieth Century*', *International Journal of Constitutional Law*, 2: 4, 724–6
Frost, Catherine M. (2001) 'Survey article: the worth of nations', *Journal of Political Philosophy*, 9: 4, 482–503
Fry, Michael (1998) 'Review of *No Gods and Precious Few Heroes*', *Scottish Affairs*, 24, summer, www.scottishaffairs.org/backiss/pdfs/sa24/Sa24_Fry.pdf. Accessed on 12 September 2011
Fry, Michael (2007) *The Union: England, Scotland and the Treaty of 1707*, Edinburgh: Birlinn
Fry, Michael (2010) 'Empire rethink would do us a power of good', *Scotsman*, 10 July
Gallagher, Jim (2010) 'Why the Scotland Bill is good news for England', *Daily Telegraph*, November 30
Gallagher, Tom (2009a) *The Illusion of Freedom: Scotland under Nationalism*, London: C. Hurst
Gallagher, Tom (2009b) 'Labour and the Scottish National Party: the triumph of continuity in a changing Scotland', *Political Quarterly*, 80: 4, 533–44
Gamble, Andrew (1974) *The Conservative Nation*, London: Routledge and Kegan Paul
Gamble, Andrew (2006) 'The constitutional revolution in the United Kingdom', *Publius*, 36: 1, 19–35
Gamble, Andrew (2008) 'A union of historic compromise', in M. Perryman (ed.), *Imagined Nation: England after Britain*, London: Lawrence and Wishart, 38–42
Gardham, Magnus (2011) 'Alex Salmond hails "independence generation" as he presses case for taking scotland out of Britain', *Daily Record*, 8 September
Gardiner, Michael (2004a) 'A light to the world: British devolution and colonial vision', *Interventions*, 6: 2, 264–81
Gardiner, Michael (2004b) *The Cultural Roots of British Devolution*, Edinburgh: Edinburgh University Press
Garton Ash, Timothy (2001) 'Is Britain European?', *Prospect Magazine*, 60: 2, 26–31
Gellner, Ernest (1964) *Thought and Change*, London: Weidenfeld and Nicolson
Gellner, Ernest (1983) *Nations and Nationalism*, Oxford: Wiley-Blackwell
Gillan, Cheryl (2010) 'Address to the National Assembly for Wales on the Queen's Speech', 16 June, www.walesoffice.gov.uk/2010/06/16/cheryl-gillans-address-to-the-national-assembly-for-wales-on-the-queen%E2%80%99s-speech/. Accessed on 12 September 2011
Glasman, Maurice (2010) 'England, my England!', *Prospect*, 175, 22 September
Goodhart, David (2006) *Progressive Nationalism: Citizenship and the Left*, London: Demos
Goodhart, David (2008) 'England arise', *Prospect*, 148, 26 July, www.prospectmagazine.co.uk/2008/07/englandarise/. Accessed 4 December 2011
Grainger, J. H. (1986) *Patriotisms: Britain 1900–1939*, London: Routledge and Kegan Paul

Grant, Matthew (2003) 'Historians, the Penguin Specials and the "state-of-the-nation" literature, 1958–64', *Contemporary British History*, 17: 3, 29–54

Grant, Wyn (2009) 'Cutting Scotland loose: a southern Briton's response to Preston', *British Journal of Politics and International Relations*, 11: 3, 352–4

Grant, Wyn (2010) 'The new look, old look Treasury under Mr Osborne', *Parliamentary Brief*, 29 October, www.parliamentarybrief.com/2010/10/the-new-look-old-look-treasury-under-mr-osborne. Accessed on 12 September 2011

Gray, John (2009) 'A mini version of the Habsburg empire', in M. D'Ancona (ed.), *Being British: The Search for the Values That Bind the Nation*, Edinburgh: Mainstream Publishing, 115–20

Greener, Ian (2005) 'The potential of path dependence in political studies', *Politics*, 25: 1, 62–72

Greenfeld, Lisa (1993) *Nationalism: Five Roads to Modernity*, Cambridge, Mass.: Harvard University Press

Greer, Germaine (2005) 'Shakespeare's the daddy of all Englishmen', *Sunday Times*, April 24

Greer, Scott L. (2005) 'The territorial bases of health policymaking in the US after devolution', *Regional and Federal Studies*, 15: 4, 501–18

Greer, Scott L. (2007) 'The fragile divergence machine: citizenship, health policy and devolution', in A. Trench (ed.), *Intergovernmental Relations in the United Kingdom*, Manchester: Manchester University Press, 136–59

Greer, Scott L. (2010) 'How does decentralisation affect the welfare state? Territorial politics and the welfare state in the UK and US', *Journal of Social Policy*, 39: 2, 181–201

Guibernau, Montserrat (2006) 'National identity, devolution and secession in Canada, Britain and Spain', *Nations and Nationalism*, 12: 1, 51–76

Guthrie, Roger and McLean, Ian (1978) 'Another part of the periphery: reactions to devolution in an English development area', *Parliamentary Affairs*, 31: 2, 190–200

Hadfield, Brigid (2005) 'Devolution, Westminster and the English question', *Public Law*, summer, 286–305

Haesly, Richard (2005) 'Rue Britannia or rule Britannia? British identities in Scotland and Wales', *Ethnopolitics*, 4: 1, 65–83

Harvie, Christopher (1991) 'English regionalism: the dog that never barked', in B. Crick (ed.), *National Identities: The Constitution of the United Kingdom*, Oxford: Blackwell, 105–18

Harvie Christopher (2000a) *No Gods and Precious Few Heroes*, Oxford: Oxford University Press

Harvie Christopher (2000b) 'The moment of British nationalism, 1939–1970', *Political Quarterly*, 71: 3, 328–40

Harvie, Christopher (2005) 'Scotland, Europe and the world crisis: regionalism and Scotland's shifting position between Britain and Europe', in Gerry Hassan, Eddie Gibb and Lydia Howland (eds), *Scotland 2020: Hopeful Stories for a Northern Nation*, London: Demos, 149–59

Harvie, Christopher (2006) 'Bad history', *Political Quarterly*, 77: 4, 439–47

Harvie, Christopher (2008) *A Floating Commonwealth: Politics, Culture and Technology on Britain's Atlantic Coast, 1860–1930*, Oxford: Oxford University Press

Hassan, Gerry (2009) 'Reimagining England: English voices, spaces and institution building', *Public Policy Research*, June–August, 103–9

Hassan, Gerry (2011) 'We need to help England find its way in the world', *Scotsman*, 28 May

Hattersley, Roy (2006) 'Home rule all round', *Guardian*, 13 March, www.guardian.co.uk/commentisfree/2006/mar/13/comment.politics. Accessed on 5 July 2008

Hattersley, Roy (2009) *In Search of England*, London: Little, Brown

Hazell, Robert (1998) 'Reinventing the constitution: can the state survive?', CIPFA/Times and Inaugural Lecture, www.ucl.ac.uk/spp/publications/unit-publications/33.pdf. Accessed on 12 September 2011

Hazell, Robert (1999) 'Reinventing the constitution: can the state survive?', *Public Law*, spring, 84–103

Hazell, Robert (2000) 'Conclusion: the state of the nations after one year of devolution', in Robert Hazell (ed.), *The State of the Nations: The First Year of Devolution in the United Kingdom*, Thorverton: Imprint Academic, 269–81

Hazell, Robert (2001) 'The dilemmas of devolution: does Wales have an answer to the English question?', St David's Day Lecture, 12 March, Wales Governance Centre

Hazell, Robert (2006) 'Conclusion: what are the answers to the English Question?', in Robert Hazell (ed.), *The English Question*, Manchester: Manchester University Press, 220–41

Hazell, Robert (2007) 'Westminster as a three-in-one legislature for the United Kingdom and its devolved territories', *Journal of Legislative Studies*, 13: 2, 254–79

Hazell, Robert (2008) 'Conclusion: where will the Westminster model end up?', in Robert Hazell (ed.), *Constitutional Futures Revisited: Britain's Constitution to 2020*, Basingstoke: Palgrave, 285–300

Heath, Anthony and Roberts, Jane (2008) 'British Identity: its sources and possible implications for civic attitudes and behaviour', www.justice.gov.uk/docs/british-identity.pdf. Accessed 7 June 2009

Heath, Anthony, Martin, Jean and Elgenius, Gabriella (2007) 'Who do we think we are? The decline of traditional social identities', in Alison Park et al. (eds), *British Social Attitudes: the 23rd Report – Perspectives on a Changing Society*, London: Sage, 1–34

Heath, Anthony, Taylor, Bridget, Brook, Lindsay and Park, Alison (1999) 'British National Sentiment', *British Journal of Political Science*, 29: 2, 155–75

Heath-Wellman, Christopher (2001) 'Friends, compatriots, and special political obligations', *Political Theory*, 29: 2, 217–36

Hechter, Michael (1983) 'Internal colonialism revisited', in David Drakakais-Smith and Stephen Wyn Williams (eds), *Internal Colonialism: Essays around a Theme*, Edinburgh: Institute of British Geographers, 29–41

Hechter, Michael (1999) *Internal Colonialism: The Celtic Fringe in British National Development*, (with a new introduction and appendix), London: Transaction

Heffer, Simon (2007) 'The Scots destroyed the Union – so vote SNP', *Daily Telegraph*, 17 January

Hekman, Susan (1999) 'Identity crises: identity, identity politics, and beyond', *Critical Review of International Social and Political Philosophy*, 2: 1, 3–26

Henderson, Ailsa and McEwen, Nicola (2005) 'Do shared values underpin national identity? Examining the role of values in national identity in Canada and the United Kingdom', *National Identities*, 7: 2, 173–91

Hennessy, Peter (2011) Interview with author

Herb, Guntram and Kaplan, David (1999) *Nested Identities: Nationalism, Territory, and Scale*, Lanham: Rowman & Littlefield

Hewison, Robert (1987) *The Heritage Industry: Britain in a Climate of Decline*, London: Methuen

HM Government (2008) 'Submission to the Scottish Commission on Devolution', www.commissiononscottishdevolution.org.uk/uploads/2008-11-10-hmg.pdf. Accessed on 12 September 2011

HM Government (2009) 'Devolution: A Decade On – Government Response', www.official-documents.gov.uk/document/cm76/7687/7687.pdf. Accessed on 12 September 2011

Hobsbawm, Eric (1992) *Nations and Nationalism since 1780: Programme, Myth, Reality*, Cambridge: Cambridge University Press

Hoggart, Simon (2011) 'Scottish independence is a win-win situation', *Guardian*, 14 May

Holtham, Gerry (2010) 'Why Wales has been hit', www.clickonwales.org/2010/11/why-wales-has-been-hit/. Accessed on 12 September 2011

Holtham, Gerry (2011) 'Wales must choose Northern Irish or Scottish devolution routes', www.clickonwales.org/2011/12/wales-must-choose-northern-irish-or-scottish-devolution-routes/. Accessed on 5 January 2012

Hope, Christopher (2011) 'Nick Clegg's Lords reform plans criticised by MPs and peers', *Daily Telegraph*, 17 May

Horgan, Gerald (2004) 'Inter-institutional relations in the devolved Great Britain: quiet diplomacy', *Regional & Federal Studies*, 14: 1, 113–35

Horton, John (2005) 'A qualified defence of Oakeshott's politics of scepticism', *European Journal of Political Theory*, 4: 1, 23–36

Hough, Daniel and Jeffrey, Charlie (2006) *Devolution and Electoral Politics*, Manchester: Manchester University Press

House of Commons Justice Committee (2009) *Devolution: A Decade On* (vol. 1), www.publications.parliament.uk/pa/cm200809/cmselect/cmjust/529/529i.pdf. Accessed on 12 September 2011

House of Lords Select Committee on the Constitution (2002) 'Second Report', www.publications.parliament.uk/pa/ld200203/ldselect/ldconst/28/2801.htm. Accessed on 12 September 2011

Howe, Stephen (2003) 'Internal decolonization? British politics since Thatcher as post-colonial trauma', *Twentieth Century British History*, 14: 3, 286–304

Hunt, Tristram (2011) 'Monarchy in the UK', *Public Policy Research*, 17: 4, 167–74

Hurd, Douglas (2007) Cited in Vernon Bogdanor, 'The quiet revolution', *The House Magazine*, 2 March, http://epolitix.com/EN?Publications/House/1208_32/ce342dal-67e5-498c-b4d6-d3. Accessed on 27 May 2009

Ichijo, Atsuko (2005) 'Civic or ethnic? The evolution of Britishness and Scottishness', in Helen Brocklehurst and Robert Phillips (eds), *History, Nationhood and the Question of Britain*, Basingstoke: Palgrave Macmillan, 112–23

Ignatieff, Michael (1999) 'Benign nationalism? The possibilities of the civic ideal', in Edward Martimer with Robert Fine (eds), *People, Nation and State: The Meaning of Ethnicity and Nationalism*, London: I. B. Tamms, 141–8

Independent Commission on Funding and Finance for Wales (2010) *Fairness and Accountability: A New Funding Settlement for Wales*, http://wales.gov.uk/docs/icffw/report/100705fundingsettlementfullen.pdf. Accessed on 12 September 2011

Irish Times (2010) 'Was It for This?', 18 November

Irvine, Lord Derry (1998) 'Government's Programme of Constitutional Reform', Annual Constitution Unit Lecture, www.ucl.ac.uk/spp/publications/unit-publications/35.pdf. Accessed on 12 September 2011

Isserlis, A. R. (1975) 'Regional devolution and national government', in E. Craven (ed.), *Regional Devolution and Social Policy*, London: Macmillan, 169–94

Jackson, Alvin (2004) *Home Rule: An Irish History, 1800–2000*, Oxford: Oxford University Press

Jacob, Joseph (1996) *The Republican Crown: Lawyers and the Making of the State in Twentieth Century Britain*, Aldershot: Ashgate

Jancic, Miroslav (2007) 'Citizen yes, but British?', in Nushin Arbabzadah (ed.), *From Outside In: An Anthology of Writings by Refugees on Britain and Britishness*, London: Arcadia Books, 147–52

Jeffery Charlie (2008) 'Memorandum Submitted to the Justice Committee – Devolution: A Decade On', www.publications.parliament.uk/pa/cm200809/cmselect/cmjust/529/529we14.htm. Accessed on 12 September 2011

Jeffery, Charlie (2009a) 'Devolution in the UK: problems of a piecemeal approach to constitutional change', *Publius*, 39: 2, 289–313

Jeffery, Charlie (2009b) 'Devolution, Britishness and the future of the Union', *Political Quarterly*, 78: 1, 112–21

Jeffery, Charlie, Lodge Guy and Schmuecker, Katie (2010) 'The devolution paradox', in Guy Lodge and Katie Schmuecker with Adam Coutts (eds), *Devolution in Practice 2010: Public Policy Differences in the UK*, London: IPPR

Jenkins, Daniel (1975) *The British: Their Identity and Their Religion*, London: SCM Press

Jenkins, Simon (2006) 'If Scotland wants partition, the British cannot deny it', www.guardian.co.uk/commentisfree/2006/nov/29/comment.scotland. Accessed on 12 September 2011

Johnson, Nevil (2000) 'Then and now: the British Constitution', *Political Studies*, 48: 2, 118–31

Johnson, Nevil (2001) 'Taking stock of constitutional reform', *Government and Opposition*, 36: 3, 331–54

Johnson, Simon (2011) 'Vernon Bogdanor: "Terrible precedent for Alex Salmond's referendum plan"', 30 May, www.telegraph.co.uk/news/uknews/scotland/8545217/Vernon-Bogdanor-Terrible-precedent-for-Alex-Salmonds-referendum-plan.html. Accessed on 12 September

Jones, Barry and Keating, Michael (1985) *Labour and the British State*, Oxford: Clarendon Press

Jones, Dylan (2010) *Cameron on Cameron: Conversations with Dylan Jones*, London: Fourth Estate

Kaletsky, Anatole (2007) 'How Scots could be better off by going it alone', *Times*, 26 April
Kaufmann, Eric (2008) 'The lenses of nationhood; an optical model of identity', *Nations and Nationalism*, 14: 3, 449–77
Kay, Adrian (2003) 'Evaluating devolution in Wales', *Political Studies*, 51: 1, 51–66
Kay, Adrian (2005) 'A critique of the use of path dependency in policy studies', *Public Administration*, 83: 3, 553–71
Kearton Antonia (2005) 'Imagining the "mongrel nation": political uses of history in the recent Scottish Nationalist movement, *National Identities*, 7: 1, 23–50
Keating, Michael (1998) 'What's wrong with asymmetrical government?', *Regional and Federal Studies*, 8: 1, 195–218
Keating, Michael (2001) 'So many nations, so few states: territory and nationalism in the global era', in A.-G. Gagnon and J. Tully (eds), *Multinational Democracies*, Cambridge: Cambridge University Press, 30–64
Keating Michael (2004) 'Stateless nations in the new Europe', St David's Day Lecture, Welsh Governance Centre, www.cf.ac.uk/euros/resources/WGC/St%20David's%20Day%20Lecture%202004.pdf. Accessed on 12 September 2011
Keating Michael (2009) *The Independence of Scotland: Self-government and the Shifting Politics of Union*, Oxford: Oxford University Press
Keating, Michael (2010) 'The strange death of unionist Scotland', *Government and Opposition*, 45: 3, 365–85
Keating Michael (2011) 'The political economy of independence', *Scotsman*, 8 March
Keating, Michael and McEwen, Nicola (2006) *Devolution and Public Policy*, London: Routledge
Keating, Michael, Stevenson, Linda, Cairney, Paul and Taylor, Katherine (2003) 'Does devolution make a difference? Legislative output and policy divergence in Scotland', *Journal of Legislative Studies*, 9: 3, 110–39
Kellas, James (1973) *The Scottish Political System*, Cambridge: Cambridge University Press
Kellas, James and Madgwick, Peter (1982) 'Territorial ministries: the Scottish and Welsh Offices', in Peter Madgwick and Richard Rose (eds), *The Territorial Dimension in United Kingdom Politics*, London: Macmillan, 9–33
Kelly, Ruth and Byrne, Liam (2007) *A Common Place*, London: Fabian Society
Kelso, Alexandra (2008) 'Review', *Parliamentary Affairs*, 61: 3, 546–9
Kenny, Mike (2010) 'The godlessness of Englishness', *Political Quarterly*, 81: 4, 648
Kenny, Mike, English, Richard and Hayton, Richard (2008) *Beyond the Constitution? Englishness in a Post-devolved Britain*, London: IPPR
Kidd, Colin (1999) *British Identities before Nationalism: Ethnicity and Nationhood in the Atlantic World, 1600–1800*, Cambridge: Cambridge University Press
Kidd, Colin (2003) 'Race, empire and the limits of nineteenth-century Scottish nationhood', *History Journal*, 46: 4, 873–92
Kidd, Colin (2008) *Union and Unionisms: Political Thought in Scotland, 1500–2000*, Cambridge: Cambridge University Press
Kim, N.-K. (2005) 'The end of Britain? Challenges from devolution, European integration, and multiculturalism', *Journal of International and Area Studies*, 12: 1, 61–80

Kineally, Christine (2004) 'The Orange Order and representations of Britishness', in Stephen Caunce et al. (eds), *Relocating Britishness*, Manchester: Manchester University Press, 217–36
King, Anthony (2001) *Does Britain need a Constitution?*, Oxford: Sweet and Maxwell
King, Anthony (2007) *The British Constitution*, Oxford: Oxford University Press
Kingsnorth, Paul (2008) *Real England: The Battle against the Bland*, London: Portobello Books
Kumar, Krishan (2003) *The Making of English National Identity*, Cambridge: Cambridge University Press
Kumar, Krishan (2006) 'English and French national identity: comparisons and contrasts', *Nations and Nationalism*, 12: 3, 413–32
Kumar, Krishan (2010) 'Negotiating English identity: Englishness, Britishness and the future of the United Kingdom', *Nations and Nationalism*, 16: 3, 469–87
Lee, David (2007) 'Debating Scottish identity – and a burning issue closer to home', *The Scotsman*, 2 March
Lee, Simon (2006) 'Gordon Brown and the British Way', *Political Quarterly*, 77: 3, 369–78
Lee, Simon (2007) *Best for Britain? The Politics and Legacy of Gordon Brown*, Oxford: Oneworld Publications
Leonard, Mark (1997) *Britain TM: Renewing Our Identity*, London: Demos
Leonard, Mark (2002) 'Introduction', in Phoebe Griffith and Mark Leonard (eds), *Reclaiming Britishness*, London: Foreign Policy Centre, i–xiv
Lewis, Greg (2003) 'Wales has nothing to lose but its chains', *Wales on Sunday*, 5 October
Lichtenberg, Georg C. (1990) *Aphorisms*, trans. R. J. Hollingdale, Harmondsworth: Penguin
Lieven, Dominic (1999) 'Dilemmas of empire: power, territory, identity', *Journal of Contemporary History*, 34: 2, 163–200
Life in the UK Advisory Group (2003) *The New and the Old: The Report of the 'Life in the United Kingdom' Advisory Group*, London: Home Office
Linklater, Magnus (2007) 'Before you start laying into those subsidy junkies...', *Times*, 27 June
Lloyd, John (2005) '1707 and all that' (review), *Financial Times*, 19 August
Lloyd, John (2008) 'Britain's four nations', *Financial Times*, 1 November
Lloyd, John (2011) 'No Union, please, we're English', *Reuters*, 29 December, blogs.reuters.com/john-lloyd/2011/12/29/no-union-please-were-english/. Accessed 5 January 2012
Lodge, Guy and Schmuecker, Katie (2007) 'The end of the Union?', *Public Policy Research*, 14: 2, 90–6
Loughlin, James (2007) 'Creating "a social and geographical fact": regional identity and the Ulster question 1880s–1920s', *Past and Present*, 195: 1, 159–96
Lovering, James (1978) 'The theory of the "internal colony" and the political economy of Wales', *Review of Radical Political Economics*, 10: 1, 55–67
Lynch, Peter (2005) 'Scottish independence, the Quebec model of secession and the political future of the Scottish National Party', *Nationalism and Ethnic Politics*, 11: 4, 503–31

Lynch, Peter (2009) 'From social democracy back to no ideology? The Scottish National Party and ideological change in a multi-level electoral setting', *Regional and Federal Studies*, 19: 4, 619–37

MacCormick, Neil (1999) *Questioning Sovereignty*, Oxford: Oxford University Press

MacCulloch, Dairmuid (2010) *A History of Christianity*, London: Penguin Books

MacDonnell, A. G. (1942) *England, Their England*, London: Macmillan

Mackie, Allan (2010) 'David Cameron vows to campaign against Scottish independence', *Scotsman*, 5 October

MacWhirter, Iain (2010) 'Scotland finds its feet: is this the first step to independence?', *Herald Scotland*, 2 December

Maddox, David (2011a) 'Independence support rises to a six-year high', *Scotsman*, 5 December

Maddox, David (2011b) 'Independence now inevitable – Alex Salmond', *Scotsman* 9 May

Madgwick, Peter and Rose, Richard (1982) 'Introduction', in Peter Madgwick and Richard Rose (eds) *The Territorial Dimension in United Kingdom Politics*, London: Macmillan, 1–5

Major, J. (2011) Mr Major's Ditchley Annual Lecture Speech, Ditchley Foundation, www.johnmajor.co.uk/page2282.html. Accessed on 12 September

Mandler, Peter (2006) 'What is "national identity"? Definitions and applications in modern British historiography', *Modern Intellectual History*, 3: 2, 271–97

Marinetto, Mike (2003) 'Governing beyond the centre: a critique of the Anglo-governance school', *Political Studies*, 51: 3, 592–608

Marnoch, Gordon (2003) 'Scottish devolution: identity and impact and the case of community care for the elderly', *Public Administration*, 85: 2, 253–73

Marquand, David (1993) 'The twilight of the British state? Henry Dubb versus sceptred awe', *Political Quarterly*, 64: 3, 210–21

Marquand, David (1997) *The New Reckoning: Capitalism, States and Citizens*, London: Polity Press

Marquand, David (1998) 'The Blair paradox', *Prospect*, 30: May, 19–24

Marquand, David (2008a) *Britain since 1918: The Strange Career of British Democracy*, London: Weidenfeld and Nicolson

Marquand, David (2008b) 'Give us a moral vision for England', http://ourkingdom. opendemocracy.net/2008/01/07/give-us-a-moral-vision-for-england/. Accessed on 3 August

Marquand, David (2009) 'Bursting with skeletons': Britishness after empire', in A. Gamble and Tony Wright (eds), *Britishness: Perspectives on the British Question*, Oxford: Wiley-Blackwell, 10–20

Martinez-Herrera, Enric (2002) 'From nation-building to building identification with political communities: consequences of political decentralization in Spain, the Basque Country, Catalonia and Galicia, 1978–2001', *European Journal of Political Research*, 41: 3, 421–35

Marwick, Arthur (2005) 'Review', *English Historical Review*, 120: 487, 807–9

Massie, Alan (2002) 'Maddest of tribunals', *Times Literary Supplement*, 9 August, 12–13

Massie, Alan (2011a) 'There is still a turn-off on motorway to independence', *Scotsman*, 17 August

Massie, Alan (2011b) 'Why the Scots want independence from the English', *Daily Telegraph*, 22 December
McCrone, David (1997) 'Unmasking Britannia: the rise and fall of British national identity', *Nations and Nationalism*, 3: 4, 579–96
McCrone, David (2002) 'Who do you say you are? Making sense of national identities in modern Britain', *Ethnicities*, 2: 3, 301–20
McIntyre, W. D. (2004) 'Clio and Britannia's lost dream: historians and the British Commonwealth of nations in the first half of the 20th century', *Round Table*, 93: 376, 517–32
McLean, Iain and McMillan, Alistair (2006) *State of the Union: Unionism and the Alternatives in the United Kingdom since 1707*, Oxford: Oxford University Press
McLean, Iain, Lodge, Guy and Schmuecker, Katie (2008) *Fair Shares? Barnett and the Politics of Public Expenditure*, London: IPPR
McNab, Scott (2011) 'Michael Moore tells Salmond: stop picking fights – do your job', *Scotsman*, 30 August
Meaney, Neville (2003) 'Britishness and Australia: some reflections', *Journal of Imperial and Commonwealth History*, 31: 2, 121–35
Mellett, Russell (2009) 'A principles-based approach to the Barnett formula', *Political Quarterly*, 80: 1, 76–83
Merrick, Rob (2011) 'It is time for Merseyside to declare independence', www.liverpooldailypost.co.uk/views/liverpool-columnists/columns/2011/06/22/rob-merrick-it-is-time-for-merseyside-to-declare-independence-92534-28917724/#ixzz1QT4bgzML. Accessed on 12 September
Miers, Tom (2010) *The Devolution Distraction: How Scotland's Constitutional Obsession Leads to Bad Government*, London: Policy Exchange
Miller, David (1995) *On Nationality*, Oxford: Clarendon Press
Miller, David (2000) *Citizenship and National Identity*, London: Polity Press
Miller, David (2005) 'Crooked timber or bent twig? Isaiah Berlin's nationalism', *Political Studies*, 53: 1, 100–23
Miller, William L. (1998) 'The periphery and its paradoxes', *West European Politics*, 21: 1, 103–29
Ministry of Justice (2007) 'Memorandum Submitted to the Justice Committee – Devolution: A Decade On', www.publications.parliament.uk/pa/cm200809/cmselect/cmjust/529/529we29.htm. Accessed on 12 September
Minogue, Kenneth (1992) 'Transcending the European state', in P. Robertson (ed.), *Reshaping Europe in the Twenty First Century*, Basingstoke: Macmillan
Minogue, Kenneth (2004) 'Oakeshott and political science', *Annual Review of Political Science*, 7: 2, 227–46
Mitchell, David (2011) 'If Scotland does secede, I won't be alone in mourning for my country', *Observer*, 15 May
Mitchell, James (2006) 'Devolution's unfinished business', *Political Quarterly*, 77: 4, 465–74
Mitchell, James (2007) 'The United Kingdom as a state of unions: unity of government, equality of political rights and diversity of institutions', in Alan Trench (ed.), *Devolution and Power in the United Kingdom*, Manchester: Manchester University Press, 24–47

Mitchell, James (2009) *Devolution in the UK*, Manchester: Manchester University Press

Mitchell, James (2010) 'A disunited kingdom', *Parliamentary Brief*, 19 May, www.parliamentarybrief.com/2010/05/a-disunited-kingdom. Accessed on 12 September

Mitchell, James and Leicester, Graham (1999) 'Scotland, Britain and Europe: diplomacy and devolution', Scottish Council Foundation Occasional Paper 12, www.scottishpolicynet.org.uk/scf/publications/oth16_diplom/contents.shtml. Accessed on 12 September 2011

Mitchell, James and Bradbury, Jonathan (2004) 'Devolution: comparative development and policy roles', *Parliamentary Affairs*, 57: 2, 329–46

Montgomerie, Tim (2011) 'Tory members reject Scottish independence even though it would increase chances of Conservative majority', 10 June, http://conservativehome.blogs.com/thetorydiary/2011/06/tory-members-reject-scottish-independence-even-though-it-would-increase-chances-of-conservative-majo.html. Accessed on 12 September

Mooney, Gerry and Williams, Charlotte (2006) 'Forging new "ways of life"? Social policy and nation building in devolved Scotland and Wales', *Critical Social Policy*, 26: 3, 608–29

Moore, Charles (1995) *How to Be British*, Centre for Policy Studies Annual Lecture, 2 October, www.cps.org.uk/cps_catalog/CPS_assets/338_ProductPreviewFile.pdf. Accessed on 12 September 2011

Moore, Margaret (2001) *The Ethics of Nationalism*, Oxford: Oxford University Press

Morgan, Kenneth O (1990) *The People's Peace: British History 1945–1983*, Oxford: Oxford University Press

Morgan, Kevin (2001) *The New Territorial Politics: Rivalry and Justice in Post-Devolution Britain*, www.iwa.org.uk/debate/Territorial_Kevin_Morgan.html. Accessed on 3 April 2004

Morgan, Rhodri (2008) 'Justice Committee – Minutes of Evidence – Devolution: A Decade On', 8 May, www.publications.parliament.uk/pa/cm200809/cmselect/cmjust/529/8050810.htm. Accessed on 12 September 2011

Morris, William (1977) *News from Nowhere*, ed. James Redmond, London: Routledge and Kegan Paul

Morrison, Blake (1995) 'The guttural muse', *Guardian*, 6 October

Morrison, Richard (2008) 'England, a nation with a history, but no destiny', *Times*, 22 October

Mullen, Tom (2009) 'Scotland – Scotland's constitutional future', *European Public Law*, 15: 1, 33–46

Murkens, Jo Eric with Jones, Peter and Keating, Michael (2002) *Scottish Independence: A Practical Guide*, Edinburgh: Edinburgh University Press

Murphy, Paul (2008) 'Justice Committee – Minutes of Evidence – Devolution: A Decade On', 29 January, www.publications.parliament.uk/pa/cm200809/cmselect/cmjust/529/8012905.htm. Accessed on 12 September 2011

Nairn, Tom (1977) *The Break-up of Britain*, London: New Left Books

Nairn, Tom (1988) *The Enchanted Glass: Britain and Its Monarchy*, London: Radius

Nairn, Tom (1989) Britain's royal romance, in Raphael Samuel (ed.), *Patriotism: The Making and Unmaking of the British National Identity*, vol. 3, London: Routledge, 72–86

Nairn Tom (2000) *After Britain: New Labour and the Return of Scotland*, London: Granta

Nairn Tom (2002) 'Disorientations from down under: the old country in retrospect', in Gerry Hassan and Chris Warhurst (eds), *Tomorrow's Scotland*, London: Lawrence and Wishart, 234–52

Nairn Tom (2007) 'Union on the rocks?', *New Left Review*, 43: 1, 117–32

Nairn, Tom (2008) 'Globalisation and nationalism: the New Deal?', Edinburgh Lectures, www.scotland.gov.uk/Resource/Doc/923/0057271.pdf 2008. Accessed 3 May 2009

Nairn, Tom and Kerevan, George (2005) 'Scotland in the global age: Tom Nairn in conversation with George Kerevan', in Geory Hassan, Eddie Gibb and Lydia Howland (eds), *Scotland 2020: Hopeful Stories for a Northern Nation*, London: Demos, 225–40

Nelson, Fraser (2012) 'Would you bet against Alex Salmond?', *Spectator*, 2 January, www.spectator.co.uk/coffeehouse/7540743/would-you-bet-against-alex-salmond.thtml. Accessed on 4 January

New Statesman (2009) 'Does the monarchy still matter?', 9 July

Nimni, Ephraim (1999) 'Nationalist multiculturalism in late imperial Austria as a critique of liberalism: the case of Bauer and Renner, *Journal of Political Ideologies*, 4: 3, 289–314

Norman, Wayne (2006) *Negotiating Nationalism: Nation-building, Federalism, and Secession in the Multinational State*, Oxford: Oxford University Press

Northern Ireland Life and Times (2010) 'Survey 2010', www.ark.ac.uk/nilt/2010/Political_Attitudes/index.html. Accessed on 12 September 2011

Northern Ireland Office (2010) 'Northern Ireland Grand Committee (Spending Review): extracts from speech by Secretary of State Owen Paterson MP', www.nio.gov.uk/northern-ireland-grand-committee-spending-review-extracts-from-speech-by-secretary-of-state-owen-paterson-mp/media-detail.htm?newsID=16947. Accessed on 12 September 2011

Norton, Phillip (2007) 'Tony Blair and the Constitution', *British Politics* 2: 2, 269–81

Norton, Phillip (2011) 'The English Question', http://nortonview.wordpress.com/2011/04/19/the-english-question/. Accessed on 12 September

Norwich, Bishop of (2008) *House of Lords Debates*, col. 1149, 19 June

O'Brien, Conor Cruise (1988) *God Land: Reflections on Religion and Nationalism*, Cambridge, Mass.: Harvard University Press

O'Donnell, Sir Gus (2008) 'Memorandum Submitted by the Cabinet Office to the Justice Committee: Minutes of Evidence – Devolution: A Decade On, www.publications.parliament.uk/pa/cm200809/cmselect/cmjust/529/529we02.htm. Accessed on 12 September 2011

O'Leary, Brendan (1987) 'The Anglo-Irish Agreement: meanings, explanations, results and a defence', in Paul Teague (ed.), *Beyond the Rhetoric: Politics, the Economy, and Social Policy in Northern Ireland*, London: Lawrence and Wishart, 11–40

O'Leary, Brendan (1996) 'Insufficiently liberal and insufficiently nationalist', *Nations and Nationalism*, 2: 3, 444–51
O'Toole, Fintan (2010) 'Abysmal deal ransoms us and disgraces Europe', *Irish Times*, 29 November
Oakeshott, Michael (1962) *Rationalism in Politics and Other Essays*, London: Methuen
Oakeshott, Michael (1975) *On Human Conduct*, Oxford: Clarendon Press
Oakeshott, Michael (1983) *On History and Other Essays*, Oxford: Basil Blackwell.
Oakeshott, Michael (1991) *Rationalism in Politics and Other Essays* revised and expanded edition, Indianapolis: Liberty Press
Oakeshott, Michael (1993) *Morality and Politics in Modern Europe: The Harvard Lectures*, ed. Shirley R. Letwin, New Haven: Yale University Press
Oakeshott, Michael (1996) *The Politics of Faith and the Politics of Scepticism*, ed. and with introduction by Timothy Fuller, New Haven: Yale University Press
Oakeshott, Michael (2004) *What Is History? And Other Essays*, ed. Luke O'Sullivan, Exeter: Imprint Academic
Observer (2006) 'As a true patriot, Mr Brown must enter the devolution debate', 2 July
Open Europe (2011) 'Two lane Europe fallacy', http://openeuropeblog.blogspot.com/2011/02/two-lane-europe-fallacy.html. Accessed on 12 September 2011
Orlie, Melissa A. (1999) 'Beyond identity and difference', *Political Theory*, 27: 1, 140–9
Orridge, A. W. (1981) 'Uneven development and nationalism', *Political Studies*, 29: 1, 1–15, 181–90
Orwell, George (1941; 2001) The lion and the unicorn – socialism and the English genius: part 1 England your England, in P. Davison (ed.), *Orwell's England*, Harmondsworth: Penguin, 251–77
Orwell, George (2000) *Essays* with an introduction by Bernard Crick, Harmondsworth: Penguin
Osmond, John (2009) 'Welsh independence in an era of interdependence', Mark Perryman (ed.), *Breaking Up Britain: Four Nations after a Union*, London: Lawrence and Wishart, 193–206
Our Kingdom (2011) 'The Scottish spring', www.opendemocracy.net/ourkingdom/collections/scottish-spring
Page, Ed (1978) 'Michael Hechter's internal colonial thesis: some theoretical and methodological problems', *European Journal of Political Research*, 6: 3, 295–317
Parekh, Bikhu (2003) 'Being British', *Government and Opposition*, 37: 4, 581–4
Parekh, Bikhu (2008a) *A New Politics of Identity: Political Principles for an Interdependent World*, Basingstoke: Palgrave
Parekh, Bikhu (2008b) *House of Lords Debates*, col. 1143, 19 June
Parker, Mike (2009) 'Independence – that's when good neighbours become good friends', in Mark Perryman (ed.), *Breaking up Britain: Four Nations and a Union*, London: Lawrence and Wishart, 172–82
Parker, Simon (2003) 'Regional government: the issue explained', *Guardian*, 23 May
Parris, Matthew (2010) 'With a shrug of the shoulders, England is becoming a nation once again', *Spectator*, 18 December

Paterson, Lindsay (2002) 'Is Britain disintegrating? Changing views of "Britain" after devolution', *Regional and Federal Studies*, 12: 1, 21–42

Pattie, Charles, Seyd, Patrick and Whiteley, Paul (2004) *Citizenship in Britain: Values, Participation and Democracy*, Cambridge: Cambridge University Press

Paun, Akash (2008) 'Lost souls in the lobbies?' Backbenchers from Scotland and Wales in post-devolution Westminster', in Alan Trench (ed.), *The State of the Nations 2008*, Exeter: Imprint Academic, 197–220

Paxman, Jeremy (1998) *The English: A Portrait of a People*, London: Michael Joseph

Paxman, Jeremy (2011) '*A Short History of England* by Simon Jenkins – review', *Guardian*, 8 September

Perryman, Mark (2008) 'Becoming England', in Mark Perryman (ed.), *Imagined Nation: England after Britain*, London: Lawrence and Wishart, 13–34

Perryman, Mark (2009) 'A jigsaw state', in Mark Perryman (ed.), *Breaking Up Britain: Four Nations after a Union*, London: Lawrence and Wishart, 14–43

Peterkin, Tom (2011) 'Independence now inevitable, says Tam Dalyell', *Scotsman*, 16 August

Pieper, Josef (1954) *The End of Time: A Meditation on the Philosophy of History*, trans. M. Bullock, London: Faber and Faber

Pittock, Murray (2001) *Scottish Nationality*, Basingstoke: Palgrave

Pittock, Murray (2008) *The Road to Independence? Scotland since the Sixties*, London: Reaktion Books

Pittock, Murray (2009) 'To see ourselves as others see us', *European Journal of English Studies*, 13: 3, 293–304

Pocock, J. G. A. (1975) 'British History: a plea for a new subject', *Journal of Modern History*, 47: 4, 601–21

Pocock, J. G. A. (1999) 'Enlightenment and counter-enlightenment, revolution and counter-revolution: a Eurosceptical enquiry', *History of Political Thought*, 20: 1, 125–39

Pocock, J. G. A. (2000a) 'Gaberlunzie's return', *New Left Review* (second series), 5, 41–52

Pocock, J. G. A. (2000b) 'The Union in British history', *Transactions of the Royal Historical Society*, 10, 181–96

Pocock, J. G. A. (2009) *Political Thought and History: Essays on Theory and Method*, Cambridge: Cambridge University Press

Popham, Peter and Portilho-Shrimpton, Thais (2008) '"I despise Islamism": Ian McEwan faces backlash over press interview', *Independent*, 22 June

Porter, Bernard (2004) *The Absent-minded Imperialists: Empire, Society and Culture in Britain*, Oxford: Oxford University Press

Powell, Enoch (1969) *Freedom and Reality*, ed. J. Wood, Kingswood: Elliott Rightway Books, 338–9

Preston, Peter (2008) 'Cutting Scotland loose: soft nationalism and independence-in-Europe', *British Journal of Politics and International Relations*, 10: 4, 717–28

Preston, Peter (2009) 'The other side of the coin: reading the politics of the 2008 financial tsunami', *British Journal of Politics and International Relations*, 11: 3, 504–17

Price, Adam with Levinger, Ben (2011) *The Flotilla Effect: Europe's Small Economies through the Eye of the Storm*, www.english.plaidcymru.org/uploads/downloads/Flotilla_Effect_-_Adam_Price_and_Ben_Levinger.pdf. Accessed on 12 September

Pulzer, Peter (1967) *Political Representation and Elections in Britain*, London: Allen and Unwin

Rawlings, Richard (2003) *Delineating Wales: Constitutional, Legal and Administrative Aspects of National Devolution*, Cardiff: University of Wales Press

Raynor, Gordon (2011) 'Cameron drums up support for royal wedding street parties as figures show north–south divide', *Daily Telegraph*, 11 April

Rees-Mogg, William (2005) 'The Battle for England', *Times*, 9 May

Resnick, Philip (2008) 'Hubris and melancholy in multinational states', *Nations and Nationalism*, 14: 4, 789–807

Rhodes, R. A. W., Wanna, John and Weller, Patrick (2009) *Comparing Westminster*, Oxford: Oxford University Press

Ribeiro, Aileen (2002) 'On Englishness in Dress', in Christopher Breward, Becky Conekin and Caroline Cox (eds), *The Englishness of English Dress*, Oxford: Berg, 15–27

Rifkind, Malcolm (1998) 'Scotland, Britain and Europe: a new United Kingdom for a new century', Scottish Council Foundation, 19 June, www.scottishpolicynet.org.uk/scf/publications/oth4_rifkind/contents.shtml. Accessed on 12 September 2011

Robbins, Keith (1989) *Nineteenth-century Britain: Integration and Diversity*, Oxford: Clarendon Press

Robbins, Keith (2005) 'Review', *English History Review*, 120: 488, 1096–7

Rojek, Chris (2007) *Brit-myth: Who Do the British Think They Are?*, London: Reakton Books

Rokkan, Stein and Urwin, Derek (eds) (1982) *The Politics of Territorial Identity: Studies in European Regionalism*, London: Sage

Romani, Roberto (2002) *National Character and Public Spirit in Britain and France, 1750–1914*, Cambridge: Cambridge University Press

Rose, Richard (1965) *Politics in England: An Interpretation*, London: Faber

Rose, Richard (1982a) *Understanding the United Kingdom: The Territorial Dimension in Government*, London: Longman

Rose, Richard (1982b) 'Is the United Kingdom a state? Northern Ireland as a case study', in Peter Madgwick and Richard Rose (eds), *The Territorial Dimension in United Kingdom Politics*, London: Macmillan, 129–30

Royce, Josiah (1995) *The Philosophy of Loyalty*, with an introduction by J. J. McDermott, Nashville: Vanderbilt University Press

Russell, Meg and Hazell, Robert (2000) 'Devolution and Westminster: tentative steps towards a more federal Parliament', in Robert Hazell (ed.), *The State of the Nations: The First Year of Devolution in the United Kingdom*, Thorverton: Imprint Academic, 183–221

Salmon, Trevor (2011) 'How independent would Scots really be if country was member of EU? The answer is – not very', *Scotsman*, 20 December

Salmond, Alex (2007) 'Only Scottish independence can solve the English Question', *Daily Telegraph*, 20 March

Salmond, Alex and Alexander, Wendy (2006) 'Is an independent Scotland economically viable?', *Financial Times*, 12 December

Sandbrook, Dominic (2011) 'Why we should be proud of being Little Englanders', *Daily Mail*, 30 July

Sanderson, J. B. (1966) 'Professor Oakeshott on history as a mode of experience', *Australian Journal of Philosophy*, 44: 2, 210–23

Sandford, Mark (2002) 'What place for England in an asymmetrically devolved UK?', *Regional Studies*, 36: 7, 789–96

Sandford, Mark (2009) 'Conclusion', in Mark Sandford (ed.), *The Northern Veto*, Manchester: Manchester University Press, 186–90

Santayana, George (1922) *Soliloquies in England and Later Soliloquies*, London: Constable and Company

Schopenhauer, Arthur (1892) *Essays*, selected and translated by T. Bailey Saunders, London: Swan Sonnenschein

Scotland Office (2009) *Scotland's Future in the United Kingdom: Building on Ten Years of Scottish Devolution*, London: Her Majesty's Stationery Office

Scotland Office (2010) *Strengthening Scotland's Future*, www.scotlandoffice.gov.uk/scotlandoffice/files/Scotland_Bill_Command_Paper.pdf. Accessed on 12 September 2011

Scotland Office (2010) *Strengthening Scotland's Future*, London: Her Majesty's Stationery Office

Scottish Executive (2007) *Choosing Scotland's Future: A National Conversation, Edinburgh*, www.scotland.gov.uk/Publications/2007/08/13103747/0. Accessed 11 April 2011

Scottish Government (2010) British-Irish Council (press release), 25 June, www.scotland.gov.uk/News/Releases/2010/06/25144630. Accessed on 15 July 2011

Scottish Government (2011) 'British–Irish Council', www.scotland.gov.uk/News/Releases/2010/06/25144630. Accessed on 12 September

Scottish Government (2011) 'Devolved governments' shared agenda', 31 May, www.scotland.gov.uk/News/Releases/2011/05/31162113. Accessed on 12 September

Scottish National Party (2011) Party Manifesto 2011, http://manifesto.votesnp.com/. Accessed on 12 September

Scruton, Roger (2010) *The Uses of Pessimism and the Danger of False Hope*, London: Atlantic Books

Sellar, W. C. and Yeatman, R. J. (1930) *1066 and All That: A Memorable History of England*, London: Methuen

Seton-Watson, Hugh (1979) 'History', in C. Maclean (ed.), *The Crown and the Thistle: The Nature of Nationhood*, Edinburgh, Scottish Academic Press, 272–305

Settle, Michael (2010) 'Cameron focused on Scotland after poor poll results', *Herald Scotland*, 26 November

Sewel, Lord (2007) 'The Union and devolution – a fair relationship', in C. Bryant (ed.), *Towards a New Constitutional Settlement*, London: Smith Institute, 74–9

Shore, Chris (2004) 'Whither European citizenship? Eros and civilisation revisited, *European Journal of Social Theory*, 7: 1, 27–44

Shulman, Stephen (2003) 'Exploring the economic basis of nationhood', *Nationalism & Ethnic Politics*, 9: 2, 23–49

Sinclair, Thomas (1970) 'The position of Ulster', in Simon Rosenbaum (ed.), *Against Home Rule*, Port Washington: Kennikat Press, 169–81

Sked, Alan (1989) *The Decline and Fall of the Habsburg Empire 1815–1918*, Harlow: Longman
Smith, Anthony D. (2001) *Nationalism: Theory, Ideology, History*, London: Verso
Southern, Neil (2007) 'Britishness, "Ulsterness" and unionist identity in Northern Ireland', *Nationalism and Ethnic Politics*, 13: 1, 71–102
Spender, Stephen (1951) *World within World*, London: Hamish Hamilton
Squires, Judith (2007) 'Negotiating equality and diversity in Britain: towards a differentiated citizenship?', *Critical Review of International Social and Political Philosophy*, 10: 4, 531–59
Stapleton, Julia (1994) *Englishness and the Study of Politics: The Social and Political Thought of Ernest Barker*, Cambridge: Cambridge University Press
Stapleton, Julia (2001) *Political Intellectuals and Public Identities in Britain Since 1850*, Manchester: Manchester University Press
Stapleton, Julia (2005) 'Citizenship versus patriotism in twentieth-century England', *Historical Journal*, 48: 1, 151–78
Stapleton, Julia (2006) 'Ernest Barker: Classics England-Britain and Europe 1906–1960, *Polis: Journal of the Society for Greek Political Thought*, 23: 2, 203–21
Stapleton, Julia (2008) 'Modernism, the English past, and Christianity: Herbert Butterfield and the study of history', *Historical Journal*, 51: 2, 547–57
Starkey, David (1999) 'By 2050 England will have recreated itself: visionary, multi-ethnic, free. Is this farewell to the bulldog breed?', www.chronicle-future.co.uk/debate2right.html. Accessed on 12 September 2011
Stewart, A. T. Q. (1986) 'The siege of Ulster,' *The Spectator*, 11 January
Stewart, A. T. Q. (2001) *The Shape of Irish History*, Belfast: Blackstaff Press
Stoker, Gerry (2006) *Why Politics Matters: Making Democracy Work*, Basingstoke: Palgrave Macmillan
Straw, Jack (2007) 'Living with West Lothian', *Prospect*, 139, 27 October
Straw, Jack (2008) 'Justice Committee – Minutes of Evidence – Devolution: A Decade On', 13 May, www.publications.parliament.uk/pa/cm200809/cmselect/cmjust/529/8051303.htm. Accessed on 12 September 2011
Sturm, Roland (2003) 'Re-reading Tom Nairn', *Scottish Affairs*, 45 www.scottishaffairs.org/backiss/pdfs/sa45/sa45_Sturm.pdf. Accessed on 11 June 2010
Sutherland, C. (2005) 'Nation-building through discourse theory', *Nations and Nationalism*, 11: 2, 185–202
Swenden, Wilfried (2010) 'Beyond UK exceptionalism? Comparing strategies for territorial management', in Klaus Stolz (ed.), *Ten Years of Devolution in the United Kingdom*, Augsburg: Wissner Verlag, 13–35
Thompson, Andrew (2005) *The Empire Strikes Back? The Impact of Imperialism on Britain from the Mid-nineteenth Century*, Harlow: Longman
Thompson, Janna (2007) 'Patriotism and the obligations of history', in Igor Primoratz and Alexsandar Pavkovic (eds), *Patriotism: Philosophical and Political Perspectives*, Aldershot: Ashgate, 147–59
Thomson, Richard (2009) 'The social-democratization of Scottish nationalism', in Mark Perryman (ed.), *Breaking Up Britain: Four Nations after a Union*, London: Lawrence and Wishart, 119–32
Tierney, Stephen (2007) 'Giving with one hand: Scottish devolution within a unitary state', *International Journal of Constitutional Law*, 5: 4, 730–53

Tilley James and Heath Anthony (2007) 'The decline of British national pride', *British Journal of Sociology* 58: 4, 661–78

Todd, Jennifer, O'Keefe, Theresa, Rougier, Nathalie and Canas Bottos, Lorenzo (2006) 'Fluid or frozen? Choice and change in ethno-national identiification in contemporary Northern Ireland', *Nationalism and Ethnic Politics*, 12: 3, 323–46

Tomlinson, Jim (2009) 'After decline?', *Contemporary British History*, 23: 3, 395–406

Torrance, David (2011a) 'The Balkans tell me that, sometimes, things fall apart for no reason at all', *The Scottish Review*, 28 July, www.scottishreview.net/BackPage150.shtml?utm_source=Sign-Up.to&utm_medium=email&utm_campaign=244317-The+night+I+intruded+into+private+grief. Accessed on 12 September

Torrance, David (2011b) Cameron must fight harder for the Union', *The Scotsman*, 19 May

Torrance, David (2011c) 'It seems that we are all unionists now', *The Scottish Review*, 19 May, www.scottishreview.net/DavidTorrance125.shtml. Accessed on 12 September

Toque (Gareth Young) (2012) 'The sanctimonious cockwaffle of David Marquand', 2 January, http://toque.co.uk/sanctimonious-cockwaffle-david-marquand. Accessed 5 January

Travers, Tony and Kleinman, M. (2003) *The Politics of London: Governing an Ungovernable City*, London: Palgrave

Trench, Alan (2004) 'Introduction: has devolution made a difference?', in Alan Trench (ed.), *Has Devolution Made a Difference? The State of the Nations 2004*, Exeter: Imprint Academic, 1–10

Trench, Alan (2005a) 'Introduction: the dynamics of devolution', in Alan Trench (ed.), *The Dynamics of Devolution: The State of the Nations 2005*, Exeter: Imprint Academic, 1–19

Trench, Alan (2005b) 'Intergovernmental relations within the UK', in Alan Trench (ed.), *The Dynamics of Devolution: The State of the Nations 2005*, Exeter: Imprint Academic, 137–60

Trench, Alan (2006) 'Learning from the lawyers?', *Regional and Federal Studies*, 16: 1, 117–24

Trench, Alan (ed.) (2007a) *Devolution and Power in the United Kingdom*, Manchester: Manchester University Press

Trench, Alan (2007b) 'Memorandum submitted to the Justice Committee by Alan Trench', www.parliament.the-stationery-office.co.uk/pa/cm200809/cmselect/cmjust/529/529we15.htm. Accessed on 12 September 2011

Trench, Alan (2008a) 'Introduction: the second phase of devolution', in Alan Trench (ed.), *The State of the Nations 2008*, Exeter: Imprint Academic, 1–22

Trench, Alan (2008b) 'Scotland and Wales: the evolution of devolution', in Robert Hazell (ed.), *Constitutional Futures Revisitied: Britain's Constitution to 2020*, Basingstoke: Palgrave Macmillan, 29–42

Trench, Alan (2009a) 'Devolution plus': what it might entail and where it might lead', *Scottish Affairs*, 68: 1, 69–74

Trench Alan (2009b) 'Issues relating to higher education and devolution' written submission to the Commission on Scottish Devolution, www.commissiononscottishdevolution.org.uk/uploads/2009-02-12-alan-trench-(no.2).pdf. Accessed on 12 September 2011

Trench, Alan (2010a) 'Wales and the Westminster model', *Parliamentary Affairs*, 63: 1, 117–33
Trench, Alan (2010b) 'Labour's failure to understand devolution', http://devolutionmatters.wordpress.com/2010/09/16/labours-failure-to-understand-devolution/. Accessed on 12 September 2011
Trench, Alan (2010c) 'Conservative-Lib Dem alliance and the Union', 9 May, http://devolutionmatters.wordpress.com/2010/05/09/a-conservative-lib-dem-alliance-and-the-union/. Accessed on 12 September
Trench, Alan (2011a) 'Fantasy and fibbing on the campaign trail', *Public Finance*, 3 May
Trench, Alan (2011b) 'Win-win strategy may yet triumph', *Scotsman*, 8 June
Trench Alan (2011c) 'We need ceasefire in Scots cold war, *Scotsman*, 29 June
Trench, Alan (2011d) 'Four options – and none of them easy', *Scotsman*, 9 December
Tully, James (2001) 'Introduction', in Alain Gagnon and James Tully (eds), *Multinational Democracies*, Cambridge: Cambridge University Press, 1–34
van Kersbergen, Kies (2000) 'Political allegiance and European integration', *European Journal of Political Research*, 37: 1, 1–17
van Kersbergen, Kies (2003) 'Welfare state reform and political allegiance', *European Legacy*, 8: 5, 559–71.
Varney, David (2007) *Review of Tax Policy in Northern Ireland*, http://webarchive.nationalarchives.gov.uk/20100808181404/webarchive.nationalarchives.gov.uk/+/http://www.hm-treasury.gov.uk/d/varney171207.pdf. Accessed on 12 September 2011
Vincent, Andrew (1997) 'Liberal nationalism: an irresponsible compound?', *Political Studies*, 45: 3, 275–95
Viroli, Maurice (1997) *For Love of Country: An Essay on Patriotism and Nationalism*, Oxford: Clarendon Press
Walden, George (2004) 'Anthropologist, study thyself' (review), *New Statesman*, 10 May
Walker, Brian (1998) 'British and Irish', *Belfast Telegraph*, 26 March
Walker, David (2002) *In Praise of Centralism*, London: Catalyst Forum
Walker, David (2010) 'Debate: problems of quality and logic in the case for devolution', *Public Money & Management*, 30: 2, 84–5
Walker Gail (2011) 'Sense of Britishness is more complicated than box ticking', *Belfast Telegraph*, 29 March
Walker, Graham (2010) 'Scotland, Northern Ireland and devolution: past and present', *Contemporary British History*, 24: 2, 235–56
Walker, Graham and Farrington, Chris (2009) 'Ideological content and institutional frameworks: Unionist identities in Northern Ireland and Scotland', *Irish Studies Review*, 17: 2, 135–52
Walker, Neil (2000) 'Beyond the unitary conception of the United Kingdom constitution?', *Public Law*, autumn, 384–404
Wallace, Jim (2011) 'Governing in coalition', in Institute for Government, *One Year On: The First Year of Coalition Government: A Collection of Views*, 18–19
Walzer, Michael (1997) *On Toleration*, New Haven: Yale University Press
Ward, Paul (2004) *Britishness since 1870*, London: Routledge

Ware, Vron (2007) *Who Cares about Britishness? A Global View of the National Identity Debate*, London: Arcadia Books
Watson, George (1973) *The English Ideology: Studies in the Language of Victorian Politics*, London: Allen Lane
Weight, Richard (2002) *Patriots: National Identity in Britain 1940–2000*, Basingstoke: Macmillan
Wheatcroft, Geoffrey (2009) 'England might yet review the state of the Union', *Financial Times*, 22 April
White, Michael (2011) 'Don't worry about future Scottish independence – we've been here before', www.guardian.co.uk/politics/blog/2011/jun/27/dont-worry-scottish-independence-been-here-before. Accessed on 12 September
Whittle, Peter (2011) *Monarchy Matters*, London: Social Affairs Unit
Wicks, Elizabeth (2006) *The Evolution of a Constitution: Eight Key Moments in British Constitutional History*, Oxford: Hart
Willetts, David (2009) 'England and Britain, Europe and the Anglosphere', in Andrew Gamble and Tony Wright (eds), *Britishness: Perspectives on the British Question*, Oxford: Wiley-Blackwell, 54–61
Williams, Glanmor (1979) *Religion, Language and Nationality in Wales*, Cardiff: Cardiff University Press
Williams, Gwyn (1991) *When Was Wales?*, Harmondsworth: Penguin
Wills, Michael (2006) 'Being British is different now', *Sunday Times*, 15 January
Wills, Michael (2008) 'The politics of identity', paper presented to the IPPR, www.justice.gov.uk/news/sp260308b.htm. Accessed on 12 September 2011
Wilson, Sir Richard (2002) Evidence to House of Lords Constitutional Select Committee: devolution: inter-institutional relations in the United Kingdom, 26 June, www.publications.parliament.uk/pa/ld200102/ldselect/ldconst/147/2062605.htm. Accessed on 12 September 2011
Wilson, Sammy (2010) 'Building a drystone wall is like working at Stormont', *Belfast Newsletter*, 3 January
Wincott, David (2006) 'Social policy and social citizenship: Britain's welfare states', *Publius* 36: 1, 169–88
Winetrobe, Barry (2011) 'Enacting Scotland's "written constitution": The Scotland Act 1998', in Phillip Norton (ed.), *A Century of Parliamentary Reform*, Oxford: Wiley-Blackwell, 85–100
Winnett, Robert (2011) 'David Cameron: Britain faces crisis of confidence', *Daily Telegraph*, 25 July
Wood, Lynn (2009) 'Greening of the Welsh dragon', in M. Perryman (ed.), *Breaking Up Britain: Four Nations after a Union*, London: Lawrence and Wishart, 86–94
Wright, Tony and Gamble, Andrew (2000) 'Commentary: the end of Britain?', *Political Quarterly*, 71: 1, 1–3
Wyn Jones, Richard (2009) 'From Utopia to reality: Plaid Cymru and Europe', *Nations and Nationalism*, 15: 1, 19–47
Wyn Jones, Richard and Scully, Roger (2009) 'The public legitimacy of devolution: Scotland and Wales compared', paper presented to the Annual Meeting of the Political Studies Association, Manchester
Wyn Jones, Richard, Lodge, Guy, Henderson, Ailsa and Wincott, Daniel (2012) *The Dog That Finally Barked: England as a Political Community*, London: IPPR

Yapp, Robin (2011) 'David Cameron "bordering on stupidity" over Falkland Islands, says Argentina president Cristina Kirchner', *Daily Telegraph*, 17 June

Young, Alison (2005) 'The British constitution in the twentieth century', *Law Quarterly Review*, 121: 1, 168–70

Young, Gareth (2007) 'Why do we need an English Parliament?', http://thecep.org.uk:80/news/?page_id=202. Accessed on 12 September 2011

Young, Gareth (2011) 'England is the country, and the country is England', http://toque.co.uk/england-country-and-country-england. Accessed on 12 September

Young, G. M. (1947) 'Government', in E. Barker (ed.), *The Character of England*, Oxford: Clarendon Press, 104–17

Younge, Gary (2010) 'A nation lost', *Guardian*, 29 June

Index

Aaronovitch, David 112
Alexander, Danny 113, 190
Alexander, Douglas 108, 113
allegiance 66–83, 87, 91, 94–7,
 104–6, 121–2, 156, 187–8, 191
 primary and secondary 96
Amery, Leo 69
Anderson, Perry 26
Andrews, R. 35, 47
Anglo-Irish Agreement (1985) 133
Anselm of Canterbury 11
Arditi, Benjamin 54
Armstrong, Karen 11
Ascherson, Neal 57
Ashcroft, Brian 179
Australia 32
Austro-Hungarian empire 13–14, 40, 70, 91, 165
Ayres, Sarah 145

'Bagehot' in *The Economist* 116, 161
Bagehot, Walter 47, 82
Baggini, Julian 59, 192
Baldwin, Stanley 9, 154–5
'banal unionism' (Kidd) 6, 16, 36, 105
Barker, Rodney 19, 72
Barker, Sir Ernest 9–18, 44, 56–7, 79, 94, 165
Barker, Thomas Jones 6
Barnes, Eddie 181
Barnett, Anthony 171
Barnett formula 162
Baumeister, Andrea 91
Bayard, Pierre 47
Bechhofer, Frank 59, 75
Belfast Agreement (1998) 71, 78, 109, 173
Benhabib, Seyla 78

Benner, Erica 68, 80
Bennett, Alan 165
Berlin, Isaiah 62, 110
Bevan, Aneurin 127
Birch, A. H. 28
Blair, Tony 9, 30, 55, 133, 136–7, 145
Blake, Lord 171
Blake, William 159
Bogdanor, Vernon 17, 22, 37, 46–8,
 65, 71, 81, 97–9, 103–8, 112,
 115–19, 130–1, 139, 149–50,
 165, 167, 183
Bonney, Norman 182
Bradbury, Jonathan 35, 87, 133, 136
Bragg, Billy 19, 158
British Empire 87–8
 see also imperialism
British Empire Exhibition (1924) 12–13
British–Irish Council 130
British Social Attitudes Survey 71
Britishness 7–19, 24, 29–30, 35–40,
 44–7, 56–8, 68, 71, 75–9, 88–9,
 94–5, 98, 116, 155–8, 163–4
 as distinct from being British 78
Brockliss, L. 15
Brook, Lindsay 70
Brooks, Libby 178
Brown, David 16, 83
Brown, Gordon 10, 16, 30, 58, 108, 172
Brown, John 15
Browne, Des 135
Brubaker, Rogers 73–4, 76
Bryant, Christopher 113, 153, 157
Bulmer, Simon 97
Bulpitt, Jim 87, 143–4, 157, 160, 165, 189

Burke, Edmund 91
Bush, George Senior 3
Butler, Samuel 12
Butterfield, Herbert 7, 44, 50
Byrne, Liam 17

Cable, Vince 173
Calman Commission 90, 119–20, 126, 140, 167, 173
Cameron, David 18, 151, 170–5, 190
Canada 97
Cannadine, David 18, 45
Canovan, Margaret 79–80, 82, 103, 149
Catterall, Peter 48
census forms 78
centrifugal tendencies 144, 170
Chandler, Raymond 3, 9, 19, 185
Charter 88 70
Chesterton, G. K. 46, 149, 158–9
Choudry, Sujit 97
citizenship 79–80, 101–2, 115, 148
'civil association' (Oakeshott) 95–6
Clark, J. C. D. 5, 24, 27, 46, 56, 76
Clarke, Kenneth 150–1
Clegg, Nick 60, 173–4
Cohen, Robin 16, 19
Cole, Laurence 70
Colley, Linda 9–10, 16–17, 57, 86–7
Colls, Robert 148
colonialism, internal 27–33, 38, 111
Columbus, Christopher 55
common standards across the United Kingdom 106–7, 120, 139, 187
'communities of fate' 78–9
Condor, Susan 78, 152–3, 156–8
consent, principle of 112
Conservative Party 170–5
  Democracy Task Force 150–1
ConservativeHome 171
'constitutional *anomie*' (Flinders) 131–2, 136
constitutional reform 55, 98
constitutionalism 19–22, 69, 188
'constructive ambiguity' 181
contract, principle of 84–6
Cooke, Edward 13, 26
Cooper, Frederick 73–4
corporation tax 176–7
Cosgrove, R. A. 80
Crick, Bernard 71, 79, 89–91, 102, 148, 163–4

Crowther-Hunt, Lord 159
Cullen, L. M. 24
cultural identity 163
Curtice, John 74–5, 103, 152, 163, 180–1

Dalyell, Tam 180
d'Ancona, Matthew 17–18
Dangerfield, George 191
Davies, Norman 9–10, 37–40, 53, 88, 187–8
Davies, Ron 33
de Breadun, Deaglan 188
decentralisation 20, 173
'declinism' 25–8, 36
decolonisation 27
Devine, Tom 38, 101, 180
'devolution paradox' 120, 122, 139, 187–9
Dicey, A. V. 46–7, 81, 109–10, 147
Dickens, Charles 7
'diffusionist tendency' (Mitchell) 127–8
dominion status 117
'dry wall' metaphor 52–62, 65, 85, 96, 99, 105, 133, 188, 192
Dyson, Kenneth 72

Eastwood, D. 15
Edward VIII 54
Einstein, Albert 91
Eliot, T. S. 4, 99
Elis-Thomas, Dafydd 41
Elton, G. R. 18–19
Elvidge, Sir John 135
'emotional quackery' 3–4, 44
'endism' 26–8, 36–7, 40, 43, 48–52, 55, 57, 62, 69–72, 180, 187, 189
English, Richard 25, 40, 152, 163
'English Question' 145–52, 159–60, 163, 171, 175, 191–2
Englishness and English identity 68, 145–64, 189
'enterprise association' (Oakeshott) 93–4
European Union (EU) 40–2, 49, 72, 96–7, 126, 189–90
Euroscepticism 190
Evans, Jill 73

Falconer, Lord 46, 168–9
Farrington, Christopher 94

Field, Frank 161–2
'fifth nation' politics 103–22, 125–30, 140, 183, 187–8
Finlay, Richard 31–2
Fitzjames Stephen, James 140
Flinders, Matthew 55, 131–2
Forsyth, Michael 145, 169
Frank Joseph, Emperor 14
free trade 8
Freeden, Michael 85
Fried, Charles 22
Fry, Michael 30–1, 34
Funeral in Berlin (film) 77

Gallagher, Jim 176
Gallagher, Tom 182
Gamble, Andrew 26, 60, 86–7
Gardiner, Michael 30
Garton-Ash, Timothy 44
Gellner, Ernest 69, 167–8
Gillan, Cheryl 174
Ginsberg, Allen 165
Gladstone, W. E. 65–6, 103
Glasman, Maurice 158
global financial crisis (from 2008) 98
globalisation 39–41, 58, 157, 189
Goethe, J. W. von 89
Government of Wales Act (2006) 173
Grainger, J. H. 10
Gray, John 14, 45–6, 58–9, 78
Greener, Ian 60
Greenfeld, Liah 68
Greer, Germaine 165
Greer, Scott 84, 101–2, 116–17

Haesly, Richard 113
Hain, Peter 113
Harvie, Christopher 10–11, 17, 19, 34–5, 38, 101, 170
Hattersley, Roy 13, 155
'Having your cake and eating it' 181
Hazell, Robert 113, 122, 127–8, 136, 145, 149, 152, 168–70, 182
Heaney, Seamus 68
Heath, Anthony 70, 75, 163
Heath, Edward 173
Hechter, Michael 27–9, 32–3, 38
Heffer, Simon 165
Hegel, G. W. F. 69, 84, 97
Heidegger, Martin 50
Henderson, Ailsa 82–3
Hennessy, Peter 153, 162

'historical past' and 'practical past' 50–1
Hobsbawm, Eric 73
Hoggart, Simon 166–7
'hollowing out' of ethos 46
Holtham, Gerry 128, 191
Horton, John 51–2
House of Commons Justice Committee 138, 149, 191
House of Lords 110
  Select Committee on the Constitution 134, 138, 142
Howe, Stephen 27–8, 38, 40, 43
hubris of the English 67–8, 178
Hume, David 82
Hunt, Tristram 82
Hurd, Douglas 109

identity
  definition of 73–4
  as distinct from identification 74
  see also cultural identity; Englishness and English identity; national identity
identity politics 65–8, 72
imperialism 8–9, 30, 88
'independence-lite' concept 181–2
Institute of Public Policy Research (IPPR) 120, 137, 162–4, 192
instrumental view
  of Scottish independence 191
  of the union 85–7, 90–5, 98–101
intergovernmental relations 130, 135, 138, 141–2, 174, 176
Iraq War 80
Irish financial crisis 42
Irish Home Rule 6, 20, 98, 103, 109–10, 144, 150
Irish Republican Army (IRA) 27
Irish unity 36, 76, 188
Irvine, Lord 46
Isserlis, A. R. 107, 114–15, 121, 140

Jancic, Miroslav 80
Jeffery, Charlie 37, 117, 120, 141–3, 175
Johnson, Nevil 61, 114, 119, 144
Julian of Norwich 42

Kaletsky, Anatole 179
Kant, Immanuel 41
'Kant's dove' syndrome 41–2, 72–3, 87, 117, 179, 182–6, 190

Kaufmann, Eric 77
Kearton, Antonia 33
Keating, Michael 35, 42, 77, 81, 142–4
Kellas, James 116
Kelly, Ruth 17
Kenny, Michael 25, 40, 153
Kidd, Colin 6, 15–16, 28–9, 49, 54, 105, 120, 170, 188
Kim, N.-K. 17
King, Anthony 156, 178
Kumar, Krishnan 37, 153, 156

Labour Party 17, 30, 138, 142, 172, 180
Lampedusa, Giuseppe Tomasi di 34, 169
Larkin, Phillip 61
Lee, Simon 159
Leicester, Graham 61
Leonard, Mark 17, 88–9
Levinger, B. 72–3, 98
Lewis, Greg 35
Liberal Democrats 151, 170, 173
Lieven, Dominic 14
Life in the United Kingdom Advisory Group 79
Lloyd, John 166, 190
Lloyd George, David 107–8
Lodge, Guy 120, 141–2, 162, 175
London, government of 146
Lovering, James 28
loyalty 73, 77
Lyttleton, Humphrey 35

Macauley, Lord 19, 71, 89
McCrone, David 43, 59, 72, 75
Macdonald Margo 141
MacDonnell, A. G. 7–9
McEwan, Ian 36
McEwen, Nicola 82–3
McGuinness, Martin 188
MacIntyre, Alasdair 24, 91
McLean, Iain 37, 92–6, 99, 116, 162–3, 178
McMillan, Alistair 37, 92–6, 99, 116, 163, 178
Macmillan, Harold 54
MacWhirter, Iain 178
Madgwick, Peter 66, 104, 121
Mandler, Peter 4, 36, 74
Marquand, David 9, 22, 30, 87, 131–2, 147–9, 159
Marr, Andrew 157
Marxism 4
Massie, Alan 181–2

Meaney, Neville 32
Miers, Tom 182
Milburn (rock band) 181
Miller, David 80, 110–11
Miller, W. L. 74
Milton, John 159
Ministry of Justice 135–6
Minogue, Kenneth 42, 52–3
Mitchell, David 122
Mitchell, James 61, 107, 110, 125–30, 136, 177, 192
monarchy 81–2
Montesquieu, Baron de 81–2
Mooney, Gerry 121
Moore, Charles 146–9, 155, 163
Moore, Michael 183
Moreno scaling 70, 155, 187
Morgan, Kenneth O. 25
Morgan, Rhodri 135
Morris, Jan 57
Morris, William 157–8
Morrison, Blake 68
Morton, A. V. 57
'moving spirit' fallacy (Scruton) 48–51
multinational statehood 16, 56, 59, 65–7, 72, 76, 82, 91–2, 105, 116, 187
Murphy, Jim 113
Murphy, Paul 113–14, 137–8
Mycock, Andrew 47

Nairn, Tom 4, 26, 37–42, 68–70, 88, 100, 152, 149–50, 163, 189
National Health Service 87
national identity 4, 15–16, 59, 61, 66–83, 95–7, 108, 152, 155–6, 159, 166, 189
nationalism 9–13, 27–42, 44, 46, 69–72, 76–80, 84–5, 88–91, 94, 97–101, 106, 149–53, 157–71, 178–84, 186, 189–90
'neo-unionism' (Keating) 143
Norman, Wayne 180
Northern Ireland Life and Times Survey 76
Norton, Philip 55, 151, 192
Norwich, Bishop of 24

Oakeshott, Michael 5, 11–12, 16, 47, 50–4, 61–2, 89, 93–100
O'Brien, Conor Cruise 32
O'Donnell, Sir Gus 134, 137
O'Leary, Brendan 111, 133

opinion polls 75, 166, 190
Orange Order 6, 92
Orlie, M. A. 76
Orridge, A. W. 28
Orwell, George 77, 161
O'Toole, Fintan 42
Our Kingdom online forum 178

Page, Ed 28, 32
Paisley, Ian 110
'paradox of externality' 189–90
Parekh, Bikhu 18, 24, 78, 80, 95
Park, Alison 70
Parker, Mike 85–6
parliamentary sovereignty 17, 21–2, 48, 65, 77, 130–1
Parnell, Charles Stewart 143
Parris, Matthew 154–61, 166, 186
Pascal, Blaise 43
Paterson, Lindsay 59
Paterson, Owen 176
path dependence theory 59–60
patriotism 5–6, 27, 42, 69, 72, 76–9, 88–9, 96, 101
  definition of 99
Pattie, Charles 71, 76
Paxman, Jeremy 186–7
Pearce, Graham 145
Perryman, Mark 157
Petranovic, Danilo 78
Pittock, Murray 29, 33
Plaid Cymru 41, 72, 137, 170, 172
Pocock, J. G. A. 4–5, 24, 26, 32, 41, 55–6, 70, 149–50, 154
political parties 108, 118, 164
  see also Conservative Party; Labour Party; Liberal Democrats
popular sovereignty 16, 21
Porter, Bernard 8, 15
Portillo, Michael 185
post-colonialism 31
Powell, Enoch 147
Preston, Peter 31, 88–9
Price, Adam 35, 72–3, 98, 186
Priestley, J. B. 57
'primordial' unionism 92–4, 98–100, 121
'project discourse' about the union 86–91, 96, 101
providentialism 7–11, 24, 47, 49, 53, 55, 68, 89, 105
public expenditure per head 162
'punctured equilibria' (Greener) 60

Rees-Mogg, William 161
referendums 109–10, 113, 145, 166, 176, 178, 182–4
regionalism, English 145
Renan, Ernest 85
Resnick, Philip 67–8
'respect agenda' 171–7, 190
Rhodes, R. A. W. 55, 133, 155
Rifkind, Sir Malcolm 22, 50, 172
Robbins, Keith 12, 35
Roberts, Jane 75
Rojek, Chris 100, 102
Rose, Richard 12, 66, 80, 97–9, 104–9, 112–18, 121, 125, 147, 157, 163
Roth, Joseph 165
Round, John Horace 80
Royce, Josiah 73
Russell, Meg 113
Ryle, Gilbert 71

Salisbury, Lord 110
Salmond, Alex 72, 127, 130, 170, 181, 186–7, 190
Sandford, Mark 146
Santayana, George 15
Schmuecker, Katie 120, 141–2, 162, 175
Schopenhauer, Arthur 126
Scotland Act (1998) 21, 152
Scottish nationalism and the Scottish National Party (SNP) 13, 15, 41, 49, 82, 94, 118, 126, 130–1, 140–1, 149, 152, 166–72, 177–84, 186, 191
Scottish Parliament 34, 71, 141, 169, 173–80, 183–4
Scruton, Roger 48–51
Scully, Roger 116, 120
secession from the union 110–12, 129
Second World War 9, 12
'self-colonization' 38–40, 49, 68, 72
Sellar, W. C. 7
separatism 168–9, 178–80
Seton-Watson, Hugh 107, 155
Sewel Convention 141
Sewel, Lord 85–6, 102
Seyd, Ben 74–5, 103
Seyd, Patrick 71, 76
Shanks, Michael 25
Shapiro, Ian 78
'shared-rule' concept 129–30, 141
shared values 59

Shore, Chris 97
Shulman, Stephen 94
Sinn Fein 170
'Slovak scenario' 116, 163, 178
social contract theory 87
social democracy 139–40
solidarity, principle of 84–6, 117
sovereignty *see* parliamentary sovereignty; popular sovereignty
'special relationship' with America 87
Spender, Stephen 6
Starkey, David 147
Stendhal 44
Stewart, A. T. Q. 29
Strathclyde, Lord 110
Straw, Jack 136, 142, 150
Sturm, Roland 26
supra-nationalism 97
Sutherland, C. 76–7
Swenden, Wilfried 129

tax-raising powers 175–7
Taylor, A. J. P. 91
Taylor, Bridget 70
Thatcher, Margaret 137, 139
Thomson, Richard 40
Tilley, James 70
Torrance, David 169, 182
transition, politics of 167–70
Trench, Alan 21, 45, 86, 90, 100, 105, 118, 129, 132, 136, 142, 169, 172, 177, 181, 184
Trimble, David 181
truth, different types of 3–5, 9, 24–5, 43
Tully, James 65–7, 187

Ulster Covenant (1912) 103–4
Ulster unionism 12–15, 20, 77–8, 106
United Nations (UN) 49
university tuition fees 142, 161
Unowsky, Daniel 70

van Kersbergen, Kies 96–7
Varney, Sir David 176–7
Viroli, Maurice 79

Walden, George 166
Walker, Brian 78
Walker, David 117, 139
Walker, Gail 78
Walker, Graham 94
Walker, Neil 131
Wanna, John 55, 133, 155
Ward, Paul 36, 95
Ware, Vron 57
Watson, George 18
Weight, Richard 31, 36–7, 125
'welfare state' provision 84, 93, 121
Weller, Patrick 55, 133, 155
Wells, H. G. 152
Welsh Assembly 71, 116, 138, 173–4, 176
Welsh Assembly Government (WAG) 135
'West Lothian question' 118–19, 146, 149, 152
Whig interpretation of history 18–20, 31, 44–51, 55, 58, 62, 69, 147, 188
White, Michael 166–7
Whitelaw, Willie 155
Whiteley, Paul 71, 76
Wicks, Elizabeth 20, 45–6, 129
Willetts, David 146–7, 163
Williams, Charlotte 121
Williams, Glanmor 34
Williams, Gwyn 15, 32
Wills, Michael 58, 89
Wilson, Harold 155
Wilson, Sir Richard 134
Wilson, Sammy 60
Wittgenstein, Ludwig 140
women's suffrage 47
Woolf, Virginia 54
Worsthorne, Peregrine 45
Wright, Tony 26
Wyn Jones, Richard 41, 116, 120

Yeatman, R. J. 7
Young, Alison 133–4
Young, Gareth 155
Younge, Gary 159
Young, G. M. 157

Zollverein union 85